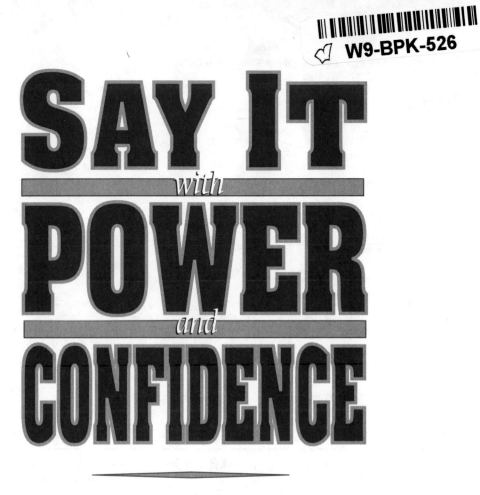

SAY IT *with* POWER *and* CONFIDENCE

PATRICK J. COLLINS

PRENTICE HALL
Paramus, NJ 07652

Library of Congress Cataloging-in-Publication Data

Collins, Patrick J.
    Say it with power and confidence   / by Patrick J. Collins.
       p. cm.
    Includes index.
    ISBN 0-13-614272-9 (case). — ISBN 0-13-614280-X (pbk.)
    1. Public speaking.   I. Title.
PN4121.C613   1997   97-29006
808.5' 1—dc21   CIP

Acquisitions Editor: *Tom Power*
Production Editor: *Eve Mossman*
Formatting/Interior Design: *Robyn Beckerman*

© *1998 by Patrick J. Collins*

Printed in the United States of America

10 9 8 7 6 5 4 3 2

ISBN 0-13-614272-9 (c)   ISBN 0-13-614280-X (p)

ATTENTION: CORPORATIONS AND SCHOOLS

Prentice Hall books are available at quantity discounts with bulk purchase for educational, business, or sales promotional use. For information, please write to: Prentice Hall Special Sales, 240 Frisch Court, Paramus, New Jersey 07652. Please supply: title of book, ISBN, quantity, how the book will be used, date needed.

PRENTICE HALL
Paramus, NJ 07652

A Simon & Schuster Company

On the World Wide Web at http://www.phdirect.com

Prentice Hall International (UK) Limited, *London*
Prentice Hall of Australia Pty. Limited, *Sydney*
Prentice Hall Canada, Inc., *Toronto*
Prentice Hall Hispanoamericana, S.A., *Mexico*
Prentice Hall of India Private Limited, *New Delhi*
Prentice Hall of Japan, Inc., *Tokyo*
Simon & Schuster Asia Pte. Ltd., *Singapore*
Editora Prentice Hall do Brasil, Ltda., *Rio de Janeiro*

Dedication

For Donna, Kristen, and Lauren

Contents

Part One
MAXIMIZING YOUR PERSONAL COMMUNICATIVE POWER

Chapter One
Developing Nonverbal Communication Skills   3

Chapter Two
Improving Your Language Power   17

Chapter Three

Becoming a Better Listener 37

Part Two

PREPARING AND DELIVERING POWERFUL SPEECHES AND PRESENTATIONS

Chapter Four

Speechwriting: How to Create a Powerful Message 51

Chapter Five

Audience Analysis: Making Sure Your Message Hits Home   71

Chapter Six

Handling Tough Questions and Tough Audiences   83

Chapter Seven

Making Effective Sales Presentations   109

Chapter Eight

Instant Speeches: Handling Spur-of-the-Moment and Special-Occasion Speeches

Part Three

SUREFIRE STRATEGIES FOR SPECIAL SITUATIONS

Chapter Nine

The Job Interview

Chapter Ten

Handling the Media   171

Chapter Eleven

Preparing to Be an Effective Witness   195

Chapter Twelve

Getting What You Want in Negotiations   213

Chapter Thirteen

Handling Crisis Communication   237

Chapter Fourteen

Conducting Successful Meetings   253

Chapter Fifteen

Thirty-one Quick Fixes to Improve Your Communicative Power

Index

Acknowledgments

Much of the information contained in this book is the product of discussions, and interactions with my colleagues and students at John Jay College, as well as those in business and government with whom I've had the privilege of working over the years. My thanks for all you have taught me.

Individual thanks go to my wife, Donna, for her constant encouragement, which was often sought and always there; to my friend and editor Sharon Nettles, for her keen eye and ready wit; to Henry Morrison, my literary agent, for his belief in this project; and to Tom Power at Prentice Hall for his vision and guidance. To Eve Mossman and Robyn Beckerman for their attention to detail. Thanks also to my good friends Anthony Garcia and Mike and Vicky Kay for being ever willing to listen. Finally, my heartfelt thanks to Jonathan Alexander and John Elefteriades for their special contributions in making this work possible.

Introduction

Why You Need
Say It with Power and Confidence

If you have ever left a meeting, a sales presentation, or even a job interview with the thought, "It could have gone better," or "The *next* time they ask me that question I'll say . . . ," you need *Say It with Power and Confidence.* If you have ever negotiated an agreement, only to say to yourself a few months later, "How did I ever agree to this?" you need *Say It with Power and Confidence.* If you have ever been halfway through a presentation only to realize that just about no one was listening, *Say It with Power and Confidence* can help you get your audience back—an audience of one or one hundred.

As skilled as you might be in some aspects of life, you are probably at a disadvantage when it comes to getting your message across with confidence, authority, and credibility—to getting what you want from an interpersonal encounter. *Say It with Power and Confidence* is a comprehensive guide to giving you the communicative edge—the advantage in *every* situation from the speaker's podium to the negotiating table and beyond.

The need to be a truly *powerful* communicator is greater than ever before. In this era of corporate downsizing, being an *essential* member of the team is a major key to survival. Strong interpersonal skills are the main ingredient in your personal survival kit. *Say It with Power and Confidence* can help you build the skills that will help make you a key member of any team. But being a truly masterful communicator is a greater challenge than ever. There was a time when turning in an adequate performance at the speaker's podium was enough. That's no longer the case. Today you must function in multiple arenas: the boardroom, the negotiation table, and even the TV studio, just to name a few. *Say It with Power and Confidence* gives you the information and provides you with the specific tactics you need—not just to *survive,* but to *prosper* in *all* of these arenas and others.

If you feel a sense of inadequacy as a communicator, you are not alone. Even if you are the beneficiary of a lengthy and rigorous education, you may also be its victim. That's because the spoken word, in spite of its impact and power on all of our lives, is still a very fleeting event, virtually impossible to systematically measure or evaluate. Therefore, educators, whose every success or failure is reflected by student performance on standardized tests, have largely ignored interpersonal skills as worthy of their attention. Sadly, such essentials as how to captivate people with your ideas or how to negotiate to get what you want are still excluded from most curricula. *Say It with Power and Confidence* will remedy that deficit.

How *Say It with Power and Confidence* Can Help You

Even after nearly thirty years as a communications educator and consultant, I still marvel at the obvious and costly communicative blunders made by people who should know better. As the chair of an academic department, I have watched highly educated people effectively demolish their chances of success in a job interview with a single and needlessly errant response. In helping senior executives prepare for major addresses, I have seen normally clear-thinking, well-intentioned people bore, alienate, or even offend the very people they wanted to touch with their message. I have observed negotiators stumble their way through sessions, making mistake after mistake and yet wondering why they failed to attain their goals. I have seen executives in the midst of a crisis struggling to manage the crisis itself and making the disastrous miscalculation of ignoring the communication of their actions.

Over the years, seeing so many people needlessly fail to achieve their communicative objectives in so many crucial situations, I sought to develop ways to help the people I worked with and taught, not by burying them in theory, but by developing specific, practical means of avoiding the communicative pitfalls that surround them. *Say It with Power and Confidence* is the result of that effort. It is a book designed to give you the advantage in virtually *every* communicative situation you will encounter.

Say It with Power and Confidence provides you with a unique combination of tips, tactics, and advice you can apply right away on the path to becoming a more powerful communicator. For example, you'll learn how to:

- Send just the right nonverbal signals in any situation

- Minimize anxiety and maximize self-confidence

- Be an effective public speaker—even if you hate public speaking!

- Use language to get and keep people on your side
- Handle tough audiences and tough questions in any setting
- Get what you want at the negotiating table
- Avoid common blunders in the job interview
- Get your message across to the media

   . . . and much more!!!

All the information in *Say It with Power and Confidence* is presented in a direct, no-nonsense style so that you can begin applying it immediately and get results. Each chapter begins with an at-a-glance summary to let you know what's covered and ends with a list of specific techniques for review. *Say It with Power and Confidence* is a book you not only will want to read from cover to cover, but will also want to use as a reference and guide through the verbal minefields we all face from time to time.

How *Say It with Power and Confidence* Is Organized

There are three elements in any communicative encounter that, if well managed, can maximize your chances of success—You, the Message, and the Situation. *Say It with Power and Confidence* examines each of these elements and shows you how to manage them in a manner that enables you to gain the communicative advantage in virtually every encounter.

Part One: Maximizing Your Personal Communicative Power

Chapter 1 of *Say It with Power and Confidence* is about *you*—that is, about the signals you send before you even say a word. You'll learn how body language, eyes, gestures, and even silence can help you gain the upper hand. You'll learn how to improve the variety and quality of your voice, an important part of making just the right impression on your listeners. Anxiety is a formidable obstacle preventing many people from attaining their goals. If you're one of the many people who would rather face death than speak in public, you'll learn how to manage your anxiety and build greater self-confidence in *all* your interpersonal encounters.

IMPROVING YOUR LANGUAGE POWER   An extremely important part of any message is the language you choose to get your point across. Making the right choices will dramatically increase the impact of your message whereas a few wrong choices will make those present either tune you out or get up and leave the room. Chapter 2 tells you what you need to know to make just the right choices. For example, what is more effective, formal or conversational language? How do you deliver highly technical material and still keep things interesting? How do you make your spoken words more colorful? More memorable? These are just a few of the questions answered in Chapter 2.

LISTENING—THE FORGOTTEN SIDE OF COMMUNICATION   Studies tell us that you remember less than 10 percent of what you hear. That's because you can process information faster than anyone can talk. Retaining more of the information you hear gives you the edge in negotiations, conducting meetings, and in any situation where getting all of the information you can is important. That's why *Say It with Power and Confidence* provides you with techniques you can use to become a better listener.

In Chapter 3, "Becoming a Better Listener," you'll learn how to break down the perceptual barriers that cause you to tune people out even when their message is worthwhile. You'll also discover ways to eliminate distractions and improve your listening environment. Applying these valuable listening tips will mean a dramatic increase in the amount of information you retain, information you can use to your advantage, information that most other listeners will miss.

Part Two: Preparing and Delivering Powerful Speeches and Presentations

Basic to effective communication is a message that will make people listen and take notice of what you have to say.

Chapter Four of *Say It with Power and Confidence*, "Speechwriting: How to Create a Powerful Message," takes you through a step-by-step method of showcasing your ideas to make them more memorable. No one listens to every word you say, but this chapter will show you how to hold an audience's interest and how to "get them back" at crucial points in your message. Many speakers leave their audiences and end their talks with a shrug. Instead, in this chapter, you'll learn how to leave them thinking.

MAKING SURE YOUR MESSAGE HITS HOME Communicators, from public speakers to negotiators and media guests, make a fatal mistake by not making their message audience-specific. Chapter 5 on audience analysis shows you how to "reach out" with your ideas to get and keep people on your side. You'll learn special tactics for highly educated or sophisticated audiences. This chapter even provides tips for effective communication in a "politically correct" environment and advice on issues of race, gender, and ethnicity.

HANDLING TOUGH QUESTIONS AND TOUGH AUDIENCES The most carefully crafted and delivered address is worthless if you can't handle the audience questions that are likely to follow. Chapter 6 of *Say It with Power and Confidence* not only shows you how to field questions from an audience, but, more important, how to handle tough questions and tough audiences. Q&A skills are the basis for a wide array of crucial communicative situations, from the media interview to the Q&A period that follows a speech, the job interview, or even the witness stand. This chapter shows you how to take control without seeming controlling, how to respond to "trick" questions, how to stall for time without making it obvious, and even how to handle the potentially awkward moment when you have to say "I don't know."

THE SALES PRESENTATION Sales presentations are really public-speaking contests in which the individual or team that does the best presentation gets the prize (the account). Having the best product or service often has little to do with the outcome.

Chapter 7, "Making Effective Sales Presentations," helps you and your team deliver the best presentation every time. You'll learn to avoid the blatant and most common errors made even by those who consider themselves "old pros," as well as how to deliver the delicate aspects of a sales presentation that so many presenters fumble badly. These include how to seem aggressive and direct *without* turning them off; how to talk about the competition bluntly and yet not offend anyone; the language of winning; and how to effectively manage a team presentation that really works. You may already know that selling is a tough game, but without the information contained in this chapter, it's a lot tougher and a lot less profitable.

SPUR-OF-THE-MOMENT AND SPECIAL-OCCASION SPEECHES   We all admire people who *seem* to be able to speak at a moment's notice on almost any subject and who somehow manage to come up with remarks that most of us consider not only adequate but bordering on eloquent. The important word here is *seem* because successful spontaneous speaking is anything but spontaneous. These apparently gifted orators are actually using a few tricks that are revealed in Chapter Eight so that you can function with equal brilliance on the spur of the moment. Many so-called spur-of-the-moment talks occur on special occasions in the form of tributes, award acceptances, nominations, toasts, and even eulogies. Chapter 8 provides the information and tips you'll need to shine at these special and *seemingly* spontaneous moments.

Part Three: Surefire Strategies for Special Situations

THE JOB INTERVIEW   With the possible exception of the public-speaking invitation and the tax audit, no other situation inspires as much agony as does the job interview. Not getting the job is painful because it so often symbolizes failure and rejection on a very personal level. Chapter 9, "The Job Interview," is about maximizing your chances of success in this all-important quest and also provides guidance on what to do if things don't go your way.

Beginning with vital preinterview steps that most job candidates ignore (their first mistake!), you'll begin building your advantage even before the interview takes place. Along with an extensive section of sample questions, this chapter tells you the *real* meaning behind often-asked questions.

There are also sample correct and incorrect responses designed to give you highly specific information on what you should and shouldn't say. You'll even learn how to handle questions that are intended to see how you deal with stress, as well as how to handle the all-important but delicate issue of how to talk about money in the job interview. If you are facing a job interview, you may forget your American Express card, but *don't* leave home without reading this chapter.

HANDLING THE MEDIA   Chapter 10, "Handling the Media," gives you the tactical material you'll need to make a credible and comfortable on-the-air appearance. Included is valuable information on how to control the agenda and get your point across in any media interview. You'll learn specific techniques for getting the most out of the various kinds of interviews: in-studio, remote camera, and even the "ambush" interview. In case you're new to the TV studio, you'll also find enough technical information (where to look, when to talk, and why all those people are standing around) to put you at ease. There is even a section on call-in radio shows.

While the emphasis is on electronic (radio and TV) journalists, print reporters present another set of problems and opportunities. Chapter 10 shows you how to get the best coverage from a more casual, lengthy, and *potentially dangerous* print interview.

THE WITNESS STAND   With the ever-increasing number of civil cases filed annually, as well as the thousands of legislative and regulatory hearings, you are more and more likely to find yourself on the witness stand.

In this adversarial setting, you can expect the opposition to be ready with some tricks and traps or at least an attempt to take you in some informational direction you'd rather not go. Chapter 11, "Preparing to Be an Effective Witness," arms you with strategies to avoid being trapped by the other side. You'll discover such valuable tactics as how to spot hidden messages in your counsel's objections and ways to maintain your comfort and credibility on the witness stand. You may not feel you need this information, but not having it could prove very costly.

GETTING WHAT YOU WANT IN NEGOTIATIONS   In most business settings, you are likely to end up negotiating at one time or another. Yet since your involvement in negotiation is only occasional, you might find yourself using a learn-as-you-go approach. Especially when the stakes are high, as many have learned the hard way, unfavorable agreements that are the result of bad negotiation are not only costly but may be with you for a long time.

Chapter 12 does away with the dangers of negotiating by instinct. Instead, you are guided through a series of proven techniques designed to get you what you want at the negotiation table. Among the topics covered are, what you should know *before* you begin negotiations; how to discuss numbers; the use of silence as a negotiation tactic; how to spot disunity on the other side and use it to your advantage; and when and how strongly to disagree.

CRISIS COMMUNICATION   Those who have been through any kind of corporate crisis will tell you that the worst time to start planning on how you'll handle things is in the midst of that crisis. How effectively an organization communicates during a crisis shapes public perceptions about the competency of its management and even whether the organization itself survives. Chapter 13, "Handling Crisis Communication," is a guide to formulating a crisis communication plan.

Included is such vital information as (1) defining the crisis, (2) getting the most from your PR and legal advisers, (3) media planning for the crisis, (4) the importance of symbolic communication, and (5) communicating recovery. You'll find this chapter extremely helpful in tackling the communicative aspects of a crisis, especially if you apply its contents *before* things have "hit the fan."

CONDUCTING SUCCESSFUL MEETINGS   If people want to assess your ability as a manager or executive, there is no need to dig out your personnel file. All they have to do is watch you run a meeting. Are things getting done? Moving along? Falling apart? At no time is your ability to manage more visible or more vulnerable than when you run a meeting. Yet there is little information on what to do—how to proceed when thrown into this potentially risky setting.

Say It with Power and Confidence fills this informational gap with a unique chapter containing all you'll need to handle meetings like a seasoned veteran and master parliamentarian. In Chapter 14 you'll gain vital information on how to control the content and tone of meetings, how to set the level of formality, and how to use rules to your advantage. You'll also learn effective techniques for holding elections, a tricky and sometimes explosive piece of business.

But meetings aren't just about issues; they are also about managing people. That's why this chapter shows you how to avoid having meetings degenerate into "gripe sessions" and how to handle conflict among those present. *All* of the information in "Conducting Successful Meetings" is geared toward getting you the most from your meetings and the people who attend them. You'll surely pass this managerial test with flying colors!

THIRTY-ONE QUICK FIXES TO ENHANCE *YOUR* COMMUNICATIVE POWER   *Say It with Power and Confidence* is intended to be the most comprehensive book of its kind, giving you all the information you need to build dramatic and tangible gains in your ability to communicate in a wide array of situations. The summary in Chapter 15 is a compilation of the skills items that are not only likely to give you the most difficulty, but is also the source of the most costly errors you are likely to make.

Reading this chapter, which covers tips on everything from the speaker's podium to the media interview, should jog your memory about other important points covered earlier. It is also offered as a kind of communicative pep talk, an intensive "lightning round" review of the essentials in making *you* a powerful and confident communicator.

Part One

MAXIMIZING YOUR PERSONAL COMMUNICATIVE POWER

Chapter One

Developing Nonverbal Communication Skills

At-a-Glance Summary

Most of this book is about helping you to get your message across and accomplishing your communicative agenda. This chapter, however, is about you.

Individuals and audiences alike decide whether to accept or reject your message from the moment you enter a room, gathering impressions about you and your message by observing everything from body language and facial expressions to eye contact and voice. How you handle these nonverbals or *signal behaviors* can make or break your performance.

This chapter provides the information you need to manage your nonverbal or signal behaviors and gives you the edge in any of the communicative situations discussed in this book, from the speaker's podium to the broadcast studio, from the negotiating table to the witness stand.

Developing Nonverbal Communication Skills

The communication process begins as soon as you enter the room, whether it's for an audience of one in a job interview or for a gathering of hundreds at the annual shareholders meeting. The one factor common to all of these situations, that transcends every tactic you employ, is you.

Sending the Right Nonverbal Signals

Your signal behaviors are an integral part of your every verbal encounter. Voice, gestures, eyes, body language, even your appearance can help, or in some cases hinder, your impact on an audience.

If you mismanage your signal behaviors, you will lack the power and impact you could and should have. You risk coming across as somewhere between boring and arrogant, uncaring or incompetent, and generally worthy of little more than an audience's polite tolerance.

If you do not have a high opinion of your communicative skills, let me provide you with some encouraging news: Having worked with thousands of speakers over the years, I have yet to meet one who does *everything* poorly. For example, those with superior verbal skills might not shine when it comes to vocal expressiveness, but none of the speakers I've met were in need of a total "communicative makeover."

As you use the techniques in this chapter, don't put together an "act." It will only come apart under pressure. Instead, concentrate on making some gradual adjustments in your signal behaviors as needed, while working with and building upon your strengths. This way, you'll come across as both comfortable and consistent, two sure hallmarks of an effective, credible spokesperson.

Now let's look at the major signal behaviors and how you can use them to boost the impact of your spoken word.

Presenting a Commanding Entrance

If you are giving a speech, your entrance and the first minute at the podium should be smooth and seamless, with a minimal but definite moment to adjust the microphone, arrange your notes, and establish your comfort level.

If you skip this step, your speech will be a bit disjointed and will not flow as freely as you wanted it to. The result? The audience will simply see a speaker who is anxious and "a bit off" and will wonder why. The lack of a commanding entrance causes you to lose credibility and authority with your audience, immediately and needlessly.

How do you smooth out an entrance and make sure that all-important first moment goes smoothly? *Manage the environment!*

Anytime you are doing a presentation, testifying at a hearing, or appearing on a TV program, get there with enough time to check out the surroundings, even the day before for a particularly important event.

Whenever necessary, have changes made in advance, be it a taller podium, a better microphone, or a rearrangement of the chairs. If you're going to be using a flip chart, make sure there are markers and that they work. Even if you arrive early just to become familiar with the surroundings, you'll make yourself more comfortable by doing so and prepare yourself to make a commanding entrance.

The comfort and psychological advantage you gain by being familiar with the speaking environment will be evident in your performance, and by taking charge of the environment you will communicate that you are prepared, competent, and worthy of their attention.

Using Silence Effectively

Yes, using silence effectively is a powerful communicator that most speakers fear. Let's say that you've just approached a podium to give a speech. If your entrance went smoothly and you sent positive signals with that entrance, you will diminish your effectiveness by starting your speech immediately.

Instead, wait a moment. Take a breath. Relax and take a look around your audience. *Let some silence happen.* This direction is as applicable to an audience of ten as it is to an audience of two hundred. This bit of silence communicates that you are in charge and that you want their attention. It also shows that you're not particularly afraid of silence.

If you ignore this direction and just dive right into your remarks, the many conversations that are going on in any audience will be interrupted. At the moment you begin, audience members are more likely to be thinking of their interrupted conversations rather than your first words, a poor set of circumstances for even the best of speakers. A few seconds of silence gives them time to shift their attention from their conversations to you. You'll build considerable authority and listenership in that brief moment.

You should also use silence to emphasize. Before and after a particularly important fact, pause. Although we have been talking about the speaker's podium, silence is an important communicator in any of the situations covered in this book. That moment of silence will cause anyone not fully listening to refocus on you and gives greater impact to the phrase punctuated at either end by silence. In a speech script, you may even want to mark your notes to make sure some planned silences occur, especially if you have a habit of speaking rapidly.

In a culture where talking is success, silence is wrongly viewed as failure. Use this powerful signal behavior to your advantage. With practice, strategically applied, silence can be a real booster of your authority, competence, and self-assurance.

Using Your Eyes to Get Your Message Across

Shakespeare called the eyes "the mirror of the soul." The eyes are a highly important communicator. In this culture, if you don't look at people when you talk to them, it's considered a sign that you might not be telling the truth.

Similarly, if your talk to an audience is interspersed with darting glances around the room, they are likely to think you are "shifty" or somehow to be distrusted. Some misguided speakers direct their eyes onto their notes and attempt to "tune out" the fact that there is an audience present. The fact is, the audience just as quickly tunes out such speakers.

The solution to sending the right signals with your eyes is simple and to the point: *Look at the person or people you are talking to.* In a courtroom, or a media or job interview, it means looking at the person who asked the question as you respond.

When speaking to a group, the best method of making eye contact varies depending upon audience size. You should either look directly at individual audience members as you speak or direct your gaze toward areas of the audience, such as left, center, and right, to give the impression that you are speaking *directly* to each member of an audience. This applies even if the glare of lighting makes your audience invisible from the podium.

I have found that with an audience of about thirty or fewer people, it's possible to make eye contact with each one as I speak. As the audience gets above this number and up into the hundreds, directing eye contact toward areas rather than individuals works as well in conveying the impression of eye contact.

At first, maintaining adequate eye contact with your audience requires concentration and practice, as well as familiarity with your notes. After a few successful outings, maintaining eye contact will become a natural part of your delivery.

Remember, the use of your eyes in speaking is one of the chief ways in which you bond with an audience or an individual and give the impression that you are caring, committed, and credible.

This final word of advice on using your eyes to communicate: Avoid those ridiculous suggestions we have all heard, such as focusing on and speaking to a distant object in the room or pretending your audience is nude. The first of these silly strategies gives you the blank look of someone who has forgotten to take his or her medication whereas the latter will give you the silly smile of someone who is overmedicated.

Making Your Point with Gestures

"But what will I do with my hands?" is a question I often hear from those who are about to deliver a major presentation or appear in a media interview. Although I'm not usually fond of answering a question with a question, I ask, "What do you do with them in conversation?"

The fact is that the hands or gestures are never given any attention except by the inexperienced speaker in a high-pressure situation who is suddenly examining each and every signal behavior in an effort to assemble the perfect act.

I don't want you to assemble an act, but to focus on a few signal behaviors. For example, if you find yourself being a particularly rigid speaker, you might want to practice a gesture or two, but the best solution is to practice your speech with the thought of including more movement, both hand movement and movement around the podium.

It would be simple here to point out a few gestures and simply tell you to mark your text and gesture at certain key points of information. But the result is usually a cue for a hopelessly wooden, staged gesture. I once saw a speaker get an unintended laugh (the worst kind) by thrusting two fingers skyward as he said, "And now for my third point . . ."

To get back to my earlier question, "What do you do with your hands in a conversation?" the answer is, "Nothing in particular." This should also be your general approach toward gestures. They will happen naturally and appropriately if you let them, in conversation or in any other communicative encounter.

You can facilitate gesturing by placing your hands at either corner of the podium, just out of the audience's sight. In an interview, place your hands on your lap, ready to gesture. While either of these positions will make it easy to gesture, folding your hands or arms will make it more difficult to gesture and will telegraph that you are rigid and uncomfortable, physically and just maybe psychologically.

Controlling and Managing
Your Body Language

The lyric from an old show tune says, "Every little movement has a meaning all its own," and although we don't need to get too theatrical here, where you stand, how you sit, and whether you move around are all manageable signal behaviors that communicate your level of comfort and authority to your audience.

In using a podium, decide how you want to manage the space and stick to that plan. You may wish to stay behind the podium during your talk (a wise move if you have a lot of notes) and then move off to one side for the question-and-answer period. Then again, once you have been through a speech a number of times, you may wish to remain in front of the podium, or even to do away with it entirely. The important step here is to decide *in advance*. This way you avoid being one of those fidgety, leaning, wandering, or rocking speakers who communicate discomfort and indecisiveness along with their message.

On the matter of posture, the days of standing with hands at sides like some sort of palace centurion are over. You might want to rest your hands on the podium (rather than latch onto it as if frozen in terror). Try standing in a comfortable position, perhaps with one arm resting on the podium, maybe a hand in a pocket. The point is, you have a stance and posture in which you are most comfortable, and it should be a part of your behavior as you speak.

Body language should communicate comfort, and you can't be comfortable when you focus on a series of planned behaviors. Instead, remember my rule for effective management of body language, which states: *Any behavior of body language, posture, or movement that you overuse or constantly repeat becomes distracting to your audience.*

Remember that what you do in a conversation works. Using that behavior as your starting point, make some decisions about body language that make you comfortable. That enhanced level of comfort will be projected to your audience.

Gaining a More Imposing Voice

How do you feel about your speaking voice? Is it too high-pitched? Monotonous? Whiny? Most of us have little problem with or concern about voice until an important speaking occasion pops into our lives; then any and all of the things we don't like about ourselves become ripe for change or adjustment.

Do I Really Sound Like That?

In evaluating the sound of your voice, remember that your speaking voice is very much a function of anatomy and that larger people tend to have deeper or lower-pitched voices whereas those of lesser stature and size will often have a higher vocal range. Even if you're not crazy about the sound of your own voice, if your listeners have no particular reaction, it means that they can focus on the message, and communicatively, that's good.

Besides, if you somehow change your normal speaking voice (a bad idea) for a presentation or interview, you'll have difficulty keeping the "act" going, especially when the going gets tough, as in a Q&A period.

Beyond that, if you feel you have a problem regarding voice pitch or quality or a voice that tires or cracks very easily, you might consider seeing a medical specialist or a qualified voice therapist.

But I Sound Monotonous

Fortunately, with practice, this is one of the more manageable signal behaviors. Monotonous voices are actually one of two types: the voice that continues at nearly the same pitch or musical note, with very little variation; or the voice that repeats a pattern of pitch and loudness so that every phrase sounds the same.

If you have the typical monotonous voice, it's probably because you are either uncomfortable with the situation or unfamiliar with the material. Your inhibition when it comes to being "vocally alive" conveys your discomfort to an audience and wrongly signals to them that you are bored, boring, or indifferent.

How to Enhance Your Expressiveness

Here are some steps you can take to enhance vocal expressiveness.

To reduce your level of "vocal inhibition," listen to a radio commercial and compare that vocal delivery to your own. You will notice that the commercial has too much variety and expressiveness for conversation; but in radio, voice is all you have, so most announcers tend to be "hyperexpressive."

Record your own radio commercial, with the same degree of emphasis as the announcer. Note that I am not referring to the announcer's voice, but to the level of vocal variety that's present in the typical broadcast commercial. Capturing even some of that vocal expressiveness will dramatically increase the level of variety in your normal speaking voice.

Once you can imitate the "announcer" style at will, you should attempt to transfer that degree of vocal variety to the text of a speech you are presenting. In practicing, record portions of your speech with this livelier delivery.

A second technique that's effective for increasing your level of vocal expressiveness is to practice a speech as if you are delivering it to a group of small children. Have you ever noticed how adults talk to young children? Even the most stentorian voice becomes gentle and varied.

No, I'm not suggesting you actually deliver your speech to an audience as if they were a bunch of three year olds, but use this exercise to explore and increase your own vocal expressiveness. Record your voice and listen to it with a critical ear toward shedding your vocal inhibitions.

Practice both these techniques, and once they become internalized, you will find that speaking with increased vocal expressiveness will go from a learned technique to one of your natural signal behaviors.

Maximizing Your Spoken Fluency

Fluency is a signal behavior that your audience uses, right or wrong, as a measure of your personal confidence, preparedness, and even competence. We all speak with varying degrees of fluency; some of us fall over words or jumble phrases more often than do others. But there are some ideas and techniques you should be aware of that will help you maximize your spoken fluency.

Remember that *perfect fluency does not happen.* Even conversational speech is actually a series of words punctuated by verbalized pauses (saying "uh" or "you know"), hesitations, and interruptions from other participants in the conversation.

Instead of focusing on trying not to flub (which only makes you nervous and less fluent), become thoroughly familiar with your notes. Read them over repeatedly. I instruct speakers I coach to read through a speech *at least* ten times before attempting to deliver it to an audience. Some speakers are more comfortable with double that number of run-throughs.

As you read over a speech—practicing aloud is most valuable—mark the places where you tend to stop or trip over a word or phrase. If you have difficulty pronouncing a word, either spend some time learning to say the word or change it.

Another technique for improving fluency is to make sure you can read your notes. This sounds like an obvious tip until you realize that when you go over your notes, you do so in comfortable surroundings, maybe at your desk or in a favorite chair. Even as you sit in an airliner going over your notes, your eyes are a lot closer to the page than they will be at the podium.

Trying to maintain eye contact from the speaker's podium while keeping your place in hard-to-read notes is virtually impossible. The speaker who attempts to do so usually ends up abandoning the notes altogether, delivering a diluted or disjointed version of the original text.

Avoid this problem with well-marked notes that you can read easily from about three feet. This way, you can maintain adequate eye contact and fluency and will communicate a heightened degree of credibility, authority, and impact.

Projecting the Right Visual Image

While it may be socially correct to say that we are generally capable of looking beyond such externals as the appearance of a speaker, there isn't an attorney in the land who would advise his or her client to show up in court wearing bib overalls. Whether you like it or not, especially in important communicative situations, appearance counts and counts big. Audiences and individuals can and do make judgments based upon our appearance.

It's not my purpose to give "dress-for-success" advice, but I would be remiss in not including appearance in any discussion of signal behaviors. I'll leave the specifics of apparel choice to your own fashion sense and to the experts in that field, but I would advise you to be attentive to two areas: (1) audience expectations and (2) minimalization of distraction.

Be Who They Expect

Examine your role in communicating with an audience. As a senior executive, witness, candidate, or any spokesperson dealing with a sensitive issue, your personal credibility and the level of personal stability you communicate become especially crucial.

Just as you're unlikely to see a 747 captain in a clown suit (and might get off the plane if you did), those with whom you will be speaking have certain expectations, not only about what you will say, but also about how you will look. Think about those expectations and attempt to meet them. In so doing you will make those listeners comfortable enough to focus on your message more than on your appearance.

Minimize Distractions

As soon as I mention meeting audience expectations concerning appearance, the more contrarian reader or anyone whose top-ten favorite songs include "I've Got to Be Me" will think things such as, I've got to make a fashion statement to get their attention. Perhaps you even have a fashion trademark, maybe a hat or a crossword-puzzle tie.

Truly effective communication enables an audience to focus on the message, which, if you are to make the sale or convince the jury or whatever your purpose, is best accomplished in an atmosphere free of distractions. Let your *message* be the focal point of your communicative effort, not your attire.

Showing Your Qualifications

Not telling an audience who you are from a credentials point of view is a missed opportunity to establish your credibility.

This is a culture loaded down with such characters as TV weathercasters who are not meteorologists, mail-order marketeers masquerading as experts, and even people who give medical advice or sell health products after delivering such incredibly absurd disclaimers as, "I'm not a doctor, but I play one on TV. . . ."

Credentials are conveniently ignored by those who don't have them, and, in what seems like some sort of false modesty, those of us with significant experience or knowledge of an issue tend not to talk about it. My advice? Never talk to an audience or participate in any serious communicative event, from the media interview to the witness stand, without mentioning your qualifications.

As a speaker who is particularly qualified to be expressing an opinion or position on an issue, you give much greater weight to your remarks and boost your credibility by telling your audience who you are from a credentials point of view. Failure to do so raises doubts in the minds of your more critical and astute listeners. So tell them, as soon as possible, what your qualifications are.

Credentials don't have to consist of a string of academic degrees. You might have served for an impressive number of years in your field—an equivalent in most listeners' minds. If you're short on time in an industry, perhaps you have some special training or have thoroughly researched the issue on your own.

The point here is to say something on the credentials issue. Most speakers don't. If you do, especially in a debate or panel discussion, you establish your personal credibility and authority and increase the impact of your message.

Reducing Your Anxiety Level

Note that I have not said, Don't be anxious. Nor am I about to present a magic formula for ridding yourself of speaker anxiety because, short of medication (which I don't advise), it doesn't exist.

If you are a victim of "stage fright" or speaker anxiety, it helps to understand why you feel this way. Many of the speakers I work with have lengthy explanations containing gobs of psycho-babble to explain their anxiety. Their anxiety is, however, more likely generated by the fact that they are ill-prepared, overtired, or have failed to implement many of the techniques outlined in this chapter.

My point is that you shouldn't become overly focused on speaker anxiety. Sure, you're under pressure, and yes, everyone will be looking at you; but beyond that, audiences are usually sympathetic and supportive, particularly with the less experienced speaker. Keep your anxiety level in perspective. At this point, overdiscussing or analyzing speaker anxiety will only heighten it.

Summary

We have been discussing various signal behaviors and tactics to help you enhance your communicative performance. Review these tactics and behaviors and focus on a few that may detract from your effectiveness as a speaker. *How* you deliver your message, rather than *what* you actually say, can greatly alter an audience's perception of how competent, authoritative, and credible you are.

If you are planning on a major overhaul of your spoken delivery skills, do so a few steps at a time. The key to success here is to put together a series of signal behaviors that send positive messages about you and your ability, rather than "an act" that will come apart as soon as you encounter a stressful situation.

Adjusting your communicative behavior gradually will mean that you can remain comfortable and behaviorally consistent, whether the climate is friendly or hostile. It is this level of comfort and consistency that will send positive signals about you and your message to an audience, making you the most powerful communicator you can be.

Quick Review:
Nonverbal Communication Skills

1. Check out the site of a presentation in advance. Familiarity breeds comfort.
2. Pause at the beginning of a speech; let your audience settle down.

3. Eye contact is important. Look directly at your audience, of one or many.

4. Don't use staged gestures; they look phony. Instead, relax and let them happen.

5. Avoid being rigid about posture. Stand or sit comfortably.

6. Practice maintaining vocal expressiveness; otherwise, don't try to change your voice, based upon some ill-defined ideal.

7. Don't focus on fluency. Know your notes, have a text you can read easily, and remember that perfect fluency is an unrealistic goal.

8. Regarding personal appearance, be comfortable but be what they expect.

9. Tell an audience, any audience, your credentials, your qualifications for being there.

10. Work on a few signal behaviors at a time, blending them into your spoken delivery, rather than putting together an "act."

Chapter Two

Improving Your Language Power

At-a-Glance Summary

This chapter helps you to increase the impact of your spoken words. The more vivid your message, the greater its impact and memorability.

Although the emphasis is on the speaker's podium, this information applies to every situation, from media interviews to sales presentations.

Improving Your Language Power

You Are What You Say

An often-heard radio commercial selling "vocabulary-building" tapes proclaims, "People can tell a lot about you from the words you use." I don't know how effective the tapes are, but I do agree that your listeners make judgments based upon your choices of language, whether in a speech you deliver, a sales presentation, or even your testimony in court.

Listeners make judgments about such vital areas as your level of knowledge, experience, and education; whether you are open and forthcoming, or might have something to hide; even whether you can be trusted and believed. Whether audience members are dressed in three-piece suits or in bib overalls, they can tell when something about your message bothers them or doesn't quite ring true.

That same audience may be bored by your speech or may find your message highly listenable and memorable, based upon your choice of language.

Despite the existence of such devices as "vocabulary tapes," there is no magical word list to guarantee results each time you talk. If there were a list of "power words," so many speakers would use all of the power words so often that, much like an overexposed celebrity, they would soon lose any power they had in the first place.

Effective use of language means using your own personal style of conversing with an audience while adapting to that audience's frame of reference. Effective language needs to be genuinely yours, not borrowed like rented formal wear. Effective language also means being as understandable as possible without being patronizing.

While maintaining your own personal style is an important element in helping you use language, building upon that style will help you increase your effectiveness by increasing the listenability and memorability of your remarks.

Using Conversational Language
to Increase Your Power

At any black-tie or formal dinner, you can usually spot the guys in the rented tuxedos. They look just a bit stiff and wooden. The garment doesn't quite fit the way it should, it's just a little bit off; but as the wearer will readily tell you, it's just a rental.

When you deliver a speech and use language you have borrowed just for the occasion—the words are someone else's or the speech contains words you wouldn't normally use—you come off like the gentleman in the rented tux: a bit stiff, uncomfortable, and generally feeling out of your element.

Whether the speech is your own or your remarks have been written for you, as is so often the case in the corporate sphere, go over your notes and delete or change phrases that sound the least bit alien to you. A good speechwriter will observe your personal style and quickly become capable of writing to match it.

Your specific speaking style, just like your personality, will be influenced by your environment and experience. Such factors as your occupation, how well read you are, your educational background, and whether you are a creature of the sciences or the arts are all factors that influence your linguistic choices and how you come across to an audience.

Many of those who write on language usage will stress the importance of being "conversational" with your audiences, and I agree with that advice. But don't do so at the expense of your usual vocabulary. If you do so, you'll be talking down to your audience, and they'll know it.

Select the Most Effective Words

I once knew a prominent college professor who seemed almost intimidated by his own stature. One reflection of his discomfort was that he spoke in language that no one else, even professors, would ever use. Instead of saying that the faculty should pay more attention to something, he made statements such as, "The faculty should lend greater consequence to the issue of . . ."

I've long since forgotten the issues of which that professor spoke, but I do remember that his language choices were a constant linguistic gymnastics exhibition. Most of his colleagues paid more attention to *how* rather than to *what* he said.

Once language becomes a performance activity, a means to dazzle rather than to communicate, the all-important message itself becomes obscured.

Following are some examples of words and phrases that are more conversational and effective than are their perfectly acceptable but less memorable counterparts. In categorizing some words and phrases as "nonconversational," I don't mean to suggest that they are not useful, but that their infrequent use in spoken language makes them unusual to the listener and therefore more likely to divert attention from your message.

Here is a list of language choices I would make in writing a speech, the Conversational words being the preferred choices:

NONCONVERSATIONAL	CONVERSATIONAL
connotes	also means
de jure	according to law
erudite	studious, learned
eviscerate	weaken
fallacious	false, misleading
forlorn	sad, miserable
faux	imitation
largesse	generosity
libation	drink
invidious	offensive, malicious
invective	insults
macro-	very large
micro-	very small
maudlin	overly sentimental
melancholia	depression
myriad	great number
obstinate	stubborn
onerous	troublesome
oxymoronic	contradictory
penurious	stingy
pedestrian	ordinary

NONCONVERSATIONAL	CONVERSATIONAL
perspicacious	wise, discerning
petulant	irritable
redouble	intensify, double
render	cause
rout	defeat
salacious	obscene
schema, scheme	plan
sensorial	sensory
sonorous	rich-sounding
torpor	sluggishness
unctuous	falsely earnest, oily
vex	annoy
wallow	roll around, luxuriate
warrant	justify, authorize

Most of us don't use the words in the left column in conversation; yet you might be tempted to use them in a speech to make things seem more formal or to impress your audience. Don't do it. Trying to boost your linguistic octane rating with words you normally don't use merely makes you uncomfortable and increases the psychological distance between you and your audience. It can also reduce their ability to comprehend your message.

An important difference between written and spoken language is that the reader can slow down or even come to a dead halt in the middle of a page in order to figure out the author's exact meaning. In spoken language, however, if your listener takes a break to ponder an obscure word, since you are still talking, part of the message will be lost.

The key is to use a level of vocabulary with which you are comfortable and yet that is fully understandable to your audience. If your vocabulary is more wide-ranging than most, remember that having such a vocabulary means more than knowing a lot of big words. It also means that you have more options and that you should use that ability to make word choices that will maximize your audience's ability to understand and retain your message.

Avoiding the Definition Trap:
Know Exactly What You Mean

Once, an undergraduate student of mine who probably didn't have time to write a speech introduction came up against one of those corollaries of education that most veteran students already know: that your chances of being called on are inversely proportional to your degree of preparedness.

She "borrowed" some words from a magazine article to begin her speech, words that went something like: "The deep purple of the predawn darkness was relinquishing its grasp on a sky that yearned to take on a more azure hue, almost as if to be in greater harmony with the burgeoning bustle of the awakening metropolis."

This description of an urban dawn was considerably more elaborate than most undergraduate students will venture for a minor assignment in a basic speech course. I suspected that she had little to do with the authorship of her opening words. Exposing this bit of chicanery consisted of nothing more than my asking the student exactly what the word "azure" meant. Of course, she had no idea, thereby learning hard and fast what Abraham Lincoln said about not always being able to fool people.

The fact is, speakers often use words they don't fully understand. Some think no one will notice; others think they know the meaning of a word but have it wrong. Don't fall into the trap of faking it. If a speech is written for you and you are not familiar with each and every word, not only in the context of the speech, but in general, look it up.

Even if it's a basic or generic term, be prepared to define it. This point was very well made to me by a longtime employee of an electric company who, after having made dozens of successful safety presentations to groups of school children, was badly stumped by the horribly obvious question that could only come from the uncluttered mind of a child: "What's electricity?"

My friend uttered one of those embarrassing but momentarily useful things we say when completely stuck, such as, "Well everybody knows that . . . and it's right there in the outlet for all of us to use." Of course, he went straight home, looked up the answer and is now a master of knowing the *exact* meaning of his remarks.

The same principle, knowing the exact meaning of what you are saying, also applies in scientific and technical circles. Often, a common term will be contained in a report, or an abbreviation will be used so frequently that everyone assumes everyone else will know what it means.

I once asked a corporate spokesperson who was talking about PCB disposal what "PCB" (poly-chlorinated-biphenyl) stood for. Although he had been dealing with the issue for some time, he had no idea. He was relieved that the question had come up in a training session and not in front of an audience.

When writing a speech or presentation, make certain that you know the meanings of any terms you'll be using and don't overlook terms or abbreviations you've used for years, the ones "everyone knows."

Managing Your Use of Abbreviations and Technical Language

Have you ever noticed that pilots and nurses talk in initials? Airplane talk is filled with such gems as the ILS, RVR, AGL, ETA, FL, and TCA.

Nurses are those people you meet in the ER who take your BP, set up an EKG and even minister CPR before sending you to the ICU. Once these people stop using initials and start using words, you almost wish they'd dump the jargon and go back to the abbreviations, but at least the initials took less time.

No matter what your chosen field, technical jargon and abbreviations have probably become a part of your vocabulary. Remember that you are shutting some of your audience out by using abbreviations or jargon. Even if they figure out what you're saying by the end of your presentation, they have not heard your entire message.

If you ignore your audience's level of knowledge and indiscriminately dump abbreviations and jargon, you will come across as smug, uncaring and inconsiderate, or ignorant of your audience's range of familiarity with your topic.

The solution? If you know that some audience members will have total familiarity with your topic and others will have none, you might begin by saying something like, "I know that some of you here are old pros in the insurance game, but others of you haven't heard me talk on this subject before. Therefore, if you pros will bear with me, I'll let the rest of you know just what all those abbreviations mean as I get to them in this presentation."

If your speech is going to contain a large number of important abbreviations and your audience contains a large percentage of neophytes, you might do the "old-pro" disclaimer and take your audience through some of the abbreviations before beginning your prepared speech.

The point here is to let the audience know that you're open, communicative, and considerate and that you want to communicate your ideas clearly and effectively to *everyone* present. The "old pros" will appreciate the fact that you have acknowledged their presence, and the new people will feel welcome and included. All will do a better job of listening.

Name Names and Speak in the First Person

Sometimes a spoken message suffers because of what you leave out rather than what you include.

Recently, in helping a senior executive prepare for a major speech, we reviewed a tape of an earlier speech in which it was his task to detail some of the serious problems his company was having. I pointed out that at no time, in a speech that lasted nearly thirty minutes, did he mention the name of the company—odd behavior for a senior executive, not exactly a display of corporate pride.

His reaction to this lapse was initially one of disbelief. Upon reviewing the tape, however, he agreed that he had tried not to associate the company name with the problems he was detailing. Nice try, but I doubt his ploy fooled the audience.

When you make such linguistic decisions in an attempt to shift or deemphasize blame, all that you communicate is your own discomfort, usually calling more attention to the very problem you were trying to minimize.

Have you ever heard a child tell his or her parents about grades? Inevitably, the conversation goes something like: "I got an A in Spanish, a B in chemistry, and *he gave me* a C in history." Our little student's intention is to take credit for everything positive ("I got . . .") and assign blame for anything negative ("He gave me . . . ").

Similarly, when things are going well, the typical corporate spokesperson's presentation is full of pronouns and references to the company: "I'm very proud, in fact all of us at American Plexon Corporation are proud to announce that the groundbreaking ceremonies for our new design center will take place on . . . "

Yet when there are problems, that same spokesperson makes the same kind of linguistic shift as did our schoolkid. The American Plexon spokesperson, on a topic much less pleasant than the new design center, is more likely to say, "The company has determined that the spill has been contained and that efforts are already under way to minimize the environmental impact."

American Plexon becomes "the company" and pronouns and specific references to the employees disappear. Notice that "efforts are under way" is a highly impersonal way of saying that the company is doing something.

While this statement gets the facts across, it also infers, by what it doesn't say, that there may be serious problems present, as signified by the lack of any reassurance.

The listener's conclusion? Something is up—if not something serious, at least something American Plexon would rather not talk about.

In contrast, the same statement delivered in a more personal style, with a more reassuring tone, can sound like this: "American Plexon has sent a team to examine the spill at our plant, and our personnel want me to reassure you that the job of minimizing the impact has already been started by our environmental safety crews."

The tone in the second statement suggests that while there is a problem, company personnel are taking care of it and that those people care enough to want to communicate the situation. In this statement, American Plexon comes across as an organization with the integrity to tell the consumer, stockholder, reporter, or whomever that audience may be exactly what is going on and what is being done about it—a tremendous improvement over the similarity to the responsibility-shifting "He gave me a C" approach of the earlier statement.

Speaking in Color, Not Black and White

The most memorable or colorful speakers are invariably those who provide descriptions in the form of images and analogies that their audiences remember.

Colorful analogies and descriptions come from a wide variety of sources, and as a speaker you'll need to be on the lookout for them. I once read a description of an automobile's cluttered dashboard as a "Tokyo by night instrument panel." W. C. Fields, in one of his films, described a gaudily arrayed old woman as being "all dressed up like a well-kept grave."

New York's previous governor, Mario Cuomo, rose to national prominence as an eloquent speaker when, in his nomination speech at the 1988 Democratic convention, he used a "shining city" as a metaphor for his vision of what America could become.

During their tough and sometimes acrimonious battle for the presidency, President George Bush derided then-Governor Clinton's economic plan as a case of "Elvis economics," on the premise that Clinton's ideas had been dead for some time. Bill Clinton, who also had good writers, accepted the description with the rejoinder that, unlike Elvis, at least his plan had been seen recently.

References to sports, the pop culture, or world events also help add that quality of color to language while they show that you have the imagination and the vision to look beyond the scope of your own field for inspiration and ideas.

Of course, your analogies and descriptions should fit your audience. Describing a failure as "a fallen soufflé" at a sports dinner is as bad as describing a success as "a triple-crown winner" to a gathering of gourmands. Similarly, the demographic profile of your audience is going to shape their definition of what is colorful and popular and what isn't.

Not reaching into literature, the arts, sports, or the less-traveled corners of your own mind for imaginative descriptors for the events and situations you present will lead an audience to describe you much the way a colleague of mine described a particularly dull job candidate after an interview: "He had a gray suit, gray hair, a gray tie . . . and a gray face."

Beware of the "Peter Piper Picked a Peck" Syndrome

One of my major objectives in helping you succeed as a communicator is getting you to be comfortable at the speaker's podium. You have learned a series of behaviors to make yourself comfortable, such as taking the time to arrange your notes, not beginning right away, even having a sip or two of water as you begin—all ways of relaxing as you begin your speech.

In the same connection, the language contained in your speech shouldn't make you uneasy. Yet, just as I am convinced that the preparers of some exotic cuisines spice their food just to see how much diners can endure, I think linguists have devised words that should never be spoken aloud, not because they are obscene or offensive, but simply because they are unpronounceable or make most speakers stumble.

Among the worst offenders in the category of unpronounceable words are such monsters as homogeneity, homonymous, magnanimity, specificity, inestimable, serendipitous, and statistics or statistical. You can probably add to this list with a selection of your own.

There are other words that speakers tend to trip over because they are unfamiliar with them. Among those I've noticed over the years are nuclear, et cetera, epitome, auxiliary, concomitant, subsidiary, prescient, and synergistic.

A good rule to follow is that *if you are rehearsing a speech aloud (which you should) and you stumble over a word more than once, change it to a more easily pronounced word or phrase.*

The alternative is to circle it and repeat the problem phrase over and over; unfortunately, this usually doesn't work. Once at the lectern, you'll more than likely flub that word or phrase, although you'll see it coming, since you've marked your notes. But having built-in flub points only adds to your discomfort.

Of course, there are times when you just can't change the language (I once gave a talk on a visual problem called homonymous hemianopsia). Then the rule is one of rehearse, rehearse, rehearse. With practice, the most difficult pronunciations can be made dramatically easier.

Remember, a nearly impossible phrase such as, "Let's examine the specific statistics in our study that show . . . " can just as easily be communicated with the words, "Let's take a look at the exact numbers in our study that show . . . " Leave Peter Piper and his pickled peppers to first graders.

Keeping Your Audience

Studies have shown that audiences tend to listen to very little of what you say, not out of malice or boredom, but because they can listen—and think—a lot more quickly than you can talk. Once a listener figures out where you are going, he or she will switch to thinking about such weighty matters as whether the dog has been fed, the car is locked, or what time the bank closes and whether you'll finish talking by then.

There are several ways to deal with the sporadic nature of listening and get the audience back on your frequency, especially when you are about to cover an important piece of information or to present a crucial argument.

The Power of "Command" Phrases

Sometimes you give a speech intended to encourage your audience to take action or to adopt your point of view. Command phrases are those that directly demand action or attention-phrases that could be delivered by a commander or a coach to gain that extra effort from those in his or her charge.

If your speech has this kind of purpose, check it for command phrases that will increase the impact of your remarks and impress your audience with the need for action. Here are some command phrases that will recapture a listener's wandering attention:

- It's *essential* that you remember
- If you leave here with only one thought
- Here is the answer you all want to know
- Let me repeat that
- It's absolutely critical to understand that
- Even if you disagree, you'll find that
- Listen to this
- The fact is this
- Regardless of what you've heard before
- It all boils down to one important piece of evidence
- The unavoidable conclusion is this

Command phrases tell an audience to "listen up," since what is to follow is especially important.

Use Ordinal Phrases

Although less dramatic than some of the other language tactics I have been talking about, ordinal phrases serve as important markers in bracketing and organizing the various parts of your speech.

They tell an audience that one area of information has concluded and the next is about to begin, and they give your audience a sense of where you are in the speech. They facilitate a listener's joining you "in progress" to pick up on the essential parts of your message. This is important, since all listeners, despite your best efforts, tend to tune in and out during a speech.

Here are some useful ordinal phrases:

- First of all
- Secondly
- The next area to consider is the fact that
- Another important factor
- In this final portion of my remarks
- Finally
- Last but not least
- Let me leave you with one final thought

Check your speech for the various types of command and ordinal phrases. A speech or presentation missing these elements of language lacks emphasis and clarity.

Effective use of these devices will not only improve an audience member's ability to listen to your message but also give you greater control over which parts of the message your audience will remember most. This is an especially important feature in a speech such as a sales presentation or any message seeking a specific outcome.

Mention Audience Members by Name

Another way to increase listenership and retention of your message is to refer to audience members by name. "As both Alice in engineering and Jared in finance will tell you, . . . " is a sure way not only to get Alice and Jared's attention, but also to present the possibility that you may be making specific reference to others present.

Perhaps the tension you create in an audience is a vestige of the terror we all felt in elementary school when we didn't have the homework and the teacher started calling names, but it works.

While I'm on the subject of naming names, the preceding technique should not be confused with the annoying habit some speakers have of constantly referring to or delivering asides to an audience member that most of those present do not know. While such references suggest a bond between you and that person, they can also create a rift between you and the rest of the audience, an inference that that audience member is privy to some exclusive information or a feeling that you'd rather be chatting with your colleague than giving a speech.

Make Your Talk Audience-Specific

Even if you don't make specific reference to members of your audience, you should still refer directly to your audience to remove any "generic" tone the speech may have. Always mention the name of the organization, not only just as you begin, but also in the text of your speech, especially before your most important points. Phrases such as "each of you" or "every one of us here today" give the talk a more personal tone, as if you were talking as much to individuals as you were to a large group.

Make Numbers Visible

If you say to an audience that twenty million people suffer from alcoholism or some other form of addictive behavior, the reaction of an audience member is likely to be somewhere between "that's mildly interesting" and "so what." If you say, however, that "Incidence figures point to the fact that two of the twenty people present here today will be afflicted by addictive behavior at some point in their lives," the reaction is likely to be a lot more personal, the impact much greater.

The problem with big numbers, especially those up there in the millions, is that we can't visualize them. Thus they have little or no impact on us. The solution is to reduce the numbers to smaller quantities, as in the preceding paragraph, or to paint a word picture of just how big a number you are talking about.

A good example of such a word picture was expressed by the late mathematician Edward Kasner in explaining the size of a number called a googol (one followed by one hundred zeroes). Dr. Kasner explained that the number of raindrops falling on Manhattan in a century is much less than a googol.

Politicians have had considerable difficulty in expressing the seriousness of the massive national debt (over two trillion dollars). From another perspective, politicians have had little difficulty in letting that debt soar, in part because the number two trillion represents an unfathomable quantity. Perhaps this is why you won't hear many of those same politicians increase the impact of that number by stating it as $60,000 for each man, woman, and child, or a debt that is growing at $13,000 per second.

Whether you are talking about sales figures, the life cycle of a product, or any set of numbers of such size as to make your listener's eyes glaze over, get out your calculator and reduce those numbers to a manageable level. Your audience will appreciate it and do a better job of remembering the facts.

What's Your Motivation?

Usually asked of actors to help them develop and intensify a character, what's your motivation is a question you should ask yourself as you review the text of any speech you are about to give.

More specifically, what is the emotional tone or mood you wish to establish in your audience with your remarks? Are you proud of an accomplishment, and do you want to instill that sense of pride in your audience? Is there a sense of urgency or crisis that must be impressed upon your audience in order to move them into action?

Establishing an Emotional Tone to Move Your Audience

Unity, anger, pride, commitment, joy, and even feelings of peace are all possible emotional responses to the language you use. If you are "proud," "excited," "delighted," or "outraged," have you told your audience in just those words? If you want your audience to share in or adopt those feelings as their own, have you said so, again in those specific terms? I call these phrases and words *E-words*.

Speakers who aren't at the podium regularly will often comment to me that they worry about boring their audiences. Using more E-words will energize any presentation. Increasing the emotionality of your talk need not mean that you jump around the stage or rant like a top-forty disc jockey announcing this week's big hit.

It is true that vocal and physical animation can enhance your perceived level of emotionality, but gaining the kind of emotional response you want from an audience begins with your choice of language.

The following E-word list not only illustrates this point but should also be helpful in determining if the emotionality of the language in your speech is compatible with your motivation or the emotional intent you wish to communicate.

E-LEVEL CHART

LOW-TO-NO E-LEVEL	HIGH E-LEVEL
I'm here to talk about . . .	I'm happy to be here to . . .
You have accomplished a lot.	I hope you're proud that . . .
There's much good news.	Let me tell you the most sensational news!
This is an important time.	During this truly great moment
We should all be concerned . . .	Let me assure you, I share your anger at . . .
We are faced with a serious situation	Make no mistake—this is a crisis.
Your immediate involvement . . .	Each of us must act now.
This isn't fair.	This is a gross injustice.
It's imperative that we act.	We can and must take action.
The decision is yours.	Here is what each of you must do.

In each case, the high E-level phrases make use of words that will evoke a greater emotional response from your audience, that is, a sense of crisis, gross injustice, anger, joy, or festivity. Also note the use of the imperative ("must") and superlative ("most sensational") whenever possible and appropriate.

Increasing the use of such E-level phrases, along with specific references to your audience ("each and every one here" instead of the simple plural pronoun "you"), are techniques that should be combined to intensify the impact of your message, making it more personal as well as having the desired emotional effect upon your audience.

Repeat Key Phrases

"That's important, let me repeat that."

Another simple yet effective technique for giving greater emphasis to certain portions of your remarks is to repeat key phrases or important facts or figures. If your speech contains a lot of numbers, pause before and repeat those that are crucial in getting your message across. Such repetition for emphasis will sound this way: "In spite of the increased sales figures, we are still three million dollars behind last year . . . three million dollars."

Watch Your Pronouns

English is a real *man's* language. (Feminists will please note the intended irony here.) One of the most offensive speeches I ever heard was given by the dean of a business college at commencement. I say offensive because, as the dean rambled on about the great sacrifices made by the men in the graduating class, I looked around and noticed that about a third of the class were women.

The problem is that we have a sexist language that most heavily favors the male side of things. Going along with the crowd, linguistically speaking, will not only be offensive to the more astute members of the audience, but you will sometimes end up discussing and explaining your error to the extent that your original message will be obscured. I've often heard sentences such as "If we get the opinion of the best attorney we can find, here is what *he* will say," thereby excluding women from the ranks of those best attorneys.

I've heard executives, usually male, innocently and ignorantly say statements such as, "All you ladies in the home will appreciate . . . ," a phrase likely to offend professional women in any audience. In the Q&A period that often follows a talk, I've heard sexual politics replace the main agenda because of such a slip.

The solution? Watch your pronouns. You will note that this book, whenever appropriate, includes both male and female pronouns. If you have the need to refer to a best attorney or surgeon or any profession or trade, I'd recommend the "he or she" form when your reference requires pronouns. The more socially aware members of any audience will take notice of such inclusion and appreciate the consideration. Male and female pronouns should be used, not as part of a crusade in the name of political correctness, but because no audience can fully listen to a message that in some way offends them.

Keep your audience focused on the message by making certain that your pronouns and your occupational examples are free of sexist references and include women, rather than excluding them as the language so often does in its usual state.

Summary

I agree with that radio commercial I mentioned at the beginning of this chapter: People do judge you by the words you use. Don't put on an act. Keep your language conversational; build emphasis and increase impact with some of the tactics outlined in this chapter. Doing so will better enable your audience to focus on and retain more of the message.

Quick Review:
Improving Your Language Power

1. Keep your language conversational; simpler is better.

2. Know the exact meaning and pronunciation of every word you use. (If you're not sure, look it up!)

3. Don't keep your company or product name a secret.

4. Explain *every* abbreviation or acronym at least once, especially the first time you use it.

5. Use examples and images to which your audience can relate.

6. Make sure your language choices convey the right emotion (pride, anger, joy, commitment) to your audience.

7. Use ordinal-phrases language to tell us where you are in a speech (first of all, second, finally, and so on).

8. Always make at least one specific mention of your audience in any speech.

9. Boil numbers down to visible quantities.

10. It's a sexist language. Watch your pronouns.

Chapter Three

Becoming a Better Listener

At-a-Glance Summary

This chapter is about making you a better listener. Much miscommunication and misunderstanding happens because the listening side of the communication equation is usually ignored.

This chapter includes tactics for improving your ability to ask the right questions, managing the perceptive barriers that impede listening, and taking effective notes.

Becoming a
Better Listener

During the early years of the *Saturday Night Live* telecasts, the late Gilda Radner portrayed a delightfully funny character by the name of Emily Litella. Emily would deliver indignant tirades on such subjects as burp control or moron poverty, only to be reminded that she was supposed to be speaking on birth control or the war on poverty. Once made aware of her error, she ended her tirades abruptly with an embarrassed gaze and an apologetic, "Never mind!"

Emily was funny because she never quite got the message right, even though she expended tremendous energy and passion expressing her concerns. Emily either couldn't hear or just didn't listen, resulting in wasted energy and lots of laughs.

Many of us suffer such lapses in listening, that, while they may not be the stuff of comedy skits, can be a serious barrier to effective communication.

Poor listening can result in costly mistakes on the witness stand, in the media interview, or at the negotiating table. On the other hand, effective listening can give you a distinct advantage as you react to a questioner, listen to a sales presentation, or at any time when remembering exactly what was said is in your best interests.

Learning to listen effectively and clearly is an often-overlooked way to improve your communication skills.

Listening, the act of hearing, perceiving, and retaining spoken information, is by nature an inefficient process. A classic study in listening behavior by Paul Rankin found that we spend nearly half (42 percent) of the business day's communicative activity listening.[1] Other studies of our listening behavior further indicate that within eight hours we forget one third to one half of what we have heard.

---

[1]Rankin, Paul T., "Measurement of the Ability to Understand Spoken Language," unpublished Doctoral Dissertation, Univ. of Michigan, 1926 reported in Adler, R. and Rodman, G. *Understanding Human Communication,* New York: Holt-Rhinehart Winston, 1985, p. 74

Identifying Barriers to Effective Listening

Thinking Too Quickly

The fact is that no one listens all of the time. Rather we engage in a kind of selective listening known to communication theorists as "out-listening." We begin by listening to a speaker and as soon as we figure out what he or she is probably going to say, we tune out and think about something else until we hear a word or phrase that gets our attention once more. This process is repeated over and over again in most listening situations.

You have experienced out-listening if you've ever sat in a meeting, listened to the speaker for a short time, realized you already saw a memo on the subject and immediately went to wondering if you brought your dry-cleaning tickets today. The major problem with out-listening is that it leaves you not with a memory of what the speaker actually said, but a memory of what you *think* he or she probably said.

Can you avoid out-listening? Not entirely, because we think faster than we speak. Most of us talk at somewhere between 120 and 150 words per minute in most situations. Studies indicate, however, that depending upon the subject and the individual, you can process information at anywhere from 500 to 800 words per minute. This disparity between rate of speech and your ability to figure out where the speaker is going is one reason your attention tends to wander.

How Expectations and Perceptions Affect Listening

Another barrier to effective listening is that our expectations shape what we hear. In a song called "The Boxer," Simon and Garfunkel sing, "A man hears what he wants to hear and disregards the rest." This lyric is a good synopsis of how selective we can be when it comes to listening. If we arrive at a meeting expecting to hear bad news, we are more likely to retain that part of the message than other portions that may mitigate the negative aspects of the message.

Perception, or your way of looking at an idea or issue, also shapes how well and how much of the message you will receive and retain. We all listen to the spoken message with a set of experiences and knowledge through which we filter what we hear. This is part of the reason that fifty people, if asked to write a synopsis of a speech they have just heard, will produce fifty different and some widely varying messages.

Avoid Becoming a "Pseudo-Listener"

Sometimes fatigue, or the wish to be somewhere else, can result in pretend or pseudo-listening. As the pseudo-listener you will look attentive, nod in agreement at appropriate times, and may even ask a question at the end of a presentation just to prove you were listening; this, after having sat through the entire presentation being tuned out and deep in thought about something else.

Another kind of pseudo-listening involves a kind of refined out-listening, so that if the speaker challenges the pseudo-listener with a statement such as, "You haven't heard a word I've said," the pseudo-listener can parrot back anywhere from the last sentence to the last paragraph.

The difference between real listening and this brand of pseudo-listening is that this pseudo-listener retains little or nothing of what was said, listening only in case there is the need to parrot back any of the information covered, information that will be forgotten immediately after the meeting ends.

Overcoming the Obstacle of Challenge-Listening

Another flawed form of listening many of us engage in is what I call challenge-listening. Whereas most audience members are there to hear a message, as a challenge-listener, you are there to have an argument based upon your expectations of what the speaker will say. This kind of prejudicially based listening means that you will wait for the speaker to make what you consider an error in content or logic or to use a term that is difficult if not impossible to define.

Once you have found the flaw, there is little reason to listen further; as the typical challenge-listener, you either cease listening altogether and sharpen your fangs for the upcoming question-and-answer period, or listen only for further "evidence" to bolster the argument you now anticipate with such glee. If you engage in challenge-listening, you will not listen to the entire message, only pieces.

If you need to refute the speaker's remarks, you won't be able to do a good job. This is because the challenge-listener's arguments are often one-dimensional and flimsy since they are based on a partial reception of the message.

Instead, try what I call "acceptance listening." This means that when you anticipate disagreeing with a speaker, make a conscious decision not to agree with but to "accept" his or her entire statement without engaging in silent rebuttal as does the "challenge listener."

Challenge listening can be seen in what passes for political debates in this culture. Typically, candidates avoid listening to and responding to the substance of each other's remarks in favor of waiting for an opponent to utter a phrase that will trigger a planned response in the hope of gaining the most media attention and thereby becoming the perceived victor.

Senator Lloyd Bentsen's now-famous debate rejoinder to then vice-presidential candidate Dan Quayle, "You're no Jack Kennedy . . . ," is a good example of challenge-listener tactics. We all remember the remark but few if any remember the context of the remark, because it was intended as a personal attack rather than as an attempt to deal with a broader issue.

Once your focus becomes so narrow as to wait for the slightest misstatement or undefinable term, you very well may have missed the point of the message and even the opportunity to engage in a more substantive rebuttal.

Managing Your "Automatic Shutoff"

Have you ever not attended a meeting because a quick look at the agenda brought you to the rapid conclusion that it would be a waste of your time? Sometimes you will sit through a speaker's presentation thinking the same thing, but since leaving would cause too big a disruption or be noticed by too many of your peers, you decide instead to take mental rather than physical leave. In other words, you employ a mode of nonlistening I call "automatic shutoff."

If you add this behavior to the degree of out-listening you normally do in any setting, be assured that you will retain virtually nothing of what is being said. Automatic shutoff behavior can take place not only because you find the topic unpalatable; perhaps it's the wrong time of day or you have a plane to catch or it's your fifth meeting of the day.

Whatever the reason, engaging the automatic shutoff means that you'll miss out on virtually the entire message, even if it contains some interesting or important ideas.

How to Avoid Being Distracted

"Is that a sports coat or did you fall through an awning on the way to this meeting?"

Sometimes you will be distracted by the speaker to the extent that you find focusing on the message difficult. You may remember that in school, if a teacher had a mannerism, students would make a point of counting how many times that mannerism occurred rather than focusing on the lesson being taught. (My high-school algebra teacher once said the word "particularly" forty-five times in one hour.) The poor listening habits I employed at that time enabled me to remember that extraordinarily useless piece of information while retaining little of the mathematical information covered.

Focusing on the style of the speaker impedes your ability to listen. Whether you focus on the presentation, as in the language used, the appropriateness of the topic, the length of the message, the speaker's appearance, voice, or nonverbals, you are taking valuable attention away from the message itself.

As you listen, you may conclude that the speaker is selling sizzle rather than steak or that there is too little substance in the message, but you can't even make that decision unless you focus on the message itself rather than on the stylistic elements that accompany it.

Control Your Listening Environment

Eliminate or minimize environmental distractions. If there is too much noise or visual distraction for you to listen effectively, politely suggest that the meeting be moved or the noise be stopped. If you, as a motivated listener, are having difficulty listening, so will anyone else present and there is little point in continuing.

Remember that noise can be visual as well as auditory. For example, if you are listening to a speaker in a hotel ballroom while in the background a work crew is quietly filling a net with balloons and hoisting them to the ceiling for a later celebration, you and other members of the audience are more likely to be captivated by this visually interesting activity than by the innards of the quarterly financial report.

Have the distraction stopped. Always attend to the environment so you can focus on the message, even if it requires a momentary disruption of the proceedings. You'll hope that the speaker will have read my words on handling distractions, and your having to take action will be unnecessary.

Get a Good Seat

If you are listening to a presentation in a room with a hundred other audience members and you're sitting in the back row, you have severely limited your ability to listen effectively by increasing your physical distance from the speaker.

Anytime anyone in that audience receives notice of a phone message, you will know about it. If anyone leaves early or arrives late, you will see their entrance or exit and perhaps be prone to speculate as to the reason for these movements. If an audience member drops his or her notes or falls asleep, if coffee or refreshments are being delivered, you will be more aware of it than anyone in the room—all because you're sitting in the back.

If listening is important, sit as close to the front as you can. In so doing, you reduce not only the distance between you and the speaker, but you eliminate most if not all of the distractions referred to here. You should be close enough to the speaker to engage his or her eye contact if at all possible.

You will notice that some of your best listening takes place in a one-on-one conversation. This is because most of the listening distractions or interferences I have been talking about are not present. Even if there is a large audience present or you are at a large meeting (more than a dozen participants, for example), by positioning yourself close enough to engage in eye contact with the speaker, you simulate the conversational setting and reduce the level of environmental distraction.

Furthermore, if you can see the speaker's eyes and he or she can see yours, just as in a conversation, it becomes highly difficult to tune out. This way you are virtually forced into paying attention, even if you might welcome a distraction or break from the subject at hand.

Take Brief Notes

Have you ever taken notes at a meeting or lecture only to throw them away later, even though they were quite detailed and required considerable effort to compile? If you have, it's likely that your notes lacked any kind of emphasis and, while voluminous, were incomplete.

The fact is (shorthand takers excepted) that you can't write down everything a speaker says. Any attempt to do so results in your writing while the speaker is still talking, which means you can't be fully listening because your perceptual focus is on trying to produce an accurate written record.

Writing extended definitions also gives little clue as to the context of the material, or the speaker's degree of vocal emphasis. I recommend that you take notes to enhance listening and retention, but I also recommend that you do so sparingly, writing down key phrases or numbers, contextual notations (for example, "numbers cited refer to state government"), or questions to be asked later.

You should also have a way of denoting important items, such as a simple check mark. At the end of the presentation, you should end up with a brief summary of what was said in phrase form, with important items noted and a list of questions if appropriate.

Just as in preparing a speech outline, it is unimportant to have the exact words of the speaker written down, but rather a list of his or her ideas in phrase form, as well as a knowledge of which ideas or pieces of information were emphasized.

Enhancing Your Listening Environment

Be Aware of Your Own Expectations and Perceptions

If you anticipate that a speaker is going to make you angry or has been offensive in the past with other audiences, also be aware that effective listening will be more difficult if you do not resolve to "listen through" those aspects of the material that you find problematical.

If terms or ideas are offensive or provocative in some other way, you might want to try writing down your expectations in advance as an ideas list and to try making another ideas list during the speaker's presentation with the intention of later comparing these ideas or areas of disagreement. In this manner, you will have your listening focused on developing an ideas list, which will counteract your tendency to sit there waiting for the speaker to fulfill your negative expectations.

Be Idea-Receptive

We have all been stuck at command-performance meetings, those at which your presence was politically expedient but otherwise a waste of your time—or so you thought.

The decision to attend but not to participate, or to be only physically present, is to shut out the possibility that you will gain any information of substance or use. You might be wrong, and in not being idea-receptive, you might never know it.

Once you have made the decision to attend a meeting or a presentation, set aside the notion of how nonproductive you expect the session to be and listen receptively. Just as with the social occasion that you dreaded attending and ended up enjoying, meetings and presentations for which you harbor advance negative feelings can be surprisingly informative or useful if you remain idea-receptive.

Ask the Right Questions

Whenever possible or appropriate, ask questions of the speaker in any meeting. By the right questions, I mean that you should ask three primary types:

1. *Repetition questions,* which are intended to have the speaker review a statement or position

2. *Probe questions,* which enable you to examine the perspectives and background of the speaker's remarks

3. *Focus questions,* which ask the speaker to better define what he or she considers most important for the listener to remember

Ask Repetition Questions

Questions that ask the speaker to review a part of his or her message should be open-ended and nonconfrontational. For example, your question should be something like, "Would you review your remarks regarding the need for a price increase?" rather than, "I don't see why we need a price increase, could you go over your reasoning once more?" With the open-ended repetition question, you will get a replay of the material that is important to you without putting the speaker on the defensive.

If the speaker resists, your response should be that you would like the repetition for clarification. If you ask for clarification while expressing your disagreement, you'll simply put the speaker on the defensive and not get the same version of the information you are seeking to clarify.

Once again, your goal should be to heighten the retention of spoken material through effective listening rather than through confrontation. A defensive speaker is not as likely to help you achieve your purpose of better understanding.

Ask Probe Questions

Probe questions are brief and to-the-point requests that ask for the reasoning behind statements. They should be directed toward parts of the message you want to know more about, or to those areas you feel the speaker has not fully explained. Such questions should be open-ended, such as, "What did you mean when you said our immediate environment?"

Probe questions should be used to flesh out and amplify a speaker's comments and to gain insight into the speaker's reasoning. Their use can lessen the misunderstanding that can occur in any setting. Asking probe questions should be a part of your job as an effective listener.

Ask Focus Questions

As the name implies, focus questions ask the speaker to get more specific and help you discern that which the speaker considers most important. You will have your own conclusions as to what was most important in any speaker's remarks, but these thoughts represent your perception and not those of the speaker.

The typical listener can always reiterate his or her own perceptions, but the truly effective listener is able to retain the message from the speaker's perspective as well.

Focus questions ask the speaker, "What aspect of your message is most important?" or "What do you believe to be the strongest or most compelling reason that we should adopt your plan?" or "Could you briefly summarize what you would like us to get out of your remarks?" With all of these focus questions, you are asking the speaker to be specific in clarifying the aspects of the message he or she considered important.

In meetings, conferences, and negotiation sessions, the strategic use of repetition, probe, and focus questions should become an internalized method in enhancing your ability to listen.

Careful notation of the speaker's responses to your questions will also serve as a listening guide that is less a product of your own biases and more an accurate reflection of that speaker's intended message.

Summary

Although the vast emphasis in communication skills is on the delivery of the message, listening remains an important and usually overlooked part of the equation. Remove as many as possible of the physical and psychological barriers that surround any communicative encounter and enhance your retention by taking notes and asking the right questions.

Sharpening your listening skills with the techniques presented in this chapter will enable you to perform at a definite advantage in any situation where a precise recollection of what was said is important.

Quick Review:
Becoming a Better Listener

1. Understand that no one listens all the time.
2. Don't let your expectations cloud your ability to listen.
3. Avoid challenge-listening, in which you seek not to hear what's being said, but to build a case against the speaker.
4. You can't listen effectively if you're angry.
5. Don't "dismiss" a speaker because you think you know what he or she will say. (I call this the automatic shutoff.)
6. Always sit near the speaker.
7. Take brief summary notes for later review.
8. Be idea-receptive.
9. Ask questions.
10. Seek repetition of important points.

Part Two

PREPARING AND DELIVERING POWERFUL SPEECHES AND PRESENTATIONS

Chapter Four

Speechwriting
How to Create a Powerful Message

At-a-Glance Summary

This chapter presents a step-by-step process for creating and writing a successful, powerful speech, from selecting your topic to writing the conclusion. You learn how to get and keep an audience on your side, whether you are presenting a short message or a major address.

Speechwriting: How to Create a Powerful Message

Among the words that strike fear in the hearts of so many, ranking right up there with the Internal Revenue Service's deceptively cheery and somehow almost lyrical, "Dear Taxpayer, we have selected your return . . . ," are the words, "We'd like you to give a speech on . . ."

Many of us barely hear the words that follow, but slip into the trancelike state we assume in the dentist's chair or at some other moment of impending pain or displeasure. Our anxiety is not only about getting up in front of an audience, but also about assembling some remarks that will dazzle them.

Many speakers start out aiming to dazzle and end up giving a highly effective verbal sedative. This happens not so much because creating a speech is all that difficult, but because it's an activity that most of us seldom perform. Thus we commit major errors and inefficiencies in the process, leading to a poor product.

Why a Well-Structured Speech Is a Powerful Speech

It's a lot tougher to get a spoken message than it is a written message across to an audience. Anyone who sits down to read has just decided to become a captive audience member. When someone reads an essay or even a novel, he or she has made a conscious decision to do so. The reader will adjust the light, find a comfortable chair, and even turn off the stereo in order to focus on the printed word. Listening to a speech is a much more passive process in which you get to choose your level of attention from total—to none at all.

Readers are much more tolerant of boring or ill-constructed messages. How many times have you heard someone say of a novel, "I've finished only fifty pages and I'm not quite sure what it's about"? Some of us (this writer excluded) even have the patience to finish an entire book and then say, "I really hated it."

Speakers don't have the luxury of tolerant audiences who will hang on to see if things get interesting. If your speech isn't interesting right away, you've lost much of your audience and won't get them back. Also, audiences don't arrange the speaking environment as they do the reading environment. Instead, it's done for them. And that environment is often filled with distractions—everything from uncomfortable chairs to rooms that are too hot or too cold, food being served (or not being served), other audience members, coughing and sneezing, erratic sound systems, and so forth.

As if all these distractions weren't enough, all of us can think faster than any speaker can talk. This fact sets up an inevitable cycle referred to by communication theorists as "out-listening"—a process in which we all engage when listening to a speaker. This means that we tend to listen until we figure out what the speaker is saying and then let some distraction take over (Was that thunder? Did I close my car windows?) and then drift back to the speaker to see if he or she is saying anything worthwhile. If the speech is well structured, you'll tend to go back until the next distraction takes you even momentarily in another direction. If the speech lacks a definite structure, you won't be able to tune back in and are more likely to give up listening altogether.

The powerful speech—the one that holds the audience's attention—is not just the one that's well written or forcefully delivered (which helps). The powerful spoken message is structured to compensate for distractions and the out-listening process. It is structured not just to capture and maintain audience attention but to let those who have wandered easily rejoin the speech in progress. By following the speechwriting steps in this chapter, you'll be able to better capture and hold the attention of your audience. Your audience will retain more of your message because your speech will be more likely to capture their immediate attention and let them know exactly which aspects of the topic you will be covering. Your speech will also let them know along the way where you are in your message and will provide a clear signal that you are ending your speech, so that they can focus on your "take-away" message.

This chapter takes you through a step-by-step process that will eliminate or greatly reduce those errors and inefficiencies and get you closer to dazzling your audience with the power of your message.

As You Begin . . .

First of all, don't sit there over a yellow pad muttering or silently pondering the question over and over again, "What should I say first?" This is completely nonproductive and usually results in hopelessly boring and usually insincere lines such as, "It is indeed an honor and a privilege to be here tonight to talk about . . ."

So for now, forget the question of what to say first (it will be covered later), and let's work on a more important beginning step . . .

Deciding What to Talk About

In some instances, the topic may be predetermined by circumstance or necessity. Otherwise, selecting a topic can be the most time-consuming part of writing a speech unless you consider these issues:

What would you *like to talk about?*

A constant goal of this book is make you a more comfortable and thus a more successful communicator. One key to being comfortable is actually having an interest in the topic you select. Can you talk to an audience effectively about a topic you don't like or believe in or don't know much about? Certainly, but it takes greater effort, is more difficult to research, and your audience will sense your discomfort.

Step #1: Select the Topic

Begin your search for a topic by making a list of five to ten subjects you enjoy talking about and edit the list according to the following criteria:

How long do they expect you to speak?

Find out how much time will be available for your speech and select a topic accordingly. This will shorten your list considerably. Too many speakers select their topic with reasoning such as they've talked about the subject before, and/or they still have their notes from last time—the only problem being that last time was a forty-five-minute sales presentation, and this is a ten-minute speech at a Rotary Club luncheon.

Consider the Audience

Look at your topic list in reference to these questions: What is the level of audience enthusiasm for your topic? Does the audience know more about the topic than you do?—a good reason to choose another topic. Will your information be genuinely useful to them? Will it be information they haven't heard before?

Where to Find Speech Material

If you have an on-line personal computer, any of the various on-line services will provide you with a wealth of topics, ideas, and information. In addition to the index materials at your local library, scanning the table of contents of a weekly news magazine can be a good start. The articles are usually of interest to a wide segment of the public and are suitable for a similarly wide range of audiences. To develop your topic-idea list, jot down each article title or a phrase that summarizes the theme of the article.

Step #2: Write an Idea List

Once you have settled upon a topic, take your topic idea and free-associate with it. This means writing down a list of ideas that come to mind as you think about your probable topic. Keep your list brief, in word or phrase form—it should contain at least ten but not more than twenty items.

The reason for the wide latitude in the length of your idea list is that some topics are easier to develop than others. For example, scientific or highly technical areas are likely to be limited in scope, whereas general topics would produce a longer list.

I have set the upper limit of the idea list at twenty because, in my experience, once an idea list gets any longer than this, the ideas become too distant from the original topic to be useful in creating your speech.

Here is an example of an idea list I generated on the topic "acid rain":

- Cloud content
- Dead trees
- Other causes
- Cars
- Specific evidence
- Clean Air Act
- Individual responses

- Paint damage
- Greenhouse effect
- Measuring acid rain
- Acid rain defined
- Power plants
- International sources
- Corporate responsibility

Warning: The idea list can sometimes produce an idea that causes you to change your entire topic. For example, in the preceding list I came up with the idea "greenhouse effect," which might easily be a topic unto itself.

If you spot an idea on your list that you'd rather talk about instead of your original topic, just generate another idea list using that new idea as a starting point and you're on your way to a better speech than you originally planned.

Step #3: Choose Your Showcase Idea

Reviewing your idea list, choose the idea that, above all others, you want to get across to your audience. I call this the *showcase idea,* because it is the idea to which all the other parts of your talk will point, just like the spotlights in a showcase.

For example, while I started out with the general topic, "acid rain," I decided that the topic was in need of definition, and that became my showcase idea: to define what acid rain is. Once you have chosen your showcase idea, write it down in phrase or sentence form. In this case, the showcase idea would be: "What exactly is acid rain?"

Step #4: Choose Your Spotlight Ideas

Spotlight ideas support your showcase idea by supplying further information that points toward or illuminates your showcase idea. So your next step is to choose two, three, or even four ideas that support or are most closely related to your showcase idea and list them. The reason for the variance in how many you choose is dependent upon two factors.

1. *The complexity of the topic.* Since some topics are more difficult to explain, you may want to limit yourself to two spotlight ideas. If your topic is easily understood, you may want to choose three or four spotlight ideas.

2. *The amount of time available for the speech.* Simply stated, the more spotlight ideas, the longer the speech. A typical speech with one showcase idea and two or three spotlight ideas will last anywhere from five to seven minutes once the beginning and ending are added.

To build an even longer speech, add another showcase idea and another set of spotlight ideas. Using this system, you can easily and systematically create a speech of one-half hour or even longer. Writing even a lengthy speech becomes a matter of creating a series of smaller units instead of the unmanageable task it can seem to be.

Step #5: Write the Text or Body of Your Speech

To begin creating the text of your speech, write the idea that you most want to get across to your audience—the *showcase idea*—in sentence form. Next, write down each of your spotlight ideas (ideas that support or amplify the showcase idea) and construct a brief essay on each spotlight idea (about 250 words).

Here is a sample of how the body of a speech on acid rain would look after following these *exact* steps (note that it is numbered II, because this is actually the middle of the speech):

II.   *Showcase Idea:* Fully appreciating the effects of acid rain on our environment begins with an understanding of exactly what acid rain is. Acid rain is defined as . . .

Spotlight Idea #1. Sources of Acid Rain
Now that you know what acid rain is, the next logical question is, Where does it come from? While some acidity may occur in nature, we make the rest of it! That's right—the major source of manmade acid rain is found in sulfur dioxide emissions (SO_2), from the burning of fossil fuels, especially high-sulfur coal. Other ways we produce acid rain include . . .

Spotlight Idea #2. Acid rain affects you personally.
Just because you can't see it doesn't mean it isn't there. Acid rain affects everything from the finish on your car to the size of your electric bill. Let's talk about car finishes . . .

If you are creating a speech that is entirely scripted, this series of brief essays, all of which highlight your showcase idea, will make up the body of your talk. A good rule of thumb is to have a minimum of two to a maximum of four spotlight ideas per showcase idea. A speech can also have more than one showcase idea, but if you get beyond two or three, remember that you run the risk of having your speech lack the focus that allows an audience to come away with a specific message. Aside from time constraints, the complexity of the topic and the attention span of your audience should be the major factors in determining the number of showcase and supporting spotlight ideas your speech will contain.

By following the steps outlined here and keeping in mind that the average speaker talks at about 125 words per minute, you should be able to plan the length of your speech with some precision. (In planning the length of your talk, don't forget to allow time for a question-and-answer session when appropriate or expected.)

If you prefer to deliver the speech from an outline instead of a script, I still recommend scripting the showcase idea, a part of the speech that you'll want to get *exactly* right and then list a few key phrases for each spotlight idea.

Here is how such an outline might look for the topic "acid rain":

II.   *Showcase Idea:* Fully appreciating the effects of acid rain on our environment begins with an understanding of just what acid rain is. Acid rain is defined as . . .

Spotlight Idea #1. Sources of acid rain
- SO_2 emissions
- Fossil-fuel combustion
- Auto emissions
- High-sulfur coal
- Natural sources

Spotlight Idea #2: How acid rain affects you
- Auto finishes
- Drinking water
- Plant life
- The economy

Text vs. Outlines

The question of whether to use a script or an outline should be answered by your level of experience as a speaker and by your knowledge of the topic. Once you have practiced and familiarized yourself with a scripted speech, you may wish to convert it into outline form.

In preparing an outline based upon your script, include not only key phrases as I have done here, but also be sure to include any pieces of information you have a hard time remembering, such as names, dates, formulas, or statistics. The outline should be used to keep your ideas on track and in sequence. Generally, the more you know about the topic and the more familiar you are with your script, the less information you'll need on your outline.

Step #6: Write the Introduction

Now that you have completed the middle or body of your speech, you'll have a considerable advantage in writing an introduction because you now know what you are going to say.

Most speakers fail to realize the crucial nature of an introduction in getting an audience focused and on their side. The introduction should be viewed as a kind of verbal curtain you draw back to reveal your showcase idea. Your job as a speechwriter at this point is to make them wonder what's behind the curtain.

Get to Them Right Away

In that first moment, as a speaker you have a unique advantage in that everyone is focused on you and your forthcoming message. It is important to get to your audience immediately in order to maximize attention to and retention of that message. As you begin your speech, don't waste your time and theirs with such words as, "Today I am going to speak to you about . . ." You're standing at a podium facing an audience and everyone present can surmise that you are going to talk about something. So dispense with the typical bland opening words and begin your message immediately.

Set the Emotional Tone

Do you want your audience to be amused? Relieved? Guilty? Anxious? Or even angry? Emotional tone is set by language, so choose language in keeping with the emotional tone you want to set.

For example, in a talk on environmental issues you might begin by saying, "Every member of this audience is guilty of a crime . . ." and then continue to talk about some of the negative impacts that all of us have upon the environment. With this statement, you have certainly gotten the attention of those in your audience, and you may have even startled them a bit with your controversial opening statement.

The emotional goal of your introduction should suit *your* purposes. Usually, a speaker attempts to write and deliver a feel-good or a "warm and fuzzy" introduction. If an amiable opening suits the speech or the audience, go ahead, but remember that you'll be sacrificing memorability.

In addition to setting the emotional tone of your speech and building audience interest, the major purpose of the introduction is to lead the listener to your showcase idea.

Continuing my "Every member of this audience is guilty of a crime" statement, I could then introduce my showcase idea—defining acid rain: "But it's easy to see how you could be guilty of a crime when you don't have any understanding of it. I am referring to acid rain, an environmental problem to which we all contribute, whether we're aware of it or not. Acid rain is . . ."

Types of Introductions

Following are some specific types of speech introductions to use as a guide in writing an introduction for your speech, along with some tips on how to make them work for you.

QUOTATIONS Use a quotation when you come across something so moving or irresistibly clever that you have to include it in your opening remarks. It should imply that you are well read and have done some research to unearth a particular pearl of wisdom for the delight of your audience. This may or may not be true, but it's the impression your audience will get with the use of a well-selected quotation.

A couple of cautions about using quotations: First and foremost, get it right and double-check it from a reliable source. Having a quotation "just a little bit off" will undo any positive impressions you had hoped to make by using it in the first place. Also, don't overintroduce a quote with statements such as, "With his usual degree of eloquence, the late and great statesman Adlai E. Stevenson once moved an audience by telling them . . . " Such long-winded phrases prior to a quotation diminish its impact by reducing any element of surprise that existed.

Either open with the quotation itself, followed by a brief phrase such as, "With these words, Adlai Stevenson . . ." or, if you want to use the author's name up front, say, "Adlai Stevenson once said . . ."

Second, *don't ever use someone else's words or wit as your own, without an acknowledgment.* Even if you do so inadvertently, the damage to your credibility can be severe. If someone finds out, *and they will,* the whole purpose for your message is likely to be obscured in the oft-justified furor that results from the appearance of plagiarism.

If you choose to begin your speech with a quotation, be certain to avoid the obvious. For example, you don't want to find yourself speaking to a group of historians and beginning with an obvious statement such as " 'Four score and seven years ago'—with these words a great American president . . ."; or before a group of baseball fans, quoting Yogi Berra's endearing but hopelessly overused, "It ain't over till it's over."

The use of quotations should reveal you to be a speaker of diligence and insight who has the generosity of spirit to recognize that others may have had interesting thoughts on your subject even before you did.

ILLUSTRATIVE STORIES In this world of scripts and teleprompters and presentations littered with slick computer-generated graphics, it is always refreshing to hear a speaker say, "Before I begin my remarks, I'd like to tell you a story." Perhaps it's a collective wish to return to a simpler time, but it's a line that invariably commands an audience's attention.

The first rule at a moment like this is to captivate, not to disappoint. Your story should be dramatic or touching, if that suits your purpose, and memorable to the extent that those present will want to repeat it.

Your story should be brief, as a general rule not much more than 10 percent of the length of your talk, and should have a direct link to your topic. Otherwise, the main reason you are there, to give a speech, becomes obscured by the entertainment provided by your story.

Following is an example of an illustrative story used at the beginning of a speech on corporate citizenship.

> Just before last Christmas, a woman came into our central-billing office with a cash payment for an overdue electric bill. As the bedraggled customer counted out the last of the one hundred twenty-three dollars and eighty-three cents she owed us, she made it known that this was her children's Christmas fund, but that she wanted to start the holiday season with her debts paid.

> Our representative asked the woman to wait in the reception area for a few minutes, and in that time, took up a collection right there in the office and returned that mom's Christmas money—a spontaneous gift from our employees to someone in need.

> More than our organized community activities and planned events I'll be telling you about, that moment tells you the kind of people we are at American United Power and why I am proud . . .

And so the illustrative story introduces the idea that American United Power is a good corporate citizen.

A question that arises with regard to an illustrative story is whether it needs to reflect an actual event or can be something you simply composed. The answer is either. While you may wish to use an event from your own experience, sometimes modifying or even embellishing a story can increase its impact. You may also want to modify a story to obscure the identity of its participants.

What's most important if you find yourself adjusting the content of an illustrative story or even creating one is that you not mislead your audience when you have done so. Tell an audience with words such as, "While the characters in my story may not be real, what happened to them has happened to all of us at one time or another . . ." or "While I've changed that story a bit, it still represents . . ."

Otherwise, especially in an adversarial situation, be assured that someone will track down your story and attempt to prove it false. If your illustrative story is modified or fictional, make sure you say so.

SPUR-OF-THE-MOMENT REMARKS   An effective device for getting into your speech is the so-called "spur-of-the-moment" or "off-the-cuff" remark. I say so-called because such spontaneity requires careful planning. Following are some typical kinds of remarks.

1. A little-known fact about the group to whom you're speaking

2. A complimentary reference to your host

3. A reference to a very recent and/or very topical news event

Perhaps the best summary of how to handle spur-of-the-moment remarks is the story of Winston Churchill, who, when asked the secret of his ability to make spontaneous remarks with such ease and eloquence, responded, "I practice them!"

DEFINITIONS OF KEY TERMS   If you don't have time to hunt down the perfect quote, or are uncomfortable making spur-of-the-moment remarks, you might consider defining a term to start your speech.

Far from a last resort, this device is particularly effective with a more sophisticated audience and works well if your talk is centered on a complex or technical topic or a term that is often mentioned but seldom defined.

One cautionary note: If you choose to open with a definition, be careful as to its source. Is the source well recognized and/or respected by the audience, or will the source of the definition merely stir up controversy?

If you choose to use your own definition, with yourself as the source, do so because you have sufficient authority to arrive at your own definition. Otherwise, it looks as if you are going your own way because you had neither the time nor the ability to do more.

RHETORICAL QUESTIONS   The rhetorical question presents a prime opportunity for one of the more awkward moments in public speaking. We have all heard speakers begin with questions such as, "How many of you have thought of visiting a tiny Caribbean island on your next vacation?"

There are a couple of flaws in this approach. The first is that *this* and *all* rhetorical questions, by their nature, create a moment of conflict as the audience wonders whether you want an answer to the question, a raised hand, or a polite affirmative nod. In those crucial opening seconds, when you should be capturing the undivided attention of your audience, you have confused them.

Aside from the momentary awkwardness, there is another danger, pointed out by the lawyer's old dictum about never asking a question to which you don't already know the answer. If the question is met with blank stares, or only four of two hundred hands are hesitatingly raised, you have just unwittingly made it apparent to all present that most of your audience doesn't care about your topic. With your own introductory words, you have created an uphill battle.

If you insist upon the rhetorical question as an introduction, make certain that you are totally sure of your audience's response.

ANECDOTES   Another type of introduction for the risk-takers among us is telling an anecdote or funny story. This can be highly effective; but whether you want to use it is a judgment call, with this author voting in the negative. I realize that there are speech occasions where beginning with some kind of joke is customary and even expected. In such cases, I'd keep the story short.

Further, if forced into the situation of beginning your talk with some witticisms, don't make the mistake of telling your audience that you will begin with "a funny story." Part of the key to getting a laugh is the element of surprise, which you will have sacrificed by letting an audience know your intentions.

Assuming you have a choice as to whether to begin your speech with an anecdote, I advise against it for several reasons. First of all, humor has an incredible capacity to amuse, and an even greater capacity to offend. As one who has done thousands of hours of public speaking, I am still amazed at the ability of the listener to misconstrue or excerpt pieces of the speaker's remarks, completely out of context, and take offense.

Second, there is always the possibility that your funny story will be a dud. This has happened to most of us, and it doesn't feel good. Public humiliation is a horrible feeling, be it in front of an audience of six or six hundred.

On the other hand, if your anecdote is received with thunderous gales of laughter, at some point—assuming your purpose is other than to deliver a comic monologue—you are reduced to saying something like, "And now to be serious . . . ," a line guaranteed to get any listener to tune you out.

HOW LONG AN INTRODUCTION?   Depending on the duration and depth of your speech, your introduction should last anywhere from one and a half minutes for a five-to-seven-minute speech, to three or four minutes for a speech of fifteen minutes or longer.

Be certain that in the introduction to a longer speech, with more than one showcase idea, you inform your audience that you will be covering several aspects of the topic. Mention each of your showcase ideas in that introduction. This way, an audience is prepared for a longer speech and has a good idea of where you are going throughout the speech.

Here is an example of an introduction to a longer speech with multiple showcase ideas.

> For most of us, understanding anything about the national debt is right up there with quantum mechanics when it comes to making sense of the issue. But I think I can make the dismal science come alive or at least make it personal for you by looking at one subject from three distinct points of view: First, why the numbers keep getting larger; second, what they mean to each and every one here today; and finally, a novel solution that just may make this coming crisis go away!

The point is to accomplish the purposes of an introduction—getting attention, setting the emotional tone, and introducing the showcase idea—without overshadowing the message itself.

Step #7: Write Your Conclusion

Speeches have been compared to relationships in that they are easy enough to begin but exceedingly difficult to end, or at least to end gracefully. I have often seen speakers end with a shrug, or by limply asking the host, "Can I sit down now?" In such cases, the speech hasn't ended, the speaker has just given up. By following a few simple steps, you can easily avoid such awkward moments and bring your speech to a smooth, successful conclusion.

Beginning the Ending

Since audiences tend to tune in and out during any speech, you'll want to provide a strong indicator that they should tune back in for the ending.

The best way of getting them to do so is with a concluding marker phrase that can vary widely but is typified by the ever-popular but overused, "In conclusion . . ."

If you're stuck, that's okay, but do try to use a variation of this phrase for your concluding marker.

Here are a few examples:

"As you can see from what I've said . . . "

"The remarks I've made today point in one direction . . ."

"I've enjoyed speaking with you today, and as I conclude, there is one particular point I'd like you to think about. . . ."

These concluding-marker phrases are significant to your audience because each of them refers to your message in the past tense. Once you begin with that marker phrase, don't mislead them by introducing further or new information.

How Long a Conclusion?

You shouldn't talk for more than two additional minutes if your talk is less than fifteen minutes long, nor more than three if your talk is more than fifteen minutes long. If you go any longer at this point, you'll lose your audience and your impact.

Writing the Conclusion

Many speakers seem to "hit the wall" creatively as they complete writing the last spotlight idea of the body of their speech. Your conclusion is too important and too memorable a part of your speech to throw away, so do some writing at this point. A strong conclusion will increase the memorability and impact of your speech, whereas a weak one will greatly diminish the effectiveness of your message.

Begin your conclusion with a concluding marker phrase and make certain that your final words accomplish one of the following goals:

1. *Summarize the showcase idea(s) of your speech.*

   Example: "In my look at the AIDS epidemic today, I have considered three areas: treatment, counseling, and research. With the information I have provided, you can readily see the very clear need for . . . "

2. *Repeat and reinforce the spotlight point that you would most like remembered.*

   Example: "Although I've covered several aspects of the AIDS epidemic, I'd like each and every one of you to remember that until we are closer to a cure, counseling people with AIDS remains an area of utmost importance."

3. *When possible or appropriate, a good technique in concluding a speech is to refer back to or repeat a part of your introduction:*

   Example: "As I said in the beginning, Dr. Helen Caldecott's statement on the horror of nuclear war that 'the living will envy the dead' is no exaggeration. I hope that I have left each of you with a deeper understanding of how her words only begin to describe this peril."

Using Linkage Words

In addition to the concluding marker phrases, a minor but important part of the speech-writing process is to insert so-called linkage or transitional phrases at various parts of your now completely written speech. These are words that bring you from one part of the speech to the next—from introduction to showcase idea, from showcase to spotlight idea, and from the final spotlight idea to your conclusion.

For example, from the introduction to the showcase idea, a linkage word might be "specifically" or the phrase "to be specific." From one spotlight idea to the next, a linkage phrase might be an ordinal phrase such as, "first of all," or "second," or "another point you should remember. . . ."

Such phrases are used naturally by the experienced speaker because they make such sense in organizing the speech for you and your audience. They are also easy to forget, however, because they are not usually considered a part of the speech itself. Linkage words also serve as signals for your audience that you are about to make another point. Linkage words and phrases serve as a kind of verbal strobe light, essential in recapturing the attention of those in any audience whose attention wanders.

Linkage words and phrases should be inserted at the following places in the text of your speech:

1. After your introduction, just before the showcase idea
2. At the beginning of each spotlight idea
3. At the start of your conclusion

to help your speech flow smoothly.

Here are some effective linkage words and phrases:

- Specifically
- First of all, second, and so on
- Another important point
- Most important
- Above all, remember that . . .
- Let's examine another issue . . .
- I'll leave you with this thought . . .
- As I wrap things up

The Final Word

Consistent with the viewpoint that a speech should be looked at essentially as an organized conversation, the last words of your speech should contain nothing more than a simple statement such as, "I've enjoyed talking with you today, and I look forward to meeting you again." Use some variation of this as your final words—thank them for inviting you, and then *stop talking!*

Quick Review:
Creating a Powerful Message

1. A well-delivered, well-received speech begins with a topic that is of *definite* interest to you and *possible* interest to your audience.

2. Grab audience attention *immediately,* with your first words.

3. Humorous introductions usually work against you, even if you get a laugh.

4. Don't use quotations to seem learned; use them because they work!

5. Don't ever use someone else's words without acknowledgment.

6. Define key terms, even if most of your audience already understands them. (Some of those present may not.)

7. Don't open your speech with a question; sometimes you get an answer you weren't expecting.

8. Arrange your ideas so that you finish up on your most important one. (Audiences tend to remember what they heard last.)

9. Once you say words such as, "in conclusion," don't talk any longer than two minutes more.

10. Check your outline for linkage words, the phrases that lead you from one part of your speech to the next.

Chapter Five

Audience Analysis

Making Sure Your Message Hits Home

At-a-Glance Summary

This chapter helps you tailor your remarks to a specific audience, a frequently overlooked way to dramatically increase the impact of your message.

Audience Analysis: Making Sure Your Message Hits Home

The importance of considering and including each specific audience while creating a speech cannot be overstated. If you make the mistake so many speakers make and ignore your specific audience by simply delivering a generic, nonaudience-specific message, your audience will return the favor by ignoring or quickly forgetting about you and what you had to say. On the other hand, if you take into account such factors as their demographics, issues perspectives, and interests as you prepare and deliver a speech, they will return the favor with increased attention to and retention of your remarks.

Matching the Topic to the Audience

Even before you begin the task of including the audience within the speech, you should first consider the question of whether the topic of your speech is compatible with the audience. For example, the most eloquent among us would be hard pressed to deliver a talk on the latest trends in midwifery practice to a group of senior citizens or recent changes in deep-sea fishing technology to a group of Midwestern corn farmers. In either case, the audience response is likely to be little more than bewildered stares followed by a collective yawn, no matter how artfully your talk is crafted.

Advertising professionals perform extensive research in order to define exactly who will buy their product, and they adjust such elements as the look, content, and language of their advertising to appeal to a specific audience. In this manner, they avoid wasting advertising dollars on audiences who don't care about their product or message or may even be offended by it.

Ignoring audience demographics can be especially embarrassing. A couple of decades ago the now-defunct National Airlines decided to sell travel from New York City to Florida and chose to do so with posters in the New York City subways. They thought this would be a good way to reach millions of commuters as they scurried about in the bleakness of a New York winter.

That, however, is where National's thinking about its audience stopped. The posters were large, simple, and offensive. Huge block letters trumpeted the words: "BOY, ARE YOU PALE!!!" and in much smaller letters at the bottom of the poster, "A reminder from National Airlines."

No sooner did the ads appear than minority groups expressed their contempt for the designation "Boy" and the highly inaccurate reference to their skin color. National goofed in ignoring the racial composition of its audience and paid the price by having to scrap an expensive advertising campaign.

It's unlikely you'll have to scrap your speech, but you should examine demographics or unique characteristics of your audience, to make your remarks audience-specific.

Making Sure You Mention Your Audience

The first step in tailoring your remarks to an audience is to mention that group, by name, within your speech. Whenever possible, include that mention in the introduction to your speech so that the speech presents both the appearance and the reality that it was created specifically for that audience.

For example, instead of saying, "Our national debt is considered by some to be a time bomb that can be defused only if we have the courage . . . ," the same line delivered in an audience-centered manner would be as follows:

> I am particularly heartened to be delivering this message to this group of accounting and finance professionals because you, as the sentinels of our nation's economic health, are in the greatest position to understand that the national debt is considered by some to be a time bomb that can be defused only if . . .

Even if your audience doesn't have a direct relationship to your topic, you can still include them in your remarks. For example, here is the same opening delivered to another audience:

> As senior citizens, you have the advantage of long experience and the perspective that comes with it. Thus, each of you has a special capacity to understand that the national debt is a virtual time-bomb that can be defused only . . .

Adjusting the Emphasis and Content
to Various Audiences

For example, if you were delivering a talk on effective résumé writing to a group of recent college graduates, your speech could be more audience-centered by increasing the amount of time spent on the inclusion of community service and volunteer work to compensate for the lack of formal experience. On the other hand, the same speech delivered to a midcareer audience might stress the construction of the objectives statement and minimize the community-service area discussed with the prior audience.

Deciding on Your Target Audience

This step is a matter of anticipating what the demographic profile of your audience will be and modifying your speech to include that "target audience." The goal in so doing is to increase the impact of your message by making your communication more intimate—more audience-centered and more in the direction of giving your audience the impression that you are really talking to each of them.

Following are some major demographic factors and audience characteristics you should consider in targeting your message, along with some samples of how to make a speech more audience-centered.

Consider the Age of an Audience

Is the audience composed of or concentrated within a particular age group? The very old and the very young are likely to be less receptive to very complex or convoluted messages.

With any audience, check to see if your examples are contemporary. For example, the death of John F. Kennedy was an unforgettable and dark moment in history for many and can be mentioned to evoke a sense of national loss and tragedy. Since it happened decades ago, however, it is as distant a memory as the Great Depression to others and has little if any emotional significance to younger audiences.

Without being patronizing ("I've got a really far-out rad talk for you today!"), be aware of the language and concerns of your audience that may be related to age. You may wish to make references to the popular music or literature of your audience, but do so only when it's relevant and appropriate. Also, if referring to any aspect of the audience's pop culture, avoid the intergenerational temptation to make the kind of critical or humorous comment that will needlessly offend rather than draw your listeners closer to you and your message.

Finally, don't refer to any age gap that may exist between you and your audience. Your appearance will have done that for you, and further commentary on how young or how old the speaker or audience is will be construed as a sign of your own discomfort, possibly increasing the psychological distance between you and your audience.

Consider the Educational Level of an Audience

It's long been my contention that education doesn't make you any smarter, but it can improve your critical and analytical ability. An educated audience may be more receptive to new ideas, but may be less tolerant of inaccuracy, poorly developed reasoning, or evidence of poor research.

Credentials are also important to more educated audiences. Questions such as who you are and what are your qualifications are more likely to be on the minds of such audiences and should be dealt with early in your message.

If your credentials don't compare to those of the audience you face, don't try to compensate by using terminology you wouldn't normally use, to try to "speak their language," just to show that you can. Also avoid making humorous references to the impressive credentials held by an audience. Both tactics will be perceived as hostile and will serve to create an issue where there was none before.

Don't be intimidated by an audience that seems more qualified than you are. Remember that you would not have been asked to speak to that audience unless those who selected you felt you had a worthwhile message to deliver.

Consider the Occupation of Your Audience

In cases where your audience is comprised almost exclusively of one occupational group, your message and illustrative examples can gain immediate and increased acceptance if they refer directly to that audience.

For example, if you are talking to a group of airline pilots, an example or a topic related to the importance of adherence to procedure or safety is likely to be well received because this occupational group relies on both these areas for the successful practice of their profession. Similarly, sharing a positive travel experience is always welcome because these highly trained professionals more often hear about missing luggage than they do about smooth, safe travel.

If you are speaking to a group of rheumatologists, examples or topics involving senior citizens would be welcome because this is the primary population served by this medical specialty, just as pediatricians would be most attentive to examples or topics involving children.

In relating to occupational activity, refer either to the activity itself or to the population served by that occupational group (as in senior citizens and rheumatologists or children and pediatricians). By looking in each of these directions, you widen the sources of examples that get your speech closer to your audience.

Some speakers, when faced with an audience composed of similar professional backgrounds, be they lawyers, accountants, engineers, and so forth, choose the occasion to use one of the tired old jokes we have all heard a jillion times. (How can you tell the number of engineers in a room? Add up the number of white socks and divide by two!) Avoid such turkeys. Your audience has heard them, and if you're lucky enough not to have offended them, you've done little more than reveal yourself as a dullard and a keeper of tired humor.

Consider Organizational Affiliations

Here is an easy way to get you and your message closer to your audience that speakers often miss.

If your audience happens to be the local chapter of Rotarians, Lions, or Jaycees or any organization that has a long tradition of community service, don't miss the opportunity to recognize their contributions even before getting to your speech. You have just enhanced the audience's receptivity to your message.

If you're speaking to other than a service organization, you might refer instead to their long history (which you looked up ahead of time) or prominent members who might be present (which you checked in advance).

Such audience references, which you can accomplish with minimal investigation, indicate to an audience that you are a sensitive and caring communicator and, at least for the time you'll be talking to them, as close to one of their own as you can get. Direct and positive references to an audience or organization can quickly move them from being neutral to being very much on your side.

Consider the Racial or Ethnic Makeup of Your Audience

Both theirs and yours should be considered here. Where there are examples to be used in a speech, or compliments to be paid to an ethnically or racially based organization, by all means do so; to ignore such realities, particularly if you are of a different background from that of the group, can be considered a snub.

If you are paying compliments to a group, do some research to acquaint yourself with such information as prominent members who might be present, or special occasions or holidays observed by that group that coincide with or even approximate the date of your appearance. Leaders of such groups or those responsible for booking your appearance will be helpful in getting you this information and will be genuinely appreciative that you bothered to ask.

Remember, the major purpose of mentioning an audience directly within your talk, or acknowledging their accomplishments, is to involve them more directly in your message and to increase its impact. Don't let your words of praise become so lengthy as to obscure your message. In short, recognize but don't patronize.

Particularly in these times of increased ethnic and racial pride and sensitivity, recognition of anything from an accomplishment to a struggle to overcome past and present obstacles is helpful in building a rapport with your audience. Avoid the trap, however, that nonmembers of an ethnic or racial group fall into with "I feel your pain/joy" remarks. As an outsider, the fact is you don't, and you haven't shared their experience. Pretending to do so will be perceived as patronizing to the edge of offensiveness.

The rule is worth repeating: Recognize, don't patronize!

Consider the Economic Status of Your Audience

This is not an attempt to get into a debate about whether the rich are different, but a recognition of the fact that there are differences both in economic status across audiences and in levels of understanding when it comes to financial matters and terminology.

On the matter of economic status, be attuned to your audience and use examples to which they can readily relate. For example, in speaking about such matters as average incomes, the mention of six-figure salaries in front of an audience that has never earned that much money or has little prospect of doing so will signal to an audience that you may be out of touch when it comes to talking about their lives. Make sure your economic examples use numbers and situations with which your audience can readily identify.

Also, in using financial and economic terminology, make sure that the audience is likely to know what you are talking about. True, most of us know that the "S&P 500" is not an automobile race, but terms such as "dollar-cost averaging" and "accelerated depreciation" can cause the eyes of many supposedly financially sophisticated audiences to glaze over.

Consider the Gender of Your Audience

Some of you may think that considering audience gender distribution is going a bit too far in audience analysis, but those of you who do probably need this information the most.

I refer particularly to speeches given before women's groups. We have a sexist language that is greatly dominated by male pronouns. Therefore, when we use examples that refer to "the best attorney" or "the most skilled surgeon," our language usually tricks us into referring to either of these accomplished individuals as a male ("If the most skilled surgeon were to evaluate this case, *he* would undoubtedly agree that . . ."). I'd suggest that you amend all such statements to include both male and female pronouns (". . . *he or she* would undoubtedly agree that . . .").

While this small linguistic adjustment may seem cumbersome at first, it will impress your audience with your sensitivity to such issues. On the other hand, failing to do so may offend female members of some audiences. Watch your pronouns!

Checklist

Use the following Audience Profile Checklist in preparing a speech to make sure you tailor your remarks for each specific audience.

AUDIENCE PROFILE CHECKLIST/SURVEY

❑ What is the gender of your audience?

_____Male   _____Female   _____Both

❑ What is their approximate average age? _____

❑ What is their approximate age *range*? _____

❏ What is the marital status of your audience?

_____Married   _____Single   _____Divorced

❏ Are there any unique cultural/ethnic audience characteristics?

_____

❏ What is their educational background?

_____High School   _____College   _____Graduate degrees

❏ What is the religious affiliation of your audience?

_____

❏ What is the professional occupation of your audience?

_____

❏ What is the political perspective of your audience (conservative versus liberal)?

_____

❏ What is their salary range?

_____$10,000–$20,000   _____$70,000–$100,000

_____$20,000–$40,000   _____$100,000+

_____$40,000–$70,000

❏ Is your audience a fraternal or sorietal organization? _____

❏ Are you speaking on the occasion of an anniversary or the celebration of an accomplishment or award?

❏ Are there famous or notable people and/or members present who should be acknowledged?

Summary

I've included this chapter because it's an area too many speakers ignore. The occasional or inexperienced speaker has a natural tendency to treat the whole speech-preparation process as a self- rather than an audience-centered-performance activity. Yet just a bit of attention spent on some of the details covered in this chapter can pay huge dividends in terms of audience appreciation of and attention to your message.

Be sure to include your audience in your speech. Think about their demographics, interests, and opinions and include them in your remarks. Make specific mention of your audience. Including each audience you speak to within your speech, often by just the very mention of their concerns, issues, or perspectives, is a simple step too many speakers neglect. One of the biggest compliments you can receive after a speech is the comment, "You were really talking to us." Tailoring a speech along the lines of the information presented in this chapter is the surest way to elicit that comment.

Quick Review: Audience Analysis

1. Make sure there are specific references to your audience in your speech.

2. When speaking to an organization, know their history and recent accomplishments and include them in your remarks.

3. Not all topics are suitable for all audiences.

4. Be careful of generation gaps in choosing your illustrative examples.

5. Don't be intimidated by audiences with greater credentials than yours.

6. Avoid stereotypic humor, especially in speaking to professional groups.

7. Be attentive to such audience demographics as age, educational level, ethnicity, and so forth.

8. Refer to individual audience members by name.

9. Recognize differing levels of familiarity with your topic, in the same audience.

10. If you are a nonmember of a minority group to whom you are speaking, don't patronize them with "I feel your pain" remarks.

Chapter Six

Handling Tough Questions and Tough Audiences

At-a-Glance Summary

This chapter is about handling tough questions and audiences. Although the primary focus is the question-and-answer period that follows a speech, the techniques covered are applicable to any Q&A situation, from the job or media interview to the witness stand.

In the pages that follow, you learn how to correct commonly made errors and avoid questioner traps.

This is not a chapter about evading tough questions. You should face the fact that the best way to handle questions is to answer them. In that spirit, this chapter provides a systematic approach to effectively answering the questions of an audience or an interviewer while expressing your informational agenda or target issues.

Handling Tough Questions
and Tough Audiences

"And now I'd be happy to take your questions." If there are any insincere words contained in this book, you have just read them. After you've conquered the demons of speaker anxiety and prepared, rehearsed, and delivered a most masterful piece of oratory, you often have to invite audience questions. At this point, most of us would rather be home trying to teach our cat to fetch.

Q&A sessions in the form of press conferences present such a significant degree of risk that presidents often avoid them under the guise of seeming "presidential." Politicians of all levels and stripes avoid spontaneous Q&A so that they can maintain control of a carefully honed image rather than have it shattered by an errant response.

The Q&A session that follows a speech means giving up control of the situation. It also means that the audience will see a version of you that is working without the safety net of a prepared text or outline—a glimpse of the real you. If poorly handled, there is the chance you'll make a spectacular blunder, inadvertently offend, forget the obvious, or even be revealed as someone who doesn't know as much as your audience initially thought you did.

But don't panic; you can exercise a lot more control over the Q&A session than you realize. In fact, if properly handled, even if you don't know the answer to *every* question asked (speakers worry about that), the Q&A session can become a real asset and positive contribution to your communicative image and impact.

By using the strategies presented in this chapter and making an honest attempt to answer the questions an audience may have for you, you can come out of the Q&A session as a more authoritative and credible communicator.

Establishing Ground Rules to Maintain Control

You might fear the Q&A session because you feel that you are giving up control of the situation. But that's only partially true.

Here are some ways you can gain greater control of the Q&A session:

Set the Length of the Session

This is done with ease and subtlety by saying, "I have a limited amount of time to take some questions from the audience." Notice that you have said "some" questions and a "limited" amount of time. The choice of these words is intentional. By saying "some questions," you have implied that the session will not go on until *every* query has been answered. Also, by saying you have "a limited amount of time" without naming a specific interval of time, you get to determine what that interval will be.

This way, you can conclude the session at your discretion by again saying that your time is limited and that you're wrapping up. If the Q&A session is going extraordinarily well, you may wish to let it continue longer than planned.

Allow One Question per Person

Another important ground rule to set up *before* the Q&A session is to limit questions to one per person until everyone present has had an opportunity to ask a question. Although announcing this rule seems like the height of fairness, and to many it is, it helps protect you from getting into a one-on-one with an audience member, which should be avoided (more on that later).

Instead, you should have one question, one response, and then on to the next questioner. When in front of a more sophisticated audience or at a press conference you may find it necessary to permit a follow-up question but these should also be limited to one. If you announce this rule in advance, you will find that audiences will happily cooperate. But if you try it halfway through a Q&A session because an audience member won't leave you alone, you'll appear evasive and authoritarian.

Have Questioners Identify Themselves

A final Q&A ground rule is to have audience members identify themselves as they begin their question. Another move toward democracy? Hardly. You are making use of the fact that people tend to behave themselves when everyone present knows their name. Stripped of his or her anonymity, the most irate questioner is a lot more polite.

You will definitely change the tone of a Q&A session by having each questioner say his or her name (and affiliation if appropriate). You may have to gently enforce this rule at first ("I'm sorry, your name is . . . ?"), but once an audience begins to conform, the results can be dramatic in terms of toning down the more hostile questioners that may be out there.

Set the Tone for Questions: Begin Aggressively

At the beginning of most Q&A sessions there is often a great deal of hesitancy on the part of both speaker and audience in getting started. Audience members tend to sit there wondering what sort of questions are permissible or expected.

An audience may need prompting from you as to what kind of questions or issues are appropriate. For example, do you intend to handle only polite "puff-ball" questions, or get into serious issues?

An audience is also often unsure about the depth and tone of questioning you expect. At this point you can and should take control by beginning with the phrase, "A question I often get is about . . ."

If you intend to deal with serious issues, your self-asked question should be on just such an issue. If you want to steer the questions toward a certain subject, your question should be on that subject.

Be certain to plan and rehearse the opening of the Q&A session, including stating the ground rules and transitioning into your start-up question. These activities will not only set the tone for the Q&A session, but, as the final portion of your speaking appearance, will play an important part in determining the impression you make.

Have an Informational Goal or Theme

You may not think you have much to learn from politicians, but communicatively you do. They tend to be very good at sticking with a message and getting it across, no matter what the occasion. As you think about the political figures you've heard, you'll realize that they keep returning to and repeating the same themes, such as the economy, the environment, or the plight of the working poor.

Similarly, you should have your own informational goals, which I refer to as *target issues*, for a Q&A session, be it a policy you're trying to implement or a sales goal for your personnel. In advance of the Q&A session, write down and internalize these target issues.

Restrict your target issues to no more than three ideas. The reason for this limit is that if you have too many, your informational goals will be ill-defined and therefore unaccomplished. You also won't be able to remember many more than three target issues and may be uncertain as to whether you are hitting the most important ones.

Later in this chapter, as a specific format for responding to audience questions is outlined, I'll also show you how to "hit your target issues" by integrating them into your responses whenever possible.

Surefire Techniques for Answering Questions

Please note that the title of this section says nothing about evasion tactics or wiggling your way out of audience questions. The most important rule of effective Q&A management—which applies as much to the media interview, the witness stand, or the job interview as to the post-speech Q&A session—is to *answer the question you are asked.*

This is a simple, basic rule that is routinely violated by speakers in all walks of life. If you take one of the usual alternate paths—such as answering a question other than the one you were asked, trying to joke your way out of it, or becoming inappropriately insulted and refusing to "dignify the question with a response"—the fact remains that you haven't answered the question.

If you don't answer the question you're asked, no matter how artful you consider the evasion, your personal credibility will suffer.

Your failure to respond may result in a few perfunctory questions because an audience has decided that any attempt to get a straight answer out of you is so remote a possibility that it isn't even worth the effort.

Answer the question you are asked.

Now that you've been sufficiently impressed with the need to be honest with an audience, you should know that there are two perceptual steps that need to occur almost simultaneously in order for you to respond effectively to most questions:

The first step is to *categorize* or codify the question into one of the usual types that people tend to ask. Doing so will make it easier to formulate a response based upon the question type itself.

The second step is to *apply the R.E.S.T. formula,* which will enable you to respond in a focused and organized manner without bringing up additional issues.

Although it will be discussed fully later in the chapter, rather than keep you in suspense, I'll point out right now that R.E.S.T. stands for *Respond, Example, Stop talking,* and *Take the next question.*

Although I realize that all this stuff about two perceptual steps may sound like quite a mouthful, or even a mindful, with practice you can carry out these steps easily and with excellent results, both in answering your audience's questions and in accomplishing your informational goals.

Codify the Question

The science of linguistics tells us that language structures or formats are really quite limited. This is especially true when it comes to the types of questions you are likely to be asked in any situation. In fact, there are only about eight basic types to consider.

Being able to "type" the question sets up a response pattern. This question "typing," combined with the R.E.S.T.-response formula, provides a system to help you through the toughest of Q&A sessions with credibility and authority.

Following are major question types you can expect to hear from the audiences you face.

Yes or No Questions

SAMPLE QUESTION: "Senator, will the taxpayers be footing the bill for your upcoming trip to France?"

ANALYSIS: A question in which the questioner provides all the information and you have only to fill in the blanks (say yes or no) and where appropriate, provide an example.

CORRECT RESPONSE: *"Yes, that trip will be paid out of taxpayer funds, but let me tell you what we intend to accomplish. . . . "*

INCORRECT RESPONSE: *"As you know, we've been concerned for a long time about building industrial bridges between the people of this region and the good citizens of France. We find that by making trips such as these we can establish contacts that . . . "*

ERRORS TO AVOID: *Not giving an immediate yes-or-no response.* Remember that the person who asks the yes-or-no question often knows the answer. By putting off an answer with a defensive statement such as the one contained in the incorrect response, you merely irritate the questioner and give the impression that you would rather not respond.

The tendency in responding to the yes-or-no question, when saying yes or no up front will be seen as bad for your side, is to begin your answer with the reasons why you're about to say something your audience won't like.

The yes-or-no question should be answered immediately and directly, or the evasiveness you display in not getting to the answer right away will be more damaging than the response itself.

But what if the answer to a yes-or-no question isn't yes or no? In such cases, simply say so. In scientific or legal areas, sometimes a simple yes or no can be an oversimplification or truly damaging. At other times, it can seem insensitive, even with a qualifier to follow. ("Did you vote against funding for the prenatal clinic?")

With responses structured such as, "While the data point in that direction, a simple yes (or no) in answer to your question wouldn't be accurate," or "Although I did cast that negative vote, you should also know that . . . ," the questioner needs to listen to the qualifier in order for the response to make sense.

You should, however, save such responses for situations in which they are really needed. Their continuous use will be ineffective and make you appear evasive.

Caesar-or-God Questions

SAMPLE QUESTION: "As a manager, which policy do you look most favorably upon—salary cuts or layoffs?"

ANALYSIS: In James 11:22, a soldier asks Christ which was more important, the laws of God or the laws of the Roman empire. In those days, the wrong answer could be fatal. Even today, those who ask you a question that requires you to choose from two alternatives almost never give you an easy choice. No matter which one you choose, the questioner or some other audience member will be back with a stinging follow-up question berating your choice.

CORRECT RESPONSE: *"As a matter of fact, I don't like either of those solutions, which is why I've put together a combined-early-retirement-and attrition program that will help us meet our goals."*

INCORRECT RESPONSE: *"Well, that's not much of a choice, but I'm afraid I'd have to choose the salary reductions as a way to go. . . . "*

RESPONSE STRATEGY: Note that in the correct response, the speaker has chosen an alternative rather than one of the choices set forth by the questioner. Therefore the correct response pattern becomes *neither*, followed by an alternative chosen by the speaker, not the audience member.

ERRORS TO AVOID: *Limiting yourself to the choices given.* It's a source of constant amazement to me that speakers who might be assertive, self-assured people in so many settings can get completely boxed in by the Caesar-or-God question, and completely forget about the words *either* or *neither*, or both. Remember that you don't have to be limited in your response to the choices given you by the questioner.

What-If Questions

SAMPLE QUESTION: "What if this division fails to meet its goals for the third quarter?"

ANALYSIS: What-if questions refer to what *might* happen, not to what has *actually* taken place. Unless the parameters described in the question are completely absurd, they are legitimate questions deserving of a response. They are also a good test of how well the speaker has analyzed a situation or issue.

CORRECT RESPONSE: *"First of all, you're raising a hypothetical issue, because our numbers don't indicate that result; but just in case, what we would have to do is reevaluate our staffing needs for the second half of the year and maybe even make some cuts. But once again, you've raised a possibility that I just don't consider realistic."*

INCORRECT RESPONSE: *"If we don't meet our goals, we'll have to look at making some reductions in the sales force, followed by a reevaluation of just how we arrived at those projections."*

RESPONSE STRATEGY: The most essential element in answering the what-if question is to keep in mind that it refers to events that have not taken place. The response should point that out both at the beginning and the end to remind the audience of the hypothetical nature of the question.

In cases where the hypothetical situation is just too absurd, or where speculation would be irresponsible, say so and don't respond further.

Such was the strategy during the Persian Gulf War when reporters, who often deal in hypotheticals in the absence of a story (what might happen, when nothing has happened), were kept from the action and thus limited to such questions as, "What if Saddam Hussein begins using biological weapons?" The constant and effective response of military officials was a refusal to speculate on what had not happened.

ERRORS TO AVOID: *Forgetting that you are dealing with a "what-if" situation.* Often speakers become so involved in placing themselves within the hypothetical scenario that they forget that it never happened. This error is compounded by the fact that audiences never listen to every word you say and will join your response "in progress," thereby getting the impression that the layoffs or the nuclear accident you're talking about have actually happened!

The Laundry-List Question

SAMPLE QUESTION: "You and your company have piled up massive losses while you continue to exploit your workers, pollute the environment, and cheat the federal government out of millions of tax dollars, all while your overpaid executives continue to rip off the shareholders. What's your comment?"

ANALYSIS: This monster of a question, often heard at annual shareholders' meetings, is not really a question at all but a statement. It's usually made by a person who is either very angry or is intent on disrupting the meeting, or both. The laundry list questioner doesn't really expect a response and should be handled carefully and systematically.

CORRECT RESPONSE: *"You've raised a lot of issues; let me try and respond. On the matter of environmental action, our company has taken a leadership role in placing the latest technology in all of our facilities. . . . " (The answer continues at length on the issue with which you are most comfortable, followed by a call for another question from another part of the audience.)*

INCORRECT RESPONSE: *"You seem very angry, if you can just try and calm down I can begin to address the many issues you have raised. Let me begin with the losses to which you refer. In the past three quarters. . ." (The speaker continues through the list, asking the help of the questioner if he or she can't remember the entire list.)*

Response Strategy

I usually advise answering the question you are asked, but in this case you will note that you haven't been asked a question. Since this audience member wants to make a statement, hurl charges, and disrupt, an answer should not be your priority. Rather, you want to attempt a response and get away from this individual quickly.

Here's what to do and what not to do: When you hear the laundry list, you will be stunned, and your audience will be embarrassed. That means they are on your side, at least temporarily.

Sometimes speakers are so stunned at this moment that they ask for a repetition of the question. This merely brings a longer version, complete with profanity from a now emboldened protester.

In responding, don't refer to the questioner's emotional state or ask for any feedback whatever. All this will bring is something like, "You're damned right I'm angry, you would be too if . . . ," and there he or she goes again.

Instead, once you hear the list, choose one issue and talk about it for a minute or so. If you get right into it, your embarrassed audience will be relieved that someone rational has taken charge.

At the end of your statement, look into a portion of the audience other than where your antagonist is seated and say, "Next question," and pause deliberately.

Usually, in the silence that follows, an easier question will be asked. If your laundry-list questioner is still in action, remember those ground rules we set up at the beginning? Now it's time to use them.

Again, if that disruptive questioner is insistent, say, "I said at the beginning, one question per person, and I'm going to stick with that rule. Let's give someone else a chance." Usually an audience will take your cue and another question will follow.

The important strategy here is to let the audience work for you and against the disrupter, which can happen only if you back off, stick to your ground rules, and use some silence.

In the unlikely event that all of these tactics don't solve the problem, invite your antagonist to get together with interested audience members after the meeting. This should mollify the disrupter. By the way, almost no one ever attends those after-meeting meetings.

Summarizing the key strategies for handling the laundry-list questioner:

1. Respond on a single issue only, and let your response be longer than usual. Choose the issue with which you are most comfortable.

2. Avoid going back to the questioner verbally or nonverbally with a glance. If you're looking for approval, you won't find it.

3. Ask for the next question from another part of the audience.

4. Stick to your ground rules of one question per person, but avoid an argument.

Practice these steps any time you expect some rough sledding in a question-and-answer setting. They really work, but should be employed smoothly and without hesitation for maximum effect.

ERRORS TO AVOID: *Commenting on the emotional state of the questioner or telling him or her to calm down.* If you have ever been asked to calm down when you were angry, you know it can have just the opposite effect. Although the questioner's anger may be a breach of etiquette, it may also be justified.

Asking for a repetition of the question. I know how dumb it sounds, but I've actually heard speakers do it, and have even evoked this response in training seminars from stunned participants.

Seeking any kind of feedback from the questioner. Generally a bad idea in Q&A sessions, especially bad here, it encourages a dialogue with the last person in the room with whom you want to have that dialogue. Maintain control and get away.

Arguing with the questioner. You can't win, so stick to your formula and get to the next questioner and question as soon as possible.

Legal or Personnel Questions

SAMPLE QUESTIONS: "Don't you think it would be reasonable if your company compensated the Braddock family for their accident on your premises? After all, your PR people invited them on the tour." Or, "Since his drug arrest, do you intend to fire John Freldoon?"

ANALYSIS: Although these questions differ in content, they have a strong common link in that responding to either of them could get you a court appearance, testifying against your own company. Such questions may be asked by the idly curious—or by investigators for potential legal adversaries.

The first question asks for your opinion on compensation in an injury case, clearly a question on a legal matter. Are you *really* qualified to answer? Probably not; but if the question is asked politely and quietly and "out of the blue," you might be tempted to respond.

Personnel matters are usually confidential and should be treated as such. As a general rule, don't publicly discuss personnel issues involving individuals.

CORRECT RESPONSE, ON LEGAL MATTERS: *"You've asked a legal question, and I'll have to decline to respond at all."*

Or, if more applicable to the situation: "That matter is currently in litigation and I cannot respond."

ON PERSONNEL MATTERS: *"It's our policy not to discuss personnel matters publicly, and I'm not going to comment further."*

INCORRECT RESPONSE: *"Sure, as an individual I feel sorry about the accident, and I'd imagine the company will take care of them."*

Or, "Mr. Freldoon has had quite a substance abuse history, and I think we will be taking some kind of punitive action, termination or otherwise."

RESPONSE STRATEGY: When you hear words such as "reasonable" or "compensation" coupled with a request for your personal opinion, be careful. Any response other than those presented here could get you into legal difficulty. Similarly, any question involving personnel policy in a corporate setting should be off limits once a name is mentioned.

ERRORS TO AVOID: *Not listening for the words that should trigger the realization that you are being asked a legal question.* Anyone who wants a corporate spokesperson to take a position against the company, particularly for use against that company, needs to be clever about it; and they will be. Be wary of overly polite or meek questioners in such areas.

Personal Questions

SAMPLE QUESTIONS: "What's your annual salary?" or "We know you're the company expert on environmental issues and you get paid to state their policies, but how do *you personally* feel about their position?"

ANALYSIS: Personal questions from audiences come in two varieties: those that seek information about your personal life, lifestyle, family background, income, and so forth; and those that seek to determine if you really believe what you're saying or are just going through the motions.

CORRECT RESPONSE: *"My salary? . . . That's a personal matter and I'm here to discuss company issues. I'll be happy to answer issues inquiries but not personal questions."*

Or, "Personally, I am happy to say that I've examined the environmental-policy studies closely, not just as a spokesperson, but as a resident of this community, and there's absolutely no difference between what I've said to you today and my personal view."

INCORRECT RESPONSE: *"Salary? . . . I'm afraid that's none of your business."*

Or, on the environmental question (after a long pause): "I haven't really given it much thought, but I don't think there would be any difference."

RESPONSE STRATEGY: Audience members often ask personal questions just to test the sincerity level and openness of the speaker; others ask them in an attempt to embarrass you. In responding to personal questions, your reaction can be more important than your answer, in that becoming angry or indignant about the question will lessen the effectiveness of everything else you've done.

Decide in advance how you'll handle such questions and stick with that policy. An audience may not like your declining to answer personal questions, but they will respect it.

One further note on the issue of salary: If yours is a matter of public record, refusing to discuss it publicly will make you look defensive and needlessly secretive. Also, if you are a senior executive with a salary higher than most, prepare your responses to such questions in advance and be able to justify your compensation level in a calm, nondefensive manner.

The second type of personal question, that which seeks your personal feelings about a policy or issue, seems simple enough on the surface but can actually be a probing and revealing query that, if not handled carefully, can be a destroyer of credibility.

The strategy here is to be prepared with a definite position on such a question and to deliver it in the most positive of terms, without hesitation. If there is any hint of doubt on your part, especially if you are slow to respond, the effectiveness of your entire effort will suffer.

ERRORS TO AVOID: *On questions that ask about you personally, becoming annoyed by the question or questioner.* This reaction accomplishes nothing. Instead, decide on how you'll handle personal questions in advance and politely stick to that policy.

On questions that seek to know more about your personal opinion ("How do you personally feel about . . . "), the biggest errors are:

1. *Being slow or hesitant in responding.* This will be seen as self-doubt even if it isn't.

2. *A bland response lacking in positive language.* Such a response will be read as equivocation and will negatively affect your credibility.

One-to-Ten Questions

SAMPLE QUESTION: "On a scale of one to ten, how would you rate your company's performance as a corporate citizen?"

ANALYSIS: Especially when you have a positive story to tell, this is a tempting question because it enables you to say all the positives you can without even having to think of any sort of elaborate response. All you have to do is blurt out, "Ten!" or the falsely humble, "Nine-and-one half and climbing!" and move on to your next questioner.

Not so fast. A second look at this question, beyond the momentary elation you feel at having been asked it, reveals that it invites you to over-simplify. Once you play this numbers game, you'll also be obliged to answer "Three" in rating a problem area. Instead, use words, not numbers, as in the sample correct response.

CORRECT RESPONSE: *"Just tacking a number on our performance would be an oversimplification and wouldn't mean much to most of our audience. I'd have to say instead that we're doing an excellent job and hope to continue."*

Or, in cases where the answer might be a very low number, "If you're refer-ring to the fact that we've had some problems in the corporate citizenship, I'll be the first to admit we could have done better. However, I'm not going to oversimplify by just tossing a number at you. Instead, let me tell you about just a couple of the initiatives we've taken to improve things. First of all . . . "

INCORRECT RESPONSE: *"Ten!" or "Three!" or any numerical response.*

RESPONSE STRATEGY: Trade the momentary joy of being able to say "Ten!" in front of an audience for the enhanced credibility of a speaker who refused to oversimplify. This way, if asked to rate a negative area or issue, you're free to respond with words, not numbers.

ERRORS TO AVOID: Numerical or flip answers to a question that invites you to oversimplify.

Being unwilling to answer this question on a negative issue if you have already answered it on a positive within the same meeting.

Stupid Questions

Those of us involved in coaching speakers and preparing media guests and witnesses, with all of our strategizing, issues analysis, and for-mulae, sometimes forget that one of the most troublesome and potentially embarrassing questions is that off-the-wall, stupid, or inappropriate ques-tion that pops up with surprising frequency in a variety of situations.

It can come from the inebriated caller to a radio or television program or from a member of a club that you are addressing as a guest speaker.

Sometimes a question is stupid or at least out of place because it's obvious to everyone (except the person who asked the question) that you have just answered that very question.

SAMPLE QUESTION: "How will the tax information you have just presented affect my geraniums?"

ANALYSIS: As you struggle to make sense of a question as bizarre as this one, or come to the reluctant conclusion that the question made no sense, an audience's initial embarrassment turns quickly to curiosity about how you'll handle this delicate situation.

CORRECT RESPONSE: *"I'm afraid I can't give you the information you might need but let's get together later and try and come up with something. Other questions?"*

INCORRECT RESPONSE: *"That's a pretty silly question in light of what we've been talking about. Could you possibly explain it a bit better? . . . I think I missed something or maybe didn't quite hear you correctly."*

RESPONSE STRATEGY: More important than the response is your reaction to the questioner and the impression you make on that audience at that moment. Being confused or embarrassed by the question is certainly appropriate on your part.

But beyond that, your only strategy should be to take the questioner seriously and respond as briefly and as sincerely as possible and get to the next question. The fact that you handled this moment with sensitivity will create a more lasting positive impression on your audience than your attempt at a response.

In cases where the question, rather than being bizarre, is merely a repetition of a question you have just answered, and it's obvious to all that the questioner wasn't listening, avoid embarrassing the questioner with such phrases as "As I just said . . ." or "If you had been listening . . ." and simply repeat your prior response.

If you feel the need to let your audience know that you are aware that this is a repetition, you might want to begin your response with a polite, "I'd be happy to go back to that issue for a moment and let you know that . . . "—a lot more subtle than "If you had been listening" or "As I just said."

Once again, more important than the response here is showing that you are a caring, sensitive communicator. Your audience will appreciate the effort.

ERRORS TO AVOID: *Seeking clarification of the bizarre or stupid question.* In the case of the bizarre question or questioner, avoid going back to that questioner for clarification or feedback; you'll only make things worse. (See incorrect sample response.) Get to the next question as soon as possible.

Commenting on the quality of the question. Don't comment in any way on the quality of the question, particularly avoiding any humorous remark made at the expense of the questioner. If you try to kid your way out of this moment, you'll come off as slick or snide—either one a very unfavorable impression.

Using the R.E.S.T. Formula to Give Successful Responses

As we begin a more detailed look at the R.E.S.T. formula, I'll restate it briefly: *Respond, Example, Stop talking*, and *Take the next question (or go to your Target issue).*

Effective communication is often comprised of applying behavior we use in conversation to the speaker's podium or media appearance.

Responding to audience questions with the randomness and spontaneity that typifies conversation, however, can get you into great difficulty in a tough-issues climate.

An audience uses the question-and-answer period as an indicator of the speaker's knowledge, authority, and sensitivity. They will also assess your credibility and skill in communicating under pressure.

Using the R.E.S.T. formula gives you the following advantages in handling the Q&A session, be it for a media interview or as guest speaker before a meeting of the local Lions Club:

1. The R.E.S.T. formula, once internalized, enables you to better organize your thoughts since it provides a definite format for each response.

2. The R.E.S.T. formula permits you to focus on ideas and issues rather than on the structure of your answer, making you more responsive to your audience.

3. The R.E.S.T. formula makes it easier to maintain a consistent length of response from question to question.

One of the key barometers of performance in Q&A is length of response. When a speaker finds a question particularly problematical, he or she either gives an extremely short answer, as if to hope that the subject and the questioner will just go away, or an extremely lengthy response, as an obviously defensive reaction in the hope of verbally stomping out any informational brush fires that might flare up in the continued presence of that issue.

Of course, the extremely short answer is perceived as evasive and causes further questions on that issue, whereas the long, multipart response brings up other issues and—you guessed it—even more questions on that dreaded issue.

A consistent length of response helps mask the difficult areas and gives you a chance to handle the Q&A session on a more level playing field.

Step #1: Respond Directly

In one line or a single sentence, give the answer to the question: simply, directly, and free of prior clarification.

SAMPLE QUESTION: "Does your company intend to raise prices over the coming year, and if so, by how much?"

SAMPLE RESPONSE: *"Yes, we are looking at a price increase in the coming year, the exact amount being between 3 and 5 percent." (This response will be added to in Step #2.)*

Note: The tendency in this type of question, particularly, is to defend yourself before responding. The result? An audience thinks you are afraid to respond directly or that you are doubtful of your own position.

INCORRECT SAMPLE RESPONSE: *"As you know, our company has had to maintain its competitive position through aggressive pricing strategies, but we also have a responsibility to our employees and our shareholders to remain profitable. Therefore, we will be looking at the possibility of raising prices in the coming year. . . . "*

Note: This speaker takes care of the company defenses for the price increase before actually answering the question, with the result that his or her audience comes to the rapid and correct conclusion that the question has not been effectively answered.

Follow the formula. Step #1 is to respond in a single sentence or phrase, directly and concisely, as in the correct sample response. Now on to Step #2.

Step #2: Explain with a Single Example

Clarify your response, using a brief, single, illustrative example. It's important here that you avoid the temptation, especially when the question is easy or it's on a topic with which you have great familiarity, to give more than one example. In so doing you cause several problems for yourself.

First of all, you are reducing the clarity of your responses. On more than one occasion in teaching the R.E.S.T. formula, as the speaker launched into his or her second example, I've interrupted and said to the audience, "What was the question?"

They seldom remember, because aside from the person who actually asked the question, audiences seldom listen to the entire response. Keep your responses brief, and audiences are better able to connect questions to your responses, increasing their retention and your impact.

In a media interview, sticking to a single example as per the formula will keep the interview focused and perhaps lessen the need for editing.

Another reason to limit yourself to a single example is to avoid bringing up additional issues. Examples other than the one you planned or the first one that occurred to you are often more tangential to the response. That's why audiences won't easily make the connection between the response and the example, resulting in those further questions.

Finally, as I mentioned earlier, it is important to balance the length of your responses. If you spend too much time on an issue, or suddenly deliver a four-second response in a sea of one-minute answers, or a two-minute answer amid a pack of thirty-second answers, an audience knows that something is up and more questions will follow, on an issue you wanted to avoid.

Instead, stick with the formula and limit yourself to a single example. I sometimes encounter some resistance to this part of the formula, as a speaker says to me after delivering a multiexampled response, " . . . but I was on a roll." I would remind any of you so inclined that things "roll" in only one direction: *Downhill!*

Here is an example of the question we started with in the first part of the formula, along with a sample response containing a single example explanation:

SAMPLE QUESTION: "Does your company intend to raise prices over the coming year and if so, by how much?"

SAMPLE RESPONSE (STEPS #1 AND #2 APPLIED): *"Yes, we are looking at a price increase in the coming year, the exact amount being between 3 and 5 percent. You should also know that the increase will be an essential part of our responsibility to both our shareholders and our employees, as well as providing the best possible products for our customers."*

Step #3: Stop Talking

Once you have completed the single example that comprises Step #2, the next thing to do is stop talking.

Including this as a step in a formula might strike you as a bit of instructional overkill, but not remembering to stop, and going into some multiple examples, is a common and often costly error.

We often equate talking with success and silence with failure—to the extent we sometimes end our phrases with connective words such as "but" or "and" or the verbalized pause ("uh"). This behavior may cover the dreaded silence, but it also causes us to say more.

If you don't learn to end your response at the conclusion of the planned single example, your response ends when you simply run out of ideas, or, put less kindly, when you run out of conversational gas. Stick with the R.E.S.T. formula.

Step #4: Take the Next Question (or Go to Your Target Issue)

At Step #4, it's decision time. After you have completed your response, you may wish to take the next question. You may, however, wish to state your target issue before doing so. It's your decision, but here are some guidelines to help you set the best course of action for Step #4.

Select as many as three target issues for use during a Q&A session. These should be themes that you want the audience to come away with, that you can integrate into your responses.

For example, if I were representing the fictional company in the sample responses regarding a proposed price increase, I might assume that customers would be disturbed by that increase. Therefore, one of my target issues would certainly be "concern for the customer." I would try to integrate that theme or target issue into some of my responses by adding it at the end of the response. Following is an example of how the *target issue* concept works.

SAMPLE QUESTION: "Does your company intend to raise prices over the coming year, and if so, by how much?"

CORRECT SAMPLE RESPONSE (WITH TARGET ISSUE):   *"Yes, we are looking at a price increase in the coming year, the exact amount being between 3 and 5 percent. You should also know that the increase will be an essential part of our responsibility to both our shareholders and our employees, and will provide the best possible products for our customers.* While I'm on the subject of our customers, once they see the product improvements made possible by the increase, they'll know that they continue to be our number-one priority."

In this response, the speaker made a smooth transition into the target issue, customer concern, after fully responding to the question asked. I would recommend that you try to get to your target issue or issues in about 25 percent, or one in four, of the responses you deliver.

With practice, you will be able to smoothly integrate your target issue(s) into your responses, while still answering the questions you are asked.

This final step embodies a couple of simple but important procedures in maintaining the control and flow of the Q&A session.

First, take your next question from someone other than the person who asked the previous question. (Remember your ground rules—one question per person until everyone has had a chance to speak.)

This is easier if you focus your eye contact on your entire audience during your response, rather than on the questioner.

Second, don't go back to a questioner for feedback on your response, such as asking, "Does that answer your question?" By doing so you invite a one-on-one exchange that will bore an audience (unless it turns into an argument).

Be careful not to react to the nonverbals of the questioner, which might range from a disgruntled frown to a negative nod. Reacting to such nonverbals will only crystallize the notion that there is dissatisfaction with your response—a sure way to turn the undecided against you.

So once again, Step #4 in the R.E.S.T. formula is either *Take the next question* or go to your *Target issue.* If you go on to the next question, do so decisively, using your ground rules to your advantage.

Using the Anecdotal Response

Once you are thoroughly practiced in applying the R.E.S.T. formula to Q&A sessions, a further step you will want to take is to include anecdotal material as responses to some questions. This essentially means telling your audience a brief story once you have responded to a question, or using the story itself as a response.

Anecdotal responses are effective because, even if their use is planned, their inclusion in a Q&A session is by chance (that of getting the right question to trigger the story). Audiences appreciate that spontaneity.

Anecdotal responses also personalize the session, as their telling gives an audience an insight into the kind of issues and situations that concern, impress, or touch you in some way, a kind of insight that is not usually gained from the standard exchange of questions and answers.

Let me give you a few cautionary notes on using anecdotal responses.

First of all, keep them brief. If they are more than two minutes long, the audience will remember the story but may forget why you told it.

Second, don't use more than one or two anecdotal responses per half hour of Q&A. If you do, your Q&A session can take on the atmosphere of a gathering around a campfire rather than a briefing by a knowledgeable spokesperson.

Stories about outstanding customer care, employee performance, or perhaps a way in which your company has not just met but exceeded a government safety standard—information that is not generally known to an external or even an internal audience—make the best anecdotal responses.

It's been my experience that most companies abound with such stories that are seldom thought of as sales and public-relations tools. Typically, they are shared at an awards dinner (often being the reason for the award) and thereafter forgotten. Think of one or two and have them ready for your next Q&A session.

Finally, if you use anecdotal responses, make sure they are factually accurate. People tend to remember these stories and may even know people who know the people in your story. If your facts are off or are embellished for dramatic effect, it can be embarrassing.

Stalling for Time

A great deal of this chapter has been spent on getting you to say certain things or at least getting you to organize your response material in certain ways. I'd like to end this chapter by telling you a few things you should never say as you conduct a Q&A session.

The first of these is that worn phrase, "I'm glad you asked me that question." It's usually uttered by a speaker who is desperately trying to buy some extra think-time before venturing a response, and no audience ever believes it.

If you need a few extra seconds to collect your thoughts, try something less obvious such as, "That's been a serious issue with us for some time, even difficult, but here is the approach we have developed."

An equally overused and never-believed phrase is, "That's a good question!" The fact is that the asker of the most moronic question thinks it was a good question, which is why he or she asked it in the first place. Once again, be honest with your audience, as in, "That's been a tough problem to solve, but here is how we are trying to manage it."

Responding When You Don't Know the Answer

It used to surprise me that even senior executives of major corporations, in a practice Q&A session for a media appearance or shareholders' meeting, would nervously say to me, "But what will I tell them if I don't know the answer?"

The illusion of the CEO's omniscience may be good for stock prices, but it's just that: an illusion. Even if you're not the CEO (or even if you are) remember that you are up there handling audience questions because you are recognized as an expert. Remember, however, that *even experts can't know everything, and the most credible ones are willing to admit it.*

If you don't know the answer to a question, simply say so. You might add that you know who does have the information, or even that you should know the answer and will have to get back to the questioner with the information. Don't view the response, "I don't know," as a defeat. If not used more than two or three times in a Q&A session, it can be a refreshing affirmation of your humanity.

Wrapping Up the Question-and-Answer Session

Once you have dealt with the major issues of concern to your audience, you will note that questions will become repetitive or too detailed to maintain the general interest of your audience. It's time to end the session. At this point you should be on the lookout for a positive question, or in a rough-issues climate, a tolerably balanced one.

If it's been a tough session, you don't want to give the impression that you are ending things and hightailing it out of town, even if that's what you'd like to do.

End the session by saying that you have time to take a few more questions. Take two, or even as many as four, until you get a friendly or easily answered tough question.

Since audiences tend to remember what you told them last, it's important if at all possible to end the session on a positive note. Therefore, you should be directive enough to say something like: "As I said earlier, our time is limited, but I'll be available for a short while to chat with you on an individual basis. Meanwhile, let me leave you with this thought: . . ."

At this time, go to your *most important target issue* and summarize it once again. Here is a sample summary touching upon a target issue:

> I've covered a lot of ground this evening, but I hope a common theme came through in just about everything I've said, from the tough issues of increasing prices to your well-justified environmental concerns. All of us at U.S. Combinatrix look forward to working with you to make this community a better place in which to live and work. We really care. Thank you

A strong closing statement will not only leave your audience with a strong positive final impression of your entire effort, but will also diminish the impact of any missteps you may have made in fielding audience questions.

Watch Your Signal Behaviors

Walk, don't run! Finally, as you leave the stage or meeting, be careful of your nonverbals—that is, don't race out of the room. If you are leaving, say goodbye to those within your gaze and be sure not to make too hasty an exit.

If you are staying to answer individual queries, don't hide in the balcony, but place yourself at a location in the room that is accessible to all those present. In this manner, all of those present, even those who leave before you do, will have the clear impression that you are communicative and willing to make every effort to tell your story to anyone who'll listen—an extremely important message to send to your audience as they assess your performance.

Quick Review:
Handling Tough Questions and Tough Audiences

1. Have an agenda or informational goal for any Q&A session.
2. Set up ground rules for your audience at the beginning of your Q&A session and stick with them.
3. Answer the question each person asks.
4. Keep your responses brief.
5. Decide in advance whether to answer personal questions.
6. Don't buy into the emotional state of the questioner (if he or she is angry or abusive, don't you get that way).
7. Don't try to "win" or look at each response as a victory/defeat situation; just answer the question.
8. Avoid saying "That was a good question," or "I'm glad you asked me that." No one believes you.
9. Remember to say "I don't know." Used truthfully and sparingly, it's a bulletproof response.
10. Practice, internalize, and use the R.E.S.T. formula: Respond, Example, Stop talking, Target issue or Take the next question.

Chapter Seven

Making Effective Sales Presentations

At-a-Glance Summary

This chapter is about planning, constructing, and delivering a powerful and successful sales presentation. In addition to helping you develop a winning attitude, it provides tactics for handling objections, putting *your* product or service at the head of the pack, and the delicate matter of talking about the competition. You also learn the special dynamics of team presentations and how to manage visual aids and sales demonstrations.

Making Effective
Sales Presentations

Few situations provide so much opportunity for spectacular success or abject failure as the sales presentation. But despite its high-risk nature, many presenters make serious mistakes that are overlooked only because the product or service is so terrific that it's sales-rep proof, or because the competition has done an even worse job of stating its case.

Establishing Your Objective

Before creating a sales presentation, decide what your specific objective is and use every part of your message to work toward that objective.

You can use the speech-building chapter as a guide to structuring your presentation, but do so with a specific objective in mind. The objective becomes your showcase idea, as illustrated in Chapter 4.

Objectives of sales presentations include:

1. New business
2. Renewing a prior account
3. Providing product or service updates
4. New-employee orientation

The sales presentation that seeks new business is the most crucial and will be the emphasis in this chapter.

Every presentation sells, however, even a seemingly less crucial one in which the purpose is to update an established customer or to train new users of your product. The people in your audience are also gathering impressions about you and your organization. Letting such presentations slide gives the competition a shot they should never get. An "Oh, it's just them" approach to an orientation session may lead the way for an "Oh, it's just you" reaction when you come in to pitch new business.

Sample Objective: Gaining a New Account

This is the traditional success/failure high-pressure situation that most of us equate with the sales presentation—all the agony of public speaking with the added possibility of spectacular failure.

If gaining new business is your objective, everything you do and say in this presentation should be geared toward accomplishing that objective.

Delivering the Presentation

Meet Your Audience Before the Presentation

This strategy is based upon the fact that audience members are more receptive to speakers they have met just prior to the presentation.

If at all feasible (if the group is fewer than twenty or so), meet and greet each one as he or she enters the presentation site. Try to remember names and even a few job titles in case you can work them into your presentation. Not only will they know who you are *before* you are introduced, but you will have communicated that you are aggressive, organized, and personable, even *before* your sales presentation has started.

Tell Them Your Goal

If you want a contract signed or an order placed, or if you are there to displace a competitor, say so. Many sales reps are apologetic about selling and are actually afraid to take the fairly confrontational stance of, "I want your business today!" They back away from this position because of the potential and immediate chance of rejection it presents.

Instead of saying what they want, such reps usually end their presentations with a quick thank-you and exit with sweaty palms. This way they can get the verdict in a follow-up phone call and face rejection in solitude. Be up-front in stating your objective (getting new business), and you'll have a clear advantage.

Deal with Objections Right Away

Not only must you anticipate objections, but you should handle them as soon as you've stated your objective (introducing the product,

product update, making a sale). Getting objections out of the way early leaves you more time to *sell* instead of fending off objections you failed to handle earlier.

EXAMPLE: "I know some of you here have some problems with Raygor Computers and may think that this is not the system for you. I'm going to give you some facts that will change your mind. Cost was a problem with some of our earlier systems, but that's changed. Sales volume and wide customer acceptance have made it possible for us to . . ."

Be direct and unapologetic in discussing objections and present a clear and concise response to each objection, as in the preceding sample statement. Avoid flip references to product problems, for example, "We really screwed up in pricing the 100 Series!" Be frank but serious: "While the 100 Series may have hit the market at a premium price, that's changed." A flip attitude about problems or a humorous approach will only damage your credibility and make prospects nervous about dealing with you in the event of a future problem.

In deciding which objections to handle, choose the major ones, or those that have the closest application to your prospect. As a general rule, limit objections to three and don't spend too much time discussing them. For example, in a twenty-minute presentation, spend no more than five minutes discussing negatives; otherwise, the objections can begin to dominate your presentation.

Discuss Problems Directly

If your product or service has suffered a major setback or received recent negative publicity, don't deal with it by not mentioning the problem at all, much the way an ostrich "avoids" danger by sticking its head in the sand.

Let's say your company has suffered a major warehouse fire that is affecting delivery dates, and everyone present knows it. By not providing some reassurance or at least a status report, you've communicated at least one of the following messages:

1. You don't know what's going on in your company.
2. You're afraid of tackling tough issues.
3. When the going gets tough, you're the one most likely to leave town.

So don't play ostrich. You have much to gain by dealing effectively with a tough objection or issue, and everything to lose by ignoring it.

As for the order in which you deal with objections, start with the one you are most comfortable discussing, perhaps the one of which you have the most knowledge. In this manner, you'll be off to a strong start and be more comfortable once you begin discussing areas with which you have less familiarity.

Selling Your Audience

Once they know who you are and what you want to get done, after you have dealt with the major objections, it's time to sell.

There are four speech formats that are particularly suited to sales presentations. These are:

1. Problem-Solution

2. Need-Product-Benefit

3. Past-Present-Future

4. Disadvantages-Advantages

The format that works best for you depends upon the nature of your product or service and the situation in which it is being sold.

For example, a high-tech product in an industry where innovation is slow to arrive would be a good place to use the historical perspective of the Past-Present-Future format. Show that your product is more evolutionary than revolutionary—an approach likely to be well received in an atmosphere where change is frowned upon.

The Problem-Solution format has a wide range of applications, while the Need-Product-Benefit format is easily adaptable to selling a service, rather than a product.

Using the Problem-Solution Format

In this format, you describe a problem of your prospect company in considerable detail. The next step is to present your product or service as the solution to that problem.

One caveat in using the Problem-Solution format is that it requires an intimate knowledge of your prospect's industry and company. Without a high degree of inside knowledge, you are not only likely to make mistakes, but may also seem presumptuous in telling your prospects their own business. The Problem-Solution format works best when you have a long-term relationship with your prospect and a strong knowledge of the company's strengths and problems.

An alternative to the Problem-Solution format is to describe the experience of another client who, by using your product or service, has had good results in solving a problem similar to that of your prospect. If you've chosen a good match or parallel situation, this approach will be effective.

Using the Need-Product-Benefit Format

This close cousin of the Problem-Solution format is a method of tying the product or service to solving a specific prospect problem and resulting in a specific benefit for that prospect. As its name suggests, you begin a sales presentation of this format by describing a need, transition into how what you have to sell will meet that need and conclude by stressing its benefit to your client.

This format is particularly useful in cases where the product or service being sold is new or has been re-engineered to meet a specific client need and thus provide a specific and unique, (when compared to the competition) benefit. In many sales minds, this format edges out the problem-solution format in that its use means that you end up talking about how your product or service will benefit the prospect—an excellent way to wrap up a sales presentation as it is more client-centered than other formats. Use of the Need-Product-Benefit format assures that you will end up talking about benefits to the client and almost certainly invite follow-up questions regarding those benefits.

Using the Past-Present-Future Format

This can be an effective approach if the evolution of a product or advanced product development is a strong selling point. You may wish to skip the historical or "past" part of this format and just go with a brief synopsis of how things are being done, followed by a detailed presentation of your product.

This format is more suited to a prospect who finds change more difficult than do others, or who has used the same systems or methods for a long time. Be careful not to be overly critical of the prospect's current way of doing things. Remember, that prospect has stuck with a competing product or service for a long time because there was, and probably still is, some positive feeling toward your competition.

If you push too hard, you'll only solidify the resistance to change that's already there. On the other hand, if you maintain an approach such as, "What you've been doing may have worked well up to now, but here are some distinct advantages to making a change," you are gaining the wedge you need to make change possible.

Using the Disadvantages-Advantages Format

If a company is starting up, or it's a new division or a totally new product, and if you don't have to deal with resistance to change, you may want to use a Disadvantages-Advantages format.

Here the initial content of your presentation, beyond introducing yourself and telling them your objective, is to be directly critical of the competition. This format is useful in a highly competitive situation where directness and a "just-the-facts" approach are appreciated and are likely to be rewarded with an order.

Some presenters make the mistake of going into too much detail about the competition in the Disadvantages-Advantages format. Balance your presentation so that you spend most of the time talking about *your* product or service. After an initial mention of the competition's name and product, you might merely refer to them as "the competition" or "other products."

One important strategic point is to cover the "Disadvantages" side first, so you end up talking about *your* product and its advantages toward the end of your remarks. Remember, those present are more likely to retain what you say *last* than what you say first. It's important to emphasize *your* company, products, and services in all their positive aspects in this final portion of the presentation.

In sales presentations, there are no absolutes about formats. Experimenting with these formats, or even combining them into more lengthy presentations will lead you to the conclusion that what works best is a matter of what you are most comfortable with, your level of product knowledge, and prospect expectations.

Regardless of the format, emphasizing your product and its advantages and ending up positively and nondefensively should be major goals in structuring your presentation.

Always Answer the Question, "What's So Good About YOUR Product?"

If asked this question after your presentation, those present should be in almost total agreement on the answer. This can happen only if you deliberately and emphatically point out the USPs (unique selling points) of your product or service.

Decide what these points are in advance and make them an integral part of the "positives" section of your presentation. That is, if you are using the Problem-Solution format, the solution should be built around those USPs or selling features.

Think of your USP as *spotlight ideas to your showcase idea* (see Chapter 4). Since we like to think in threes, this is a good number of USPs to include in your presentation. If yours is a complex product or service, you may want to expand to as many as five; but if you go beyond this, you will dilute the impact of your message.

Sales features or USPs should be brief and in headline form. For example: "Calculon computers have the highest reliability rating in the industry," or "Calculon maintains the largest support and maintenance staff in the computer business," or "Only Calculon has 1-800-COMPUTE, a 24-hour toll-free hotline for service and information."

Once again, the USPs take on the role of spotlight ideas, all in support of that showcase idea or objective for your presentation. Thus, these USP's serve as headlines that put the focus on your objective.

Concluding Your Sales Presentation

Usually, sales presentations end up with a brief Q&A session followed by your closing comments. Your summary statement should contain the following elements:

1. *Thanks for the opportunity of meeting with the prospect.* A brief and sincere thanks will suffice. Don't grovel, as in thanking them for the "privilege" of meeting with them. They won't believe it.

2. *Features summary.* In briefest headline form, repeat your USPs or spotlight ideas. Be sure to use the *exact* language used in your presentation; repetition builds retention.

3. *Repeat the objective or showcase idea.* Tell them that you'd very much like their business (all customers like hearing that) and then restate the objective with which you began the presentation. If you are seeking an order, say so; a sales contract, say so.

Close to Win

The point here is to be direct and say that you welcome a positive result. In wrapping up your sales presentation, you are thus linking the positive features of your product with the action you want that prospect to take, an important association to end up on.

Using the Language of Selling

Although presentational language is covered in Chapter 2, the sales presentation requires special consideration and some additional pointers.

Use Client-Centered Language

"It's new." "It's state of the art." "It's at the cutting edge." Aside from their being dreadfully overused, these phrases say nothing client-centered.

If you are making a claim about a product, try to do so from a client, or WIFM ("What's in it for me?") perspective: "It's easier to install," "Requires less down time," "Increases productivity 15 percent"—these are all WIFM phrases that give the prospect a benefit he or she can readily relate to.

Many salespeople are in the habit of making product-centered rather than prospect-centered claims because such statements require thinking only about the product. Prospect-centered claims require thinking about that specific customer and linking his or her needs directly to the product.

If the claim doesn't mention the customer, reexamine it and see if you can inject some customer-centered or WIFM language.

Be Definite, Not Tentative

What would be your reaction if you were on an airliner and the captain said over the intercom, "I hope we'll be landing safely in Cleveland at 7:30 tonight"? If you hadn't taken off yet, you'd get off the plane. Why? Because the captain's choice of the phrase "I hope" suggested some doubt about a safe arrival. Such tentative language doesn't belong in the airline cockpit or in the sales presentation.

If you are in the habit of saying, "I think you'll find our products to be . . ." you're being too tentative. Prospects prefer a more positive approach, such as "I know you'll agree that . . ."

Tentative language is a normal part of polite conversation and can easily slip into a sales presentation if you're not careful. If your language choices are tentative rather than positive, that tentativeness will be associated with you and your product. Use definite, positive phrases in your presentation and save the "maybe's, might be's, and I think so's" for polite conversation.

Here are some examples of "tentative" versus more effective "positive" or definite phrases:

TENTATIVE	DEFINITE
It might be possible to	I'll make sure that
I think that	I'm confident that
In the past	My experience tells me
You might want to consider	I know you'll be happy if
I really hope	I'm certain that
If we do business	As our customer, you
We've been pretty happy about	We've been tremendously proud of
Please note that	It's vital to remember
If there's anything I can do	I'm here to help!
We've been pretty fortunate	Business has been phenomenal!

Use Superlatives Freely

Your prospect isn't interested in signing up with a firm that has a "pretty good" track record or in buying products that are "among the finest." If you're the best, say so. If you're not, find another reason why buying from you is advantageous and make it a focal point of your presentation.

Don't Apologize for Selling

The sales presentation is no place for apologies. Yet if everyone in the room has a bigger title than yours or the CEO unexpectedly plants himself or herself in the room to hear what you have to say, you might find yourself apologizing for taking up their time.

If you're new to the sales business, you might be both surprised and intimidated by the fact that all these people have gathered to hear from you and may be spending a lot of money based upon what you have to say.

Some salespeople deal with their anxiety by apologizing for selling. Such phrases as, "I know your time is valuable, so I'll try to keep my remarks brief," or "This is a busy time of year for you, so I'll hurry," indicate that you aren't entirely convinced of the value of your products or service.

Name Your Competition

If you are comparing your product to another, particularly in the Disadvantages-Advantages format, it will be necessary to mention the competition. There was a time, in sales as well as in advertising, that direct mention of the competition was taboo. Now, Coke can mention Pepsi, Chrysler can mention Ford, and if Gimbels were still in business, they'd be fair game for Macy's.

Take advantage of this new freedom and mention the competition by name, at least in the early part of your presentation. It shows that you are direct and that you've done your homework, particularly if you know the competition well.

One cautionary note, however: In mentioning the competition, be truthful. Don't be afraid to say what they do well and don't exaggerate their flaws, or your prospect will know what you're up to and you'll lose your most valuable sales tool, your personal credibility.

Also remember that sales presentations have a parallel to negotiations sessions in that you should be setting the stage for your next presentation. Your prospect may already have decided to go with the competition, and although you may not know it at the time, your whole presentation may be moot. In such cases, if you are too caustic in your mention of the competition, you are merely making your prospect edgy and defensive about his or her decision. If you go too far, there won't be a next time for you or your company.

Let Them Look First, Then Touch

You may feel that, like that certain brand of "squeezably soft" bathroom tissue, having them touch the product will make them more likely to purchase. In fact, it may be a crucial factor. Wait until you have finished the presentation, however, to give out "touchables."

Otherwise, the person who is doing the touching; the person who just gave up the touchable (who feels he or she let it go too soon and is watching the current toucher); and the person who is about to get the touchable ("He's had it long enough!"), as well as the row of listeners behind this trio ("Why did it start in their row?") are not listening to your presentation.

You should be the focus. Let them know they'll get the chance to examine the product later. The same is true for any kind of handouts. Let your audience know they're coming later, but don't give out supplementary material or premiums before or during your presentation. If you fall into this trap, you'll lose the attention of your audience as they distribute the material and then will divide their attention between your presentation and the handout.

Using Visual Aids for Maximum Impact

I have included this discussion here because it is in sales presentations that most of us need to use visual aids.

Visual aids are just that, a supposed help for your presentation, a visual supplement that should amplify the points you want your audience to remember. Yet, to many speakers, they become an impediment, a distraction that reduces rather than enhances the effectiveness of the presentation.

Tell Before You Show

Your presentation should star *you*, featuring a few visual aids to enhance your major points, not the other way around. You should go on first, not a slide or transparency. Even if you're using that simple but highly effective visual, the flip chart, the contents of the initial page should be covered by *two* blank pages and hidden from view as you begin your remarks. (The audience can see through one page.)

Don't Stay in the Dark

Dim the lights if you must, as you show your slides or transparencies, but stay in a lighted area rather than becoming the anonymous "offstage announcer" for your own presentation. Eye contact, body language, and visual impact of the speaker are all communicative elements that are shrouded by darkness and are all elements that increase the impact of your presentation if you leave the lights on.

Put Up and Shut Up

When you put up a slide or transparency, or as you flip your flip chart to the next page, no one is listening, so don't talk. Instead, give them about five seconds to look at the visual and then tell them what it represents.

After telling them what the visual is, direct them to the portion you want to talk about and wait a few seconds for your audience to find your point of reference. Follow these steps with each visual, and the visuals work for you. If you don't, you'll be constantly competing with your own visuals, and neither you nor the visuals will win.

Talk to People, Not to Slides

One sure way to be overrun by your visuals is to talk to them instead of your audience. Make sure that your eye contact remains with your audience. Know *exactly* what each slide contains, and it will make it easier for you to keep your eye contact where it belongs: on your audience.

As for the visuals themselves, keep them simple and keyed to the text of your talk. Copy should be in headline form, and diagrams should be understandable at a glance. More complicated material such as system diagrams or contract language should be handed out later (which you'll tell your audience).

The Presentation Should Begin and End with You

At the end of a sales presentation, your audience should have the impression that they just saw and heard a sales presentation with you as the presenter, not a slide show with you as the narrator. This means that your talk ends as it began: projector off, screen blank, and you as the dominant figure.

Organizing Your Visual Aids

Visuals should enhance your presentation, and having them out of order or handling them poorly will chop up your presentation or even give it an unanticipated comic tone. Double-check the order of your visuals before *each* presentation and become familiar enough with your projection equipment to keep things running smoothly.

Have a Spare Bulb, an Extension Cord, and a Spare Presentation

You've probably already heard that it's important to carry a spare projector bulb (and it is, just in case). Many projectors come with one placed in the lid for such an emergency. Experience and a few awkward moments have caused me to add these tips:

First, I've seen as many presentations disrupted by the lack of a near-by electrical outlet as I have by the lack of a spare bulb. Carrying even twenty-five feet of extension cord in an unopened package (it takes up very little room this way) just might save your presentation, or might at least help it go the way you planned.

Second, you should be fully capable of smoothly delivering your talk *without visuals,* just in case projection equipment is suddenly unavailable. As an alternative, you might be able to re-create some of your visuals on flip charts; but be ready to go without them.

Your audience, never having seen your presentation or visuals, doesn't really care or isn't all that distracted by the sudden unavailability of the visual end of your presentation—unless you keep saying, "If I only had my slides you'd see that . . ."

Pointers About Pointers

Pointers are just that, pointers—meant to guide your audience to a specific part of a visual. They are not riding crops, conductors' batons, leg scratchers, or walking sticks, just to name a few of the alternate uses I've seen speakers devise over the years. Use the pointer only at the time you need it, provide the required visual guidance for your audience, and then fold it or otherwise get it out of sight.

If you are using one of the new laser pointers that put a focused dot of light on the desired part of your visual, don't overdo it. A laser pointer is an excellent tool if used judiciously, but in the hands of the overzealous user, it can become a distraction.

Speaking of hands, if the hands holding a laser pointer are just a bit shaky, the light spot dances furiously. Solve this problem by resting the pointer on the podium or on your folded arm.

Using a Product Demonstration

Many sales presentations can have their impact heightened by a demonstration of a product or process in action. Such demonstrations can turn to disaster if you don't take a few precautions.

If you're an old hand at these things, you might think you need just one or two run-throughs. You may be right, but you're gambling—an activity that should be reserved for the casino or the track, not the conference room, where you really can't afford to lose.

A jewelry wholesaler wanted to impress his prospects with a dramatic demonstration of the impact-resistant crystals on an expensive line of watches. At the presentation, he put the watch on the table and hit it squarely with a hammer. The audience spent the rest of the presentation stifling their laughter as our beleaguered salesman scooped up the parts of the smashed watch. The crystal remained intact.

If a demonstration is to be part of your presentation, go over it at least ten or twenty times and get the bugs out in private. There is really no way to recover from a failed demonstration, so don't risk it. Practice!

Making a Successful Team Presentation

If your product or service involves complex technical and/or financial or even legal data, it may be necessary and desirable to make the presentation a team effort, with each member of the team handling the portion of the presentation in which he or she is most expert.

Keep the Presentation Team Small

In planning the team presentation, don't have too large a team—no more than three or four presenters being a good rule of thumb. A larger team will inevitably have varying degrees of presentational skill and experience that will dilute the impact of the message. The mere logistics of more than three or four speakers getting up and down to speak will make things cumbersome.

Going on stage or up to the dais with a large entourage can make it look as if you're intimidated by the size or importance of the account to the extent that you brought along everyone but your receptionist to paper the house.

Instead, use a core team of three or four members with additional support personnel in the room—not as presenters, but as specialists who should be introduced as experts to handle any questions beyond the scope of the presentation team.

Maintain Unity in Your Team

Competition may be healthy among sales-force members working solo, but competition among members of a sales-presentation team is a formula for failure. For the sake of organizational and communicative clarity, the team should have a leader who will act as chief presenter and introduce the other team members.

All of the team members should support each other! This means that disagreement in front of your audience is to be avoided at all times. Make sure your team knows not to interrupt or correct a team member. A unified team also means not disagreeing with the response of a team member to a question from your audience, certainly not publicly.

A technique in bolstering the impression of a harmonious team is to deliberately refer to and reinforce each other's remarks. ("As Linda pointed out in the cost calculations . . .") Of course, use first names only, and once again, *never* publicly contradict or recast each other's remarks.

Rehearse Your Team

A team presentation generally means that it's an attempt to capture a substantial account. The best-planned presentation, if not practiced as a team effort, can come off looking as if the team has never played this game before (which might be the case).

Don't just meet, hand out team assignments, and gather at the presentation site. Practice and coordinate such items as:

1. Order of presentation
2. Introductions
3. References to each other's segments (which should be planned and included)
4. Distribution of the subjects in the Q&A session
5. Closing summary

If each of these elements is planned and coordinated and the entire presentation is practiced with the entire team present, you will give the appearance of a unified and winning team rather than a bunch of people with names like Larry, Curly, and . . . who was that other guy?

Summary

What makes selling a tough game is the fact that most sales presentations don't have positive outcomes. If they did, you could become fabulously successful with just a few days' work. Realize that each presentation is a fresh start—a new chance at a positive outcome.

Remember that each new prospect is seeing your presentation for the first time and deserves that "opening-night" level of energy. That level of enthusiasm, along with a truly prospect-centered approach, will mean more positive outcomes for more of your sales presentations.

Quick Review:
Making Effective Sales Presentations

1. Know your objective (gaining new business, renewing a prior account, providing informational support) and construct your presentation to meet that objective.
2. Deal with objections right away.
3. Don't play "ostrich" on product problems. Being open about them builds credibility.

4. Don't be ashamed of selling, or subtle about the desired outcome.

5. Every presentation should specifically say why your product or service is best.

6. Be prospect-centered, not product-centered (what's in it for them rather than what's in it for you).

7. Avoid tentative language. Say what *will* be rather than what might be.

8. In discussing the competition, be direct and factual but avoid cheap shots.

9. If prospects go with another vendor this time, follow up by remaining in touch as you work toward next time.

10. *You* should be the focus of your presentation, not your visuals.

Chapter Eight

Instant Speeches

Handling Spur-of-the-Moment and Special-Occasion Speeches

At-a-Glance Summary

This chapter is about how to give successful extemporaneous or spur-of-the-moment speeches and speeches for special occasions such as nominations, awards ceremonies, toasts, and eulogies—the rhetorical equivalent of fast food—minimal, but with just the right ingredients for getting the job done.

Instant Speeches: Handling Spur-of-the-Moment and Special-Occasion Speeches

The spur-of-the-moment speech is communication's answer to fast food. Like fast-food meals, impromptu speeches may never win awards, but they do get the job done and quench your ideational appetite, even if only momentarily.

Once you have made a few speeches, your level of terror begins to subside as you realize that you are not only capable of functioning in the public-speaking arena, but you can actually learn to enjoy it. Unfortunately, that state of enjoyment can be extinguished instantly when you hear your name in the same sentence as the phrase, ".... will now say a few words about ..."

Impromptu or extemporaneous (of the moment) speaking with little or no notice can be made a lot easier if you employ a few simple strategies.

Use Your Mind—Instead of Losing It

Former Vice President Dan Quayle was right: A mind is a terrible thing to lose—which is exactly what happens to many of us when we learn that we're about to give an impromptu speech.

You may find yourself thrown into a fit of saying something to yourself like, "Oh my God! What will I say first?" ... "What if I go blank?" ... "I'll tell a joke; no, that might not work," and on and on.

Such rapid-fire thinking is totally nonproductive and misdirected. The fact is you do need something to say, but on the spur of the moment your tendency is to focus on the exact words to use. You don't need words; you need an idea.

Remember, Language Is Automatic

That's a simple statement, but in gaining the confidence to successfully deliver the impromptu speech, it's an extremely important statement to grasp. When you think about it, you'll realize that almost all of the speaking you do is impromptu, without prior planning as to *exactly* what you'll say.

When you have a reaction to a situation, or wish to cause an action by saying something to someone, you do it—no notes, no outlines, just some words generated by an idea or a need.

Think about it. If you're waiting to board an airplane and someone walks over and deliberately picks up a piece of your luggage and starts for the exit, you don't stand there and have a debate with yourself about what to say: "Maybe I'll yell 'Police!' or an expletive . . . No, that would be too strong and this is a public place . . . but then it's an expensive piece of luggage . . ."

The fact is, you react immediately, both verbally and maybe even physically, to get back your luggage. If you did stand around thinking what to say, nothing would happen, nothing, that is, but the loss of your luggage.

Yet, when they are being introduced to "say a few words," most inexperienced speakers will focus on *exactly* what to say and as a result will say very little. The solution to avoiding this mental logjam is in that statement: *Language is automatic.*

"If you build it, they will come," said a ghostly voice to the Iowa corn farmer in the film *Field of Dreams,* exhorting him to build a baseball stadium there on the farm. An impromptu talk works much the same way in the presence of an idea. If you have an idea, don't worry about the exact words, they will come.

The point of what I've been saying thus far is to stop focusing on the exact words and focus instead on an exact idea. If I were to stop right here, you might accuse me of having substituted one problem for another. Even if you agree that language is automatic, you may be saying, "So what, unless you have an idea?"

You're quite right, so now let's talk about ways to organize your ideas for the impromptu or spur-of-the-moment speech.

Eight Idea Formats for Building Instant Speeches

If you are given the topic on short notice, an effective approach is to place the topic into one of the formats presented hereafter. As you will discover, an idea format organizes the information for you, and you can flesh out your idea based upon your knowledge of the topic. You'll also come to prefer certain of these formats so that their application to a wide range of topics becomes routine, a kind of "formula speech."

Let's say that you are a sales executive at a trade-association meeting and you are suddenly asked to speak on the topic, "Handling Customer Objections." Admittedly, this is not a tough topic for a sales executive; but unless you have a specific direction to go in, you are forced back to the "What will I say?" logjam. Instead, apply one of these formats to the topic and you will have an instant idea as well as a format for your speech.

Format #1: Teach a Lesson

No, I don't mean putting on your professorial robes and launching into an extended dissertation. But what have you learned in dealing with customers that most salespeople either never knew or simply forgot? What valuable conclusion or insight has your experience brought you? Simply answer either of these questions for your audience and your impromptu speech is done.

Format #2: Define a Term

This format is one in which you are varying the topic to suit your own ideas. Given the topic, "Handling Customer Objections," you might want to define the difference between a real objection and a negotiating ploy that you've heard from customers. Perhaps there is another customer base out there that has been largely overlooked by those in your audience, and you may wish to redefine "the customer."

Look at your own area of expertise and topics you are likely to end up talking about. There are usually terms to define or redefine, including, as in the preceding example, terms we use every day. The "Define-a-Term" format works well in that it gives you a chance not only to talk about something you know about, but even to talk about the obvious—you'll hope with a perspective your audience hasn't heard before.

Here is how the opening of a "Define-a-Term" format would sound for the sample topic "Handling Customer Objections":

> I could talk to you today about handling customer objections, but before we have the opportunity to handle those objections, we have to know who those customers are. So today I am instead going to offer you an expanded definition of the term "customer," to include some people you haven't previously thought about as potential customers. In the past, we used to define customers as . . ."

Format #3: Describe the Past, Present, and Future

This is a format particularly well suited to the senior spokesperson, and conversely less useful to those of you in the earlier stages of a career. If you have been in a field or with an organization long enough to know its history, the "Past-Present-Future" format is well suited to a wide array of topics.

For example, with our sample topic, "Handling Customer Objections," you could talk about changes in the nature of and type of customers in the past, present, or future, or the same aspects of customer objections.

Almost any idea can be put into this format, if you have the background to use it effectively. It's also simple to apply because its sequential nature organizes the talk for you more definitely than most formats. The only caution to be applied on this format is that it can easily become too long for an impromptu talk, which should generally last between three and five minutes.

Format #4: Change the Topic

The formats presented thus far will work well on topics within your own field of interest or expertise. It's possible, however, that you'll be asked to speak on a topic with which you're not totally comfortable. Perhaps you sense that the audience might have more knowledge than you do, or there is a much more pressing issue in need of discussion.

In such cases, you might feel hemmed in by the moment and the pressure to speak on a subject of which you have little knowledge. The speech that follows usually shows it. On the other hand, you don't want to embarrass your host ("I'm sorry, there must be a mistake, because I don't know much about that topic") or yourself ("I'd like to speak about customer objections, but so many of you know so much more than I do . . .").

Instead, gracefully but directly change the topic to one with which you are more comfortable and proceed with your planned remarks. Here is an example of a deft switching of topics:

> "Handling Customer Objections" is an important subject we all spend a lot of time considering, but because we spend that time, we might begin to lose sight of keying our presentations to the latest marketing campaign; so today, with your indulgence, I'm going to take a detour into what I'm sure you'll find to be useful information on that marketing plan."

Format #5: State a Problem and Give a Solution

This format is particularly suited to political, community, or personnel-management issues, or when combined with the "Define-a-Term" format, in which you may wish to organize your talk not just by stating a problem but also by defining it and proposing a solution.

Format #6: Agree/Disagree

This is a simple means of doubling the number of options available to you on a topic to be discussed that has pro and con sides.

For example, if you were asked to speak to a consumer group on selecting the best used car, you might instead speak on why purchasing a new car is a better alternative, effectively "disagreeing" with the assigned topic. If asked to speak on the need for continued levels of defense spending by the federal government, you might instead speak on the need for reallocation of resources brought about by world political changes.

Anytime you go with an "Agree/Disagree" format, the rule is diplomacy. In presenting another perspective on an issue, one other than your audience or host expected, the idea is not to say, "I'm right and you're wrong." Rather, the objective, aside from giving you another idea option for this impromptu speech, is to present your thoughts in an, "Even if we disagree with it, here is a perspective we ought to be familiar with" tone.

The objective is to increase your number of options for speaking material, not to embarrass your host or needlessly turn an audience against you.

Format #7: Base Your Speech on a Quotation

The reason there are literally dozens of books with thousands of quotations is because other people, either through the gift of eloquence or through an accident of timing (they got there first) have said something better than most of us have said it.

Just as many of us have a favorite joke or story, you may have a favorite quotation that is particularly memorable, if not for its humor, for its appropriateness to an issue or situation. Perhaps its use of language is particularly clever.

Regardless of the reason it holds your favor, the "Quotation/Comment" format is comprised of your opening your remarks with that particular quote and then offering an impromptu commentary. Although this format may seem spontaneous to an audience, it requires that you be prepared to cite a particular quote, usually from memory.

One cautionary note about using a quotation: Make sure you do so accurately and that you cite the proper source. Audience members rightly become disturbed by a quotation that's just a little bit off or is attributed to the wrong author, especially an audience that knows your subject area and might have more than a passing acquaintance with the quotation.

Also, if you use a quotation, don't use one that will be most obvious to your audience. I once sat in an audience listening to a speaker try to wow an audience with his literary acumen by quoting some of the better-known words of Charles Dickens. The literary scholar sitting next to me whispered, "If only he had used some good Dickens!"

Format #8: Begin with an Interesting Fact

Did you know that there are more radios in the United States than people; or that pasta, that staple of Italian food, originated with the Chinese? . . . Or that, well, you get the idea. If there is an unusual statistic or other piece of information that will amaze or at least momentarily captivate your audience, it can be a good starting point for your talk.

Using a bit of trivia as a starting point can be a helpful attention getter, especially when it has a close relationship to your audience, or it can be a fun way to get started even if getting to your topic is somewhat of a stretch.

For example, if I were giving a talk on how quickly the public forgets, I might begin my speech by saying, "Can you name an American President who served in the twentieth century and yet was *never* elected to office?" (The answer is Gerald Ford.)

By making use of these formats, you are far beyond survival and well on your way toward prospering in the impromptu arena.

Preparing for the Impromptu Speech

Now let's talk about developing ideas to plug into those formats. For impromptu speeches that really sparkle, you should be on an almost constant state of alert for information you can use.

Keep an Index-Card File

Clip newspaper articles that contain possibly useful information; when listening to another speaker, be ready to jot down a brief note should an especially quotable utterance occur. Another excellent and yet under-used source of speech material is the radio, especially with the increased popularity of talk programming. Much of this programming, whether local or national, is rife with useful information on everything from personal finance to household tips.

In a month of casual information gathering, you will have quite a collection of quotes, stories, and articles that you can apply to a wide array of impromptu speaking situations.

Being ready for the impromptu speech isn't a full-time job, but more a way of thinking. You hardly notice seashells on the beach, unless you're collecting seashells. The same is true of ideas for speeches, quotes, and stories. They are all around you, and once you start collecting, it will take surprisingly little time to become a highly proficient impromptu speaker.

As I pointed out earlier, once you have the ideas, the words will come.

Relax Before You Speak

That is, until you're comfortable at the speaker's podium. The normal tension of an impromptu-speaking situation pushes many speakers into the "talking is success, silence is failure" mode, and so they just launch into things immediately and are nervous throughout the talk. Instead, take a moment, establish eye contact with your audience, glance at your notes if necessary, take a breath, and then—and only then—get started.

Consider the Pros and Cons of Using Notes

A question rather than a tactic, but an important decision you'll need to make in accordance with your own comfort level. The general rule in making some "off-the-cuff" remarks is not to use notes; but then the existence of the phrase "off the cuff" originated with British Parliamentary speakers who were said to deliver their orations from notes scrawled hastily on their starched cuffs.

Making yourself comfortable should be the guide in whether you use notes or not, at least when you're relatively new to the impromptu-speech situation. Eventually, you should be able to dispense with notes, secure in the knowledge that your idea will get you through. Notes might be useful if you will be reading an involved quotation and it's essential to get it exactly right.

The same rule would apply to a set of statistics whose accurate citing is essential to your message. Think of notes as an even more minimal version of the phrase outline discussed in Chapter 4: a word or two, a format name, but no more.

Think on your feet, not off a card.

Closing Your Speech

Those of us who purport to help you, the speaker, pay plenty of attention to getting started, being organized, and not going blank, but we don't say enough about stopping.

This problem is especially apparent in the impromptu speech. You have your idea, plug in a format, and away you go. But how and when do you stop? Unless you plan your closing, your talk will end with the all-too-familiar shrug followed by an awkward glance in the direction of your host that says, "Get me out of this!"

Instead, plan your wrap-up and rehearse it. The key is to use a direct closing phrase such as, "That concludes what I have to say about customer objections. Thank you for inviting me." Or, "In ending my remarks, let me leave you with one thought that I hope will be with you well beyond this evening . . ."

You may wish to turn the proceedings back to your host with a line such as, "That wraps up my remarks for now, and in saying goodbye, I give you once more to our gracious host . . ."

Conclusions for the impromptu talk need not be elaborate, but they should be direct, and, most important, be there. Otherwise, your talk will end either on an abrupt note or on a silence that indicates you have run out of ideas and verbiage.

Practice your conclusion and, especially if you're new to the impromptu-speaking game, learn to rely on one or two stock closers such as the aforementioned. This way, you can better focus on delivering the speech, assured that a smooth conclusion is to follow.

Remember, Audiences Are on Your Side

This is a comforting piece of information to bear in mind as you are faced with the prospect of presenting an impromptu talk. The fact is, everyone present is glad that you are the one walking toward the podium instead of him or her.

This "better you than me" attitude doesn't seem all that comforting at first consideration, but audience members know you are speaking on the spur of the moment and therefore don't expect the same degree of fluency of word or thought. Nor are they expecting an extensive and prepared address complete with visuals. Instead, it's just you, an idea or two, some words, and maybe an interesting insight.

Under these circumstances, knowing that an audience wants you to succeed, you might even come to prefer the informality, the conversational style, and the freedom of the impromptu setting.

In summary, to maximize your degree of success in the impromptu talk, internalize the idea that language is largely automatic and that the only real search you need be on is for an idea. Practice using some of the formats covered earlier in this chapter, feeling free to combine them and even invent some of your own.

Finally, get lots of practice. Try an exercise such as turning to the table of contents of a news magazine and randomly selecting various topics. Try giving three-minute impromptu speeches on some of these topics, even if some of them seem unrelated to your sphere of knowledge or interest. In words that will undoubtedly be someday attributed to Yogi Berra (I said it, he didn't), it's easy to speak spontaneously, *if you're prepared.*

Preparing Special Speeches for Special Occasions

A close cousin of the impromptu speech is the special-occasion speech—it pops up on short notice and is often delivered with minimal preparation. This category includes introductions, award presentations and acceptances, nominating speeches, eulogies, and toasts.

Following are some guidelines for the various types of special-occasion speeches, and some common errors you should avoid.

Presenting Introductions

Introductory speeches, as the name suggests, introduce a speaker to an audience or a new employee or executive to his or her organization. The major elements in the success and effectiveness of the speech of introduction are clarity of purpose and brevity.

In introducing someone, perhaps the main or featured speaker, *immediately* state the purpose of your remarks to your audience in language as simple and direct as, "It's my role this evening to introduce our featured speaker . . ." followed by the body of the introductory speech.

Within the body of the speech itself, you should include two subject areas: the purpose or topic of the guest speaker's remarks and some biographical information on your guest. Since a speech of introduction should not exceed three minutes in length, biographical items should be limited to those areas that are of some importance to your audience.

Thus, if you are introducing a new head of the corporate legal staff, you should be talking more about his or her legal/educational credentials than the person's reputation as a high-school basketball star. Of course, if you're at a sports-awards dinner, you might make just the opposite selection.

When possible, check with the person you're introducing for the inclusion (or exclusion) of items from the introduction. You also might want to examine one of the many *Who's Who* guides for further information on your guest.

Ending the introduction can be accomplished by a call for applause, for example: "I'd like you to join me in welcoming . . ." (you raise your hands to start the applause and turn toward the guest speaker). In a more intimate setting or where applause is not appropriate, a simple "Ladies and gentlemen, our guest . . . (title and name)," followed by your turning toward the guest, will make it obvious that your introduction has ended.

ERRORS TO AVOID: *Excessive length.* An introduction, especially if it is for the featured speaker, should not exceed about three minutes in length. If it's much longer, it will lack focus and not serve your guest all that well, and all your audience will remember is its excessive length. If much more needs to be said, it should be done in written form and included in programs for the event or material to be distributed later.

Stealing the limelight. The introduction is for the guest; yet some speakers try to get in on their glory by talking about their close relationship to the person they are introducing; for example, while introducing a former astronaut, saying, "At one point in college I considered joining the space program, but our guest really did!" Leave yourself out of the introduction. The reason you were chosen to do it is that the audience already knows you.

Flowery language. It's an introduction, not a eulogy. Keep your language real and down to earth even in praise. For example, "Christina

Bleeker has been nationally recognized as the authority when it comes to knowledge of foreign markets," rather than, "Her performance as a foreign markets analyst has placed Christina Bleeker among the true legends of our civilization, a true oracle in a sea of muted voices . . ."

Such flowery language will do nothing more than embarrass your guest and may even get you a few stifled laughs.

Making Award Presentations

Speeches made to present awards are similar to introductory speeches in that they will also serve that purpose if the audience is not well acquainted with the recipient. In this case, however, the focus shifts from the biographical to the specific reasons, accomplishments, or traits for which the award is being given.

If your audience, or the recipient, is not all that aware of the purpose or the history of the award, you should divide your remarks into two portions: the first to explain the award, and the second, a brief biographical sketch of the recipient centering on the accomplishments or traits that culminated in the presentation of the award.

If the audience is familiar with the award, as in a monthly presentation to a sales force, you should focus on the recipient. Three or four minutes should mark the outer boundaries of duration for the presentation speech. Local or organizational custom may dictate a longer presentation, but these suggested guidelines will help keep the focus appropriately on the recipient and the award itself.

ERRORS TO AVOID: *"It was a close call!"* This is not the time to point out how tough it was for the judges to reach a decision, giving the recipient and the audience the idea that he or she barely scraped through. It's an award, not a qualifying exam, so feel free to praise the recipient.

Don't talk procedure. With all due respect to the accounting profession, one of the low moments for me during the notoriously lengthy telecasts of the Academy Awards is the introduction of the accountants from the firm that certifies or tabulates or does whatever it is they do with the results. This is a classic example of explaining the workings of the jeweled-lever watch movement in answer to the question of what time it is.

Audiences care about the award and who is getting it, not how many ballots, what kind of computer, or how many cigars were smoked in order to arrive at a decision.

Flowery language. Once again, this error makes the list because speakers tend to overpraise in an attempt to be gracious. The award itself should be sufficient praise. Avoid the temptation to speak of living legends, and so forth.

Accepting an Award

Is it just me, or does the line, "I'd like to thank the members of the Academy" immediately come to mind when you hear the phrase "acceptance speech"? Over the years, Hollywood has given us plenty of ideas of what not to do; here is what you should be doing as you speak to an audience to accept an award.

Prepare in advance. If you have any idea that you are to receive an award, even if chances are relatively remote, prepare some remarks and practice them in advance. It's dumb not to prepare, especially since audiences don't believe that most people who receive an award are truly surprised. All that "Gee, I really didn't expect this" stuff comes off as false modesty. Particularly in a corporate setting, an acceptance speech is a magnificent opportunity for self-promotion that you shouldn't overlook.

The acceptance speech should begin by thanking the speaker who presented the award for his or her gracious remarks, followed by mentions of the people by name and title who helped you with this accomplishment. Next thank the judges or whomever was directly responsible for the decision to present you with the award.

A great deal of what happens next is determined by the traditions and rules of the award-givers. For example, if yours is one of a series of awards, you may have time only for the aforementioned thank you. If yours is the major presentation of the gathering, you should describe, from your perspective, the genesis and history of the accomplishment that led to the award. Finally, you should inform your audience of what the award means to you personally; perhaps how it will change or affect your future work.

Speech contents such as describing the award-related accomplishment(s) or what an award means to you personally are interesting to audiences and are best delivered when prepared in advance. So, if at all possible, prepare and practice the acceptance speech; use minimal but legible notes to guide you; and enjoy the moment.

ERRORS TO AVOID: *Being unprepared.* As I stated earlier, people don't believe your surprise, even when it's genuine. At best you'll look disorganized.

Being shocked. If you receive an award, don't demean yourself by saying you didn't deserve it or expressing your disbelief that the award went to you. If there was any competition for the award, there will be those in the audience who will agree that you didn't deserve it, and you'll just be confirming their feelings.

Dragging out your soapbox. I said before that the Academy Award telecast has given us ample instruction on what not to do in awards ceremonies. Nowhere is this more true than when some ungrateful clown decides to use the award as a forum to bemoan the disappearance of the passenger pigeon or demand justice for those who are alleged to have captured Amelia Earhart.

If you have a cause to espouse, don't embarrass everyone present by launching into it at this moment. You'll do little to help your cause, and you'll end up making your remarks to an instantly hostile audience.

Making Nomination Speeches

Nomination speeches are usually very planned events, and the fact that you have been asked to give one means, or at least your audience will assume, that you are highly supportive of the person whose name you are placing in nomination. Therefore, your personal commitment to that candidate should be expressed in the speech. If absent, it could be taken as a signal that your remarks are less than sincere. If you know the nominee, say so, stating the basis and character of that relationship in a manner that supports his or her candidacy.

The nomination speech should highlight the accomplishments and positive characteristics of the nominee as they relate to fulfilling the demands of the position being sought. In addition, if there is a single overriding trait that makes the candidate deserving of the nomination, be it heroism, leadership ability, prominence in his or her field, a proven track record, or any such defining characteristic, you may want to build the speech around that particular trait, making it a recurring theme as you describe the office being sought.

If there is a negative issue that will be brought up during the nomination speech of an opposing candidate—for example, if your nominee has been in his or her field a short time—face that issue briefly but squarely, and do so just before the halfway mark in your speech. Audiences tend to remember best what they hear last and will retain more of your positive points.

Here is an example of how a possible negative might be handled:

> Before being completely overtaken with my deep enthusiasm for this candidate, let me say that I know some of you might feel that Art Crane should be with us a while longer before seeking this office. I'd invite any of you to take a close, detailed look at the record of *exactly* what Art has accomplished since joining us. If that record is measured, as it should be, in achievement and ability, Art Crane will *most definitely* be your nominee.

Note that while dealing with a potential negative, the language is positive, nondefensive, and enthusiastic. If this were a three-minute speech, you should not spend more than thirty seconds dealing with negative issues.

A good rule of thumb for the best length for nomination speeches is that they not exceed 20 percent of the length of the acceptance speech, with a three-minute length being the minimum.

ERRORS TO AVOID: *Outshining the nominee.* During the 1992 Democratic Convention, there was considerable concern about having Governor Mario Cuomo, certainly among the foremost contemporary political speakers, deliver the nomination speech for then Governor Clinton. Governor Cuomo turned in his usual sparkling performance and fortunately, Governor Clinton performed well in beginning his successful quest for the presidency. This was a case in which, if the nominator outshone the nominee, the outcome of the election might well have been different.

Know the skills level of the nominee and remain compatible with it. If your reputation is that of a master orator, you might consider leaving some of your rhetorical armaments at the door. Otherwise, you'll risk the politically embarrassing predicament of having an audience that prefers the nominator to the nominee.

Exaggeration. Yes, we know you like the candidate, and we're glad you said so, but that "born in a log cabin that he built with his bare hands" is the stuff of comedic caricature and should not in any way slip into nomination speeches.

Also remember to keep your facts straight. The opposition will be listening, and an error of fact could create a decidedly disruptive side issue.

Giving Eulogies

A eulogy, or speech of tribute to a deceased friend or colleague, is a type of speech many senior managers and executives end up having to deliver at some point during their careers. Such farewells are speeches of tribute, a remembrance of the positive and endearing aspects of that colleague, and definitely a time to minimize if not ignore any negatives.

In many ways the eulogy parallels the nomination speech in that it is one of tribute, minus the obligatory call for a vote. It is also a time to define and characterize your relationship with the deceased in a caring tone.

Unlike the nomination speech, since there is no election in the balance and no strategy other than the creation of a fond memory, a good framework for the eulogy is to define the most noteworthy and endearing trait of the deceased and then tell a story of an encounter you had with the deceased that defined that characteristic.

If there is a glaring negative, it's best left unmentioned, but if you must include it, do so with the greatest delicacy. A good strategy here is to point out the good that was accomplished for many, despite what may have been perceived as a negative. Even if you are talking about the company taskmaster or someone who was known around the office as "the bean counter from hell," remember that reverence for the deceased and sympathy for his or her family rules in such situations.

If, in your judgment, the atmosphere and the subject of your eulogy invite mentioning a negative, be certain to balance it with a positive in the same sentence. For example: "There isn't one of you here today who escaped what some considered 'the wrath of Fred' as he reviewed your expense accounts, but there is also no one here who would argue that Fred's dedication and concern for our well being and success always exceeded his decibel level."

Whenever possible, consult with the family of the deceased in planning your remarks. Perhaps there is a trait or an event that they would like to have highlighted. The length of a eulogy is usually proportionate to the depth and length of your relationship with the deceased, but it would be wise to make your judgment out of consideration for those present.

You should also be attentive to the overall length of the services, as well as the wishes of the family of the decedent. In a service where there are to be a series of speakers, limiting your remarks to no more than five minutes is a good rule of thumb. If you are the major eulogist, ten to fifteen minutes in length is more appropriate.

ERRORS TO AVOID: *Excessive sentimentality.* Your communicative goal should be to create a fond moment for those paying final tribute to the deceased, not to depress those gathered with tearful good-byes and sentences that begin with phrases such as, "Never again will we . . ."

Humor. Be it a case of denial in helping you deal with your own grief or a misguided attempt to honor the wishes of the deceased who, let's say, was a firm believer in irreverence, the reality and terrible finality of such an event makes humor of any kind a strict taboo for most of us. So let solemnity be the communicative order of the day.

Brutal candor. Eulogies are meant to instill fond memories, not to do a "tell it like it is" biography. As I pointed out earlier, if there is a glaring negative to be dealt with, do so ever so briefly, balancing your remark with a positive. If there are several negatives, you are better off leaving them to be dealt with by a higher authority!

Offering Toasts

Drink (alcoholic or nonalcoholic) has long been the preferred conversational lubricant in many business and social settings. In the more formal or important of these occasions, you may be asked to present that short but potentially tricky speech known as the toast. The toast is an ancient ritual said to have originated in England shortly after the time of Christ.[1] In ancient Rome, men were expected to toast their mistress with as many glasses of wine as there were letters in her name.

Happily, things have toned down quite a bit, and this ritual is much less complicated today than it was in Roman times. In a business setting, however, the toast can be a tricky assignment because it requires the best of wit, brilliance, and memorability, all in an interval brief enough to prevent participants' arms from getting tired as they raise their glasses skyward.

It should be said, however, that making the challenge a bit less daunting is the fact that the memory of a less than sterling performance may be somewhat dimmed by the libation that immediately follows.

The keys to successful toasts lie, as in so many speech situations, in a keen knowledge of the audience: what their tastes are in humor—George Bernard Shaw or Lenny Bruce—their tolerance of or fondness for irreverence, or the high-mindedness or low-mindedness of their wit.

Toasts have a better chance of being remembered if they are not only suited to your audience but also chosen with the occasion in mind. For a complete selection of toasts, I'd recommend the Paul Dickson book cited earlier. Otherwise, you might want to look at one of the many books of quotations for ideas. Meanwhile, to help you get started, here are a few toasts of the all-purpose variety:

---

[1]Dickson, Paul, Toasts: over 1,500 of the best toasts, sentiments, blessings and graces, revised ed. (1991), Crown Publishers, 256 pp.

"May life bring you an abundance of friendship, love,
accomplishment, and good health in amounts that exceed
your grandest expectations."

"L'chaim—to life!"

"You have deserved high commendation, true applause and love."
(Shakespeare, *As You Like It,* Act I)

"May the very best days and happenings of your past
pale in comparison to the best days of your future."

"May the road rise to meet you, the wind be always at your back, the sun
shine warm upon your face, the rain fall soft upon
your fields and until we meet again, may God hold you
in the palm of his hand." (Traditional Irish toast.)

"To our very best friends, who know of our faults
and love us in spite of them!"

ERRORS TO AVOID: *Long toasts.* Especially if there is a series of toasts, more than three sentences is the kiss of death for any toast. Keep it short and make it memorable.

Offensive toasts. Even if you're in a crowd where ribaldry and profanity are not taboo, they are still unnecessary. Playing "Can you top this" with vulgarity is the worst kind of pandering to your audience and a losing game for any speaker. Besides, even with what you might consider to be the most bland of humorous remarks, you would be amazed by the ability of people to be offended, even when you aren't trying.

If you are in a setting where you are regularly called upon to perform such ritual communication, you will find that you'll soon develop a repertoire of favorite toasts that with minor adjustment are largely suitable to any occasion.

Summary

Instant speeches are the fast food of oratory, and, like fast food, they work well when the time for both preparation and consumption is limited. Begin with an idea and remember that language will occur automatically. Practice using some of the formats and techniques included in this chapter; and when you are finished, stop talking!

Quick Review:
Spur-of-the-Moment and
Special-Occasion Speeches

1. Remember, language is automatic, so seek an idea and the words will happen.

2. Have a few idea formats in mind, for example, teaching a lesson or defining a term.

3. Collect interesting quotes and trivia; they make excellent starting points for spur-of-the-moment speeches.

4. Pause as you start, to collect your thoughts and settle your audience.

5. Keep notes to a minimum, no more than a phrase or two.

6. Remember that audiences are supportive of the impromptu speaker (they're glad you and not they are up there).

7. During introductions, talk about your subject, not yourself.

8. Giving an award, the recipient is the star, so keep your remarks minimal.

9. Accepting an award, thank them and clear out; stay off your soap box and avoid false modesty.

10. In delivering a eulogy, err in the direction of excessive praise over excessive candor.

Part Three

SUREFIRE STRATEGIES FOR SPECIAL SITUATIONS

Chapter Nine

The Job Interview

At-a-Glance Summary

This chapter presents tactics to help you succeed in the job interview. It looks at many of the questions you will be asked, as well as the reasons behind them, and gives you specific tactical information on how to deliver the best responses.

Other topics covered include preparing for the interview, having the right attitude, and avoiding the errors job candidates commonly make.

The Job Interview

Whether it's one of your first attempts or you've played the job interview game before, it's not a game that changes all that much from entry level to executive position. Any job interview is a highly structured encounter in which you are questioned in a formal atmosphere, speaking mostly when spoken to, in response to a series of largely predictable questions. Some of the questions are strictly informational and relevant, others trivial and maybe even illegal. Some will be asked in an attempt to trip you up or to see how you react to stress.

Interviews are stressful for most of us because we control neither the content nor the outcome. Our lack of control of the situation is underlined by the fact that it is one of the few conversations we have in our adult life in which we are literally dismissed from the room at its conclusion.

The pressure is intensified if you have been through a series of interviews in which the outcome has not been positive. In such cases, you are probably aware that certain errors can be "fatal," and a sense of desperation may creep into your performance and make matters worse.

If you are beginning to feel that the deck is stacked against you in the interview, it is. This chapter will show you steps you can take, however, to improve your odds and even turn them in your favor.

Avoid the Usual Pre-interview Blunders

Blunder #1: Gaps and Glitches in Your Résumé

Make sure your résumé adds up chronologically. Often, job candidates omit a negative career experience or fail to account for some time in which they "stopped out" of the workplace, leaving a gap in the résumé that they don't expect people to notice. I've interviewed people with such gaps and have yet to see one who wasn't surprised that anyone noticed.

Have Dates in Your Résumé

Some résumés avoid dates altogether, or merely list a starting year for a job with no reference to how long the position was held. Your reasons for such vagueness might be to mask your age or to blur the amount of experience or time spent in a series of positions. Such evasiveness raises only more questions and gives the impression that you have something to hide.

Even if such gaps and glitches in your résumé don't keep you from getting to the interview, which they might, your interviewer will have to start off by clarifying your omissions or mistakes and you will begin the interview on the defensive—a very poor starting posture.

Blunder #2: Your Objectives Statement Is Not Compatible with the Position Being Sought

Many résumés contain an objectives statement such as; "To obtain an executive-level position in the public-relations field that will enable me to use my media-management experience and high level of interpersonal skills for the benefit of client companies."

This statement is fine if you are seeking a position in the public-relations field, but will not serve you well if sent to an aerospace manufacturer. Employers like to feel that they are unique and that you want to work only for them.

Job seekers, especially those engaged in an extensive search, can seem especially lazy from an employer's perspective if their objectives statement has a generic ring to it. In this age of computers and word processors, there is no reason why your résumé shouldn't be tailored for a particular position or career area, especially when it comes to the objectives statement.

Blunder #3: I Thought You Said East Broadway!

Woody Allen once said that 80 percent of success is showing up. You know how to dress and to be on time for an interview, but do you know *exactly* where the interview is going to be held? You may go to great lengths to prepare for an interview and then undo all your good work by being in the wrong place at the appointed time.

Double-check the location of the interview, and make sure you have the correct address. This seems like a minor detail, but Woody Allen was right. If you don't show up, or you show up late because you've been stuck in crosstown traffic (and look it!), it can really steal the thunder from all those remarks you had planned to make about yourself as being terrific at handling small details.

Blunder #4: Being Underprepared

Just who are these people, anyhow? What are the objectives of the company? What does it produce? How many divisions are there? How is the organization doing—last year, or this quarter? What are the major issues facing management? Just who is that management?

Answers to all of these questions are contained in the company's annual report. Most interview candidates read it in the reception area just before the interview. You should read it well in advance of your interview. (Annual reports may be obtained from the shareholder relations office or public affairs departments in publicly held corporations.)

Even if you don't understand all the financial data, you will come away with a good sense of the company's issues climate and future outlook. Just in case your interviewer has the same last name as the CEO (chief executive officer), by asking if they are related, you will have made it obvious that you have done your homework.

A further source of information not too often examined by job seekers is the employee newsletter or bulletin. Seek to learn the level of employee public service, recent promotions, and major internal issues from an employee perspective.

It is a mistake to submit to a job interview without having read this material in advance. Having a sense of the major issues facing a company, its new programs or products, or even the names of its senior executives or board members (one of whom might be present at your interview), is an easy way to differentiate yourself from other candidates. You will use such knowledge in your responses to interview questions and will leave the impression that you are organized and interested in them and their company.

Communicate a Winning Attitude

Know Your Strengths and Be Sure You Communicate Them

An essential part of communicating a winning attitude is telling your interviewer what you like about yourself—the positive traits that will make you an asset to that employer. Decide *in advance* which positive traits about you, your experience, or your background you want to highlight in the interview.

Pick three or certainly no more than four items about yourself that are most compatible with that position or company. Write these traits down and internalize them. Practice including these traits in your responses.

Avoid the Competition

Don't show up too early for your interview. They'll think you have nothing better to do with your life, which may be true, but it is not an impression you want to convey.

Another disadvantage of being there too early is that you will see and sometimes talk with other candidates. These conversations never provide you with an advantage. You may find yourself talking with someone who says something like, "You mean you don't have a law degree and you're still bothering to go through with the interview?" or "I hear the whole thing is rigged and none of us has a chance."

Such discouraging souls may have the wrong information, but they can still throw you off your game plan by causing you to compete with them.

Show up for the interview about five minutes before you are scheduled, and you will not only minimize the anxiety-provoking waiting time, but you'll also avoid the competition and be better able to concentrate on the task at hand.

Making a Commanding Entrance

As you enter the interview area, be aggressive enough to shake hands with your interviewer, or each member of the interviewing committee if feasible.

In formal interview settings where the interview is conducted by committee, you can expect an introduction by the committee leader, followed by some introductory remarks of your own.

Let Them Know You Want The Job

To armor themselves against what they perceive as a stacked deck, some interviewees steep themselves in an attitude of resentment toward the interviewer. This is conveyed by behavior that says, "I really don't need this job," or "I may even be too good, but I'll consider taking it."

For example, I once interviewed an individual who was, at least on paper, the most highly qualified candidate for a position. Perhaps it was those strong qualifications, as well as the attitudinal factors mentioned earlier, that prompted this poor soul to open the interview with: "Before we get started, let me tell you how I define this job and what I will and will not be doing if I get it." While I vividly remember this opening statement,

I remember little else of this encounter, because for me, it ended with those unfortunate words.

Don't act as if you don't want the job, because you just might succeed in convincing your interviewer to buy your act! Actually wanting the job and being willing to say so is an important part of winning at the interview game.

The Interview Begins

After introductions and the ritual comments about such items as the weather, your trip to the interview site, and so forth.—avoid stories here, they really don't care—the interview will begin with its first substantive question.

The interview has a specific purpose (to see if you're suitable for the job) and you have a specific objective (to seem more than suitable for the job). There is no one perfect answer to every question, nor can every possible question be anticipated. Most of the questions are quite predictable, however, and, with practice, can be handled effectively.

The following section of this chapter contains a series of interview questions and variations you can expect to encounter, along with analysis, advice, and sample responses for the most difficult or crucial questions. Remember always to respond with your own words and use the sample responses as a guide.

Handling the First Question

Tell me about yourself

ANALYSIS: Not really a question but a pleasantly delivered command, this common interview opener seeks to look beyond your résumé and get a picture of "the real you." Unfortunately, many candidates stumble here because they fail to anticipate the question and therefore have difficulty deciding what to include and what to leave out.

You want to demonstrate with your response that you are career-focused. Therefore you will want to center your response upon recent job or educational experience. Personal items such as marital status, hobbies, birthplace, and so on, should be mentioned briefly and only in positive terms.

SAMPLE RESPONSE: *First of all, I'd like to thank you for the opportunity for this interview. About myself, I'm a recent graduate of Regency College with a degree in marketing. At Regency, I worked at the college radio station and developed a real interest in the music business, which shaped my career plans and in many ways shaped my interest in your business. I've had two successful jobs in the record industry, as a talent coordinator and a distribution manager, and I'm looking to build on that success. On the personal side, I grew up in Los Angeles, I'm single and I have lived here all my life. My hobbies are sailing and collecting big-band records. Does that answer your question?*

ERROR TO AVOID: BEING TOO PERSONAL OR TOO NEGATIVE   Since most interview candidates fail to anticipate this question, the tendency is to make a snap decision about what to include and just ramble for a minute or so. This is how such items as a nasty divorce or your mother's diabetic condition end up in a response that makes the interviewer as uncomfortable as you are.

Keep your response business- and credential-oriented with only minimal personal information. If the interviewer wants a more personal response, he or she will ask.

Personal Questions

Any potential employer is going to be making a substantial investment in you, and you will be expected to perform as an asset to that employer. Part of that equation is usually fitting in as a member of the employer's team. Therefore, you can expect a number of personal questions that seek to know more about the person behind the résumé. For example:

Why should we hire you?

ANALYSIS: This question is really an invitation to market yourself. I have already suggested that prior to the interview you develop an agenda that consists of about three or four positive points about yourself that you want to include in your interview. If you haven't used any of these positives yet, here is the place to start.

SAMPLE RESPONSE: *As I've said earlier, I have a proven track record and a long-term interest in this business, which isn't just professional but personal.*

At the risk of sounding immodest, I've gotten real results for anyone I've worked with, and I'd very much like the opportunity to make that kind of commitment to you. I know I have the ability and am certainly among the best qualified.

ERRORS TO AVOID: *Arrogance,* including the mistaken notion that no one else can possibly do the job or that the organization cannot survive without you. They can.

How does your experience compare to most people interested in this position?

ANALYSIS: This question is really another way of finding out what you think of your own ability. Also, if you have some obvious deficit in your résumé, such as lack of a required credential or particular type of experience, this is the time to deal with it in a positive way.

SAMPLE RESPONSE: *I'm probably among the few with experience as wide-ranging as mine over a relatively short period of time. In fact, just in case you are concerned about the fact that I've worked in the industry for fewer years than some of the other people you will be talking with, I should let you know that I didn't include any of my apprentice time in college in my résumé. I limited the résumé to paid experience, but I think those internships should certainly be counted. So to summarize, I believe that my overall qualifications can definitely be characterized as second to none.*

ERROR TO AVOID: Knocking the competition. Be gracious here and don't belittle candidates with experience or credentials that differ from yours.

What are your special qualifications? or What particular trait makes you uniquely qualified to handle this job?

ANALYSIS: This is one of those questions that, because of its simplicity and the reluctance of many of us to engage in blatant self-promotion (even if requested), can be difficult if your response isn't planned. It's also another chance to accomplish your agenda and reinforce one of your positive traits.

SAMPLE RESPONSE: *I'd have to say that my industry knowledge sets me apart from most of the people you'll be seeing. I've spent years on a consistent career track that's given me the opportunity to view this field from many perspectives, and I believe that makes me really effective.*

ERRORS TO AVOID: *Not having a planned response* to this often-asked question can result in an answer that lacks focus.

Why did you leave your last job? or
Why are you looking to leave your present job?

ANALYSIS: On the surface this question seeks the information it asks. But it is also asking if you are running from a problem, or whether there is some pattern of instability in your occupational behavior.

SAMPLE RESPONSE: *For me, changing jobs is a matter of seeking career growth and advancement. As you might know, the Sell-Quest chain has had its problems over the past few quarters and the outlook was not good. I needed room and opportunity for advancement that just wasn't there, and so I decided to make a change.*

ERRORS TO AVOID: *Excessive negativity or lack of candor.* Your response should not be an attack upon a prior or present employer, no matter how justified or appropriate you might find it.

What are your personal goals?

ANALYSIS: This open-ended question can provide a wealth of information in such areas as how driven or ambitious you might be, how important family life is in relation to your career, and how willing you are to talk about yourself. This is a question that cannot be effectively answered without prior planning and thought. Your response may even give the interviewer an indication of your attention to detail as well as your analytical skills as indicated by the thoughtfulness of your response.

SAMPLE RESPONSE: *Accomplishment and the rewards that go with it. I am referring not just to the monetary rewards but the deep sense of personal satisfaction that comes from looking back on a career and realizing that you've made a difference, not just for yourself, but for your colleagues as well.*

ERRORS TO AVOID: *Failure to anticipate the question.* This is a question that requires prior thought or the result will be a vague or rambling answer that will create doubts about everything from your sincerity to your analytical ability. Plan ahead!

Humorous responses. Some respondents use humor in an attempt to mask their ability to deliver a substantive response. So avoid the "I want your job" sort of response. An attempt at humor here will fail, especially if you do want your interviewer's job.

Other personal questions you can expect

Do you consider yourself a team player?
What do you like best about yourself?
What do you like least?

In responding to any of these personal questions, you already know enough to present your best side when they ask for a positive. In discussing what you like least about yourself, however, keep your response brief and try to present a negative they'll like, such as overattention to detail or even a small degree of workaholism.

Loyalty Questions

From entry level all the way to the executive suite, almost every member of a company gains access to confidential information. While there is no sure way to predict your level of integrity in keeping such information to yourself, a good indicator is the terms in which you discuss your former employer or the one you are about to leave. The assumption is that if you are going to bad-mouth them, you might do it to this potential employer in the future.

Sample question: I hear your former company was a really crummy outfit—what do you think?

ANALYSIS: This seems like a straightforward and simple question, but it's actually a potential trap. If you left your last job under unpleasant circumstances or harbor some negative feelings toward that employer, you'll be tempted to pay them back with a few nasty comments. Don't do it. You'll come off as spiteful and untrustworthy, even if your remarks are accurate.

On the other hand, by declining to comment on problems at another company, you'll communicate an ability to be loyal, even to a former employer, and gain the trust of your interviewer(s). Of course, if there are large issues that are public knowledge, you may be asked to comment, but stick to what everyone has read in the newspapers and decline to provide any "inside information."

SAMPLE RESPONSE: *I really don't agree with your terminology. As you know, Sell-Quest had some problems and was reorganizing its marketing department, but they were a decent employer and even wanted me to stay on longer.*

ERRORS TO AVOID: *Being too quick to criticize a former or present employer.* They'll assume you'll be doing it to them in the near future. Also avoid revealing confidential information, even if you think you're showing your worth by doing so. Nobody likes a traitor, much less hires one.

Other loyalty questions

Tell me the inside story on your former boss.
Is the drug problem at that company as bad as I've heard?
Are you glad to be getting out of that place?

ERRORS TO AVOID: *Disloyalty.* Loyalty questions present the occasion to show your degree of loyalty and personal integrity. Don't use these questions as an opportunity to take shots at companies or individuals in your past, no matter how legitimate your gripes may be. If pressed, discuss only matters that are public information and then only briefly and in polite terms.
Revealing confidential information. Avoid going "off the record" or discussing trade secrets. If you are willing to betray a past employer, they'll assume you'll be willing to do the same to them in the future.

Stress Questions

Grace under pressure is often a key ingredient in any job situation, especially those that involve problem solving with clients and even dealing with difficult people and situations in the workplace. In a competitive environment or in the sales world, you are also likely to face rejection or negative outcomes along the way. By asking stress questions, or questions that might even ask you to discuss a negative aspect of your own performance, your interviewer is seeing how you react when the going gets rough.

Sample question: Tell us about your worst on-the-job mistake or error in judgment

ANALYSIS: This is the job interview equivalent of the question, "When did you stop beating your wife?" It clearly asks for a negative, but it is also a test of your humanity and honesty. Anticipate this question and be prepared to talk about a negative. The key here is to discuss an error that you made that was not overwhelmingly negative or catastrophic, but one that shows that you're human and even willing to admit it. If you can, as in the sample response, try to discuss a negative that you were able to turn into a positive. Also, after you've clearly admitted a mistake, politely and non-defensively redirect your response to a positive.

> SAMPLE RESPONSE: *Well, I once ordered a month's supply of stationery with our company's old address, but after some initial embarrassment, we ended up giving it to a charity and even getting a tax deduction in the bargain. Obviously, I'd rather focus on what I did well at Fereton Industries, which included running a department for three years that became known for its high morale and even higher productivity.*

Other stress questions

Why should we hire anyone who admits to mistakes?
Why have you had so many jobs?
Why should we hire a new graduate like you when we can get an "old pro" for similar money?
or
Why should we hire an "old pro" when we can get a new graduate with fresh ideas for less money?

ERRORS TO AVOID: Angry or defensive responses, even if the question is seeking them. Admitting errors but then blaming others or the equally fatal, "I never make mistakes." Also, resist the temptation to knock other candidates, as in knocking the old pro or the new graduates. Instead, state that you both have strengths and then talk about your own. This is particularly true if you're a new graduate being interviewed by an old pro or even the reverse.

Judgment Questions

These are questions that force you to make a choice and in so doing, to reveal some aspect of your personality. Such questions are often asked to assess how big a priority your career is or whether you are flexible or dogmatic when it comes to applying company policy. Judgement questions are difficult because the correct answer is determined by the corporate culture and the type of person they are looking for. Your attempt to gain information on either of these areas in advance by talking to other employees is the best clue to performing well on judgment questions.

In constructing and practicing your responses, be certain to include your real feelings in your response. If you don't, you'll only be tripped by your inconsistency with other parts of the interview.

What's more important, your family or your career?

ANALYSIS: A classic among unfair questions. If you immediately blurt out "Family!" you've just placed your potential employer in second place, not a good move during the job interview. On the other hand, if you relegate those whom you usually profess to love like life itself to second place, even for the moment, you come off as an expedient cad.

For most of us, both family and career are important at times, and herein lies the nucleus of an effective answer to this question.

For women, this question can take on a sharply sexist edge as a not-too-veiled, "So will you be having a baby and leaving us?" question. While no amount of legislation can prevent such blatantly sexist questions from being asked behind closed doors, remember that your true feelings here are none of your prospective employer's business.

SAMPLE RESPONSE: *I think that they are both important, each requiring major expenditures of thought, time, and effort. To succeed at both sometimes requires the shifting of those priorities from one to the other. Regardless of the answer you'd prefer to hear, I think that choosing either would be, at best, a half-truth and an oversimplification as well.*

Other judgment questions

Suppose a company policy seemed unreasonable, would you be willing to bend the rules?

If you catch an employee in a dishonesty, would you warn him (or her), or report the matter to senior management?

How to Talk About Money

Like the waiter who leaves the check face down on your table, most of us are a bit sheepish when it comes to discussing this most essential part of any job and job interview. After all, money or the need to earn more of it may be the very reason why you're having the interview in the first place.

Put aside any discomfort you may feel as you discuss your salary and be direct and above all honest about your worth and your needs. Also, in this initial interview, keep your responses simple and to the point. Avoid mentioning benefits and retirement plans or stating demands at this time. If they are interested, all these details will be worked out later.

If you are asked for the least amount you'll take, state that you'd rather not think in terms of minimums and then name your target number. Such questions may be intended to see how badly you need the job or to see how you'll react to being put on the defensive.

Sample question: What salary do you deserve?

ANALYSIS: This is a perfectly straightforward question that many respondents overcomplicate by failing to answer directly. The question asks for a number, and that's how it should be answered. That number should be realistic and fair to both sides.

> **SAMPLE RESPONSE:** *I believe that a salary of $45,000 is fair to both of us. I believe you'll agree that both my qualifications and my past salary history indicate that I merit that amount.*

> **ERRORS TO AVOID:** *Failure to respond directly and succinctly.* If you don't respond with a number or you give a lengthy justification of your qualifications along with your number, you'll communicate your discomfort and fail to get what you want.

Aiming too high or too low on the salary issue. Remember, your interviewer is probably an expert on the value of your services and may have a specific number in mind. Your goal should be to approximate that expectation or to have a truly overpowering reason if you don't.

Also, note that undershooting your worth in an attempt to beat the competition is just as serious as an error in the other direction. If your salary expectations are well below the standard or average for your field, a low bid will be looked at as an expression of doubt about your own ability or self-worth.

Speaking in ranges in response to a direct salary question. Stating a range is a way of saying that you're willing to work for the lower number, and it's exactly what you'll get.

Questions They Shouldn't Ask

You are probably aware that no one is supposed to ask you questions about your racial or ethnic background, politics, sexual preference, family life, age, or social life. In simulated sessions, I've asked such questions and invariably the interview subject has said, "You can't ask that question; it's illegal or has nothing to do with the job."

While such questions are inappropriate, if not illegal, an interview is often held behind closed doors without witnesses, and offensive questions can and do get asked.

How you react is a matter of judgment and conscience. But you should plan your approach to such questions in advance. I would certainly advise putting the interviewer on notice any time you are asked a question that you find offensive or that you suspect may be illegal.

The strength and tone of your reaction to such problem questions must be an individual judgment call. Some effective ways to express your concern about a particular question include, "Is this question a standard part of your company's interview practices?" and "Exactly what does this line of questioning have to do with the position for which I've applied?"

If the interviewer backs off when met with such responses, or apologizes, it's probably wise to assume you're dealing with an individual rather than an organizational problem. If he or she persists, you will have to consider whether this is an environment of which you want to be a part.

The Closing Question

If you are the successful candidate, when can you start?

ANALYSIS: Don't gloat once you hear this question. Note the "If" clause in the question and realize that in a search process involving a large number of applicants, it may be a standard item, no matter how the interview goes.

Your response should indicate that you would like to leave your prior position and employer in good order and that you'll need time to do so.

ERRORS TO AVOID: *Any sort of flip answer.* The interview is wrapping up once you're asked this question, and there can be a tendency to relax to a greater extent than you should. At a time like this, an answer such as "How about after lunch?" or some sort of gratuitous shot at your prior employer could damage your credibility.

SAMPLE RESPONSE: *I'd like to give the Way-Rite people a bit of time to seek a replacement and to finish up a few projects I was working on. Would two weeks be okay?"*

Handling Rejection

A couple of weeks after the job interview, you may get a letter that begins with a phrase such as "We are sorry to inform you that . . ." and continues on to explain in the most vague generalities that you were rejected and someone else was hired.

Reading such worn phrases as "While your qualifications made our decision a difficult one, it was felt that . . ." can produce feelings ranging from anger to the deepest of disappointment, which are all understandable and perfectly normal. It's important, however, that you not begin blaming yourself when you don't achieve the desired result.

An interview is in many ways a sales call, and as any veteran salesperson will tell you, most meetings end in no sale or a rejection, no matter how well the meeting seems to go. The fact is that most job interviews end in rejection notices for most people. Don't alter your interview behavior just because you receive one or two rejections.

In the job-hunting process, you may be interviewed by a firm that has no intention of hiring you. For example, a company may wish to promote an individual from within an organization for a particular position; however, company policy or even law may require that the position be advertised and an extensive search be conducted. That requirement will be fulfilled, and the internal candidate appointed.

This scenario happens all the time, but you may be unaware of it and blame your own interview performance for the rejection. A more constructive approach would be to contact a personnel officer of that corporation to seek an evaluation of your interview performance. Not every one will be willing to meet with you under these circumstances, but those who do should provide valuable information.

Practice but Don't Rehearse

You should practice a mock interview at least five and perhaps as many as ten times before you face an interviewer. Use the questions covered in this chapter as a beginning and add any situation or industry-specific questions you can anticipate.

Practice your responses and even record, listen to, and critique your performance. Internalize your personal positive points and be certain to include them in your practice responses whenever possible.

Avoid either scripting or memorizing your responses. If you do, they'll seem staged, and you'll lack the flexibility you'll need if the interview strays in directions you didn't anticipate.

Also, be certain not to do all of your practicing the day before or on the day of the interview. Such cramming for an interview, will only heighten your anxiety and hinder the fluency of your performance.

Summary

I began this chapter by pointing out how little control you have over the job interview. Using the information in this chapter and developing your own versions of the sample responses should level the playing field if you are new to the interview game, and even tilt it slightly in your direction as you gain experience. If one interview doesn't go as well as you expected, learn from your missteps and you'll do better next time. Now, tell me about yourself!

Quick Review:
Job-Interview Strategies

1. Make sure your résumé adds up chronologically and contains dates.

2. Study an annual report or any other material that gives you advance knowledge of the company, its objectives, and its issues.

3. Don't act as if you don't need the job (unless you don't want it).

4. Practice your answers but don't ever memorize.

5. Be ready to nondefensively explain gaps in your résumé.

6. Know your major strengths and don't be modest in discussing them.

7. Be prepared to discuss a weakness or deficiency of yours with regard to the job, but be brief, nondefensive, and matter-of-fact in doing so.

8. Never bad-mouth a prior employer.

9. Don't avoid numbers in discussing salary.

10. Don't let mistakes on past interviews affect your performance on future interviews. Learn from them and move on.

Chapter Ten

Handling the Media

At-a-Glance Summary

This chapter covers the tactical side of the media interview—television, print, or radio—and provides tips to smooth out your performance and make you more comfortable and effective in the various kinds of media interviews.

You learn everything from where to look to how to be an assertive and directive interview subject, and you find out how to get the best coverage while avoiding many commonly made errors.

Handling the Media

What You Need to Know
About *All* Media Interviews

In any media interview—television, radio, or print—there are some general rules you should keep in mind to increase the chances of *your* version of the story being reported, rather than theirs.

Have an Agenda for Your Media Interview

You would never run an important staff meeting without having an agenda. You wouldn't even sit through an important dinner with a client without making a carefully worded pitch for future business. Yet corporate spokespersons routinely subject themselves to media interviews assuming that their expertise will carry them through, and they do little more than wing it despite the fact that their words will ultimately be heard by thousands or even millions of readers, viewers, and potential customers.

This "seat of the pants" approach to the media interview is why so many corporate spokespersons have a favorite "How I got burned by the media" story. The solution to avoid such a burning is to decide *exactly* what message or issue you want to get across and get to it at every opportunity.

Having an agenda, an issue you want to get across, will give you a focus and a goal and also will give you a direction in which to take the interviewer. Otherwise you'll be making the mistake of relinquishing control to the interviewer. And remember to express that agenda at every opportunity. For example, you'll often be asked by reporters and talk-show hosts before a media interview begins, "What would you like to talk about?" This question is a golden opportunity to get started on getting your point across. *Never* throw that opportunity away by saying, "Anything you'd like." If you do, you'll be headed for an informational destination chosen by the interviewer. And since media interviewers in general avoid "feel-good" stories and issues, you might find yourself blurting out some things that will depress everything, including you, your future sales, and even your stock price.

Be Directive During the Interview

An interview is a conversation sustained by the interviewer, that is, he or she keeps it going by asking you questions. Interviewers often don't know where they are going next or how much longer they should spend on a certain topic. At a moment like this, the subject brought up by the interviewer may not always be that pertinent and you have a good opportunity to take the conversational ball. Here is an example of how this move would transpire:

Host: "Will the new packaging developed by Blexon Industries mean more convenience for your customers?"

Guest: "Yes, we think the convenience will be appreciated, but we should also be looking at the very significant benefit to the environment . . . ," followed by a single example of environmental impact.

This kind of aggressive approach is not only permissible within the interview, but a necessity if you are to be effective in terms of accomplishing your informational goals.

Sometimes guests leave interviews thinking that they did not reach their informational goal or get to their target issues because the host did not ask them the right questions. Remember that the host has different goals from yours and you are unlikely to get asked "just the right questions."

By being directive with your responses, using the R.E.S.T. technique (see Chapter 6), especially on key questions, and actually naming the issues that should be discussed, you exercise a greater degree of control over the structure and direction of the interview.

Always Have an Answer to the Question, "Anything You'd Like to Add?"

As the interview comes to a close, another question is, "Anything you'd like to add?" or "Any final comments?"

This question represents your chance to present a take-home point, or to restate your target issue. Yet many interviewees throw away this opportunity. Once again, audiences remember most what they hear last. With this in mind, you may want to consider repeating your most important target issue.

Plan and rehearse your response to this question in advance, and yours will be a more powerful interview.

How Long Should My Answers Be?

We are not used to seeing long speeches or long responses on television. We have been conditioned to seeing information delivered in short bursts. Long or multilayered responses are one of the fastest ways to get a viewer to tune out.

As a general guide, answers to questions should range from fifteen to no more than thirty seconds, with no more than ten seconds on follow-up responses. In fact, in the stand-up TV interview, I recommend shortening your response to about fifteen seconds. Don't feel hamstrung by this rule, but use it as a guideline.

Learn to systematize your response technique following the R.E.S.T. formula. In this manner, you'll cover the material, get to your target issues, and appear concise and knowledgeable.

Certainly, there are issues of such complexity that a ten- or fifteen-second response becomes impractical. Remember, however, that your ultimate audience, the viewer, is right or wrong, accustomed to being fed a diet of short answers (also known as sound bytes).

Getting Comfortable on Television

One of the most insidious phrases in media is one that used to open countless TV shows in the early days of this medium: "And now, through the magic of television, we bring you another episode of . . ."

Today, one of the reasons you'd prefer four hours of dental drilling to sitting through a five-minute media interview is that you still think there's something magical about television. It seems like a world in which everything is perfect or close to it. Most of the people you see on television meet the cultural norms of attractiveness and are articulate to the point that you'll almost never hear them flub a word or go blank or seem anxious or even seem to have suffered a bad day.

Commercials are perfect and perfectly timed. No news anchor ever reads a story and says, "I didn't understand that story either; let me try and explain it so we can both understand it." A weekly moment like that on network TV would cost millions of dollars annually in time that could have been sold to sponsors.

And so, with few exceptions, the spontaneity—the imperfections, and, some would argue, the humanity—has been drained out of TV programming. Newscasters read teleprompters between commercials and chat with unparalleled awkwardness ("Great story, Judy!") only when the show is running short. For me, the starched world of TV journalism is summarized in a line uttered by the late actor Ted Knight, the vapid but well-meaning news anchor Ted Baxter on the *Mary Tyler Moore Show,* who said, "In this just handed me, there is something on your tooth."

The only thing that television shares with the world of magic is that they are both based on illusion. In this section, with the objective of making you comfortable on-camera, the medium of television will be demystified so that you can use this important medium effectively rather than buying into the passé notion of the "the magic of television."

At the Studio

If you have not visited a television studio before, you will be in for a few sensory surprises. It will be much smaller than it appears on the air. The rest of what happens while you are there has little to do with your comfort and everything to do with making your appearance look and sound as good as it can, so don't be put off or unnerved about what you are going to experience.

To begin, you will be asked to sit on a cramped platform in a chair on the set next to a host's chair or desk that is often higher than yours. You will be told to relax, but not to move or move the chair at any time during the interview. Then they'll pin a microphone to your clothing, sometimes running wires and bits of tape around, under, and behind you to hide the microphone cord, while someone else offers you a bit of makeup regardless of your gender.

In the midst of all this, you may or may not meet the host, who will hardly say two words to you. Suddenly, someone yells "ten seconds," the chaos becomes silence, some lights come on that you will think are hot enough to bleach your hair, and the host, who snubbed you two minutes ago, is looking engagingly into your eyes and welcoming you to *Action News.*

Just as you begin to gain your composure, you hear the host thanking you for being on *Action News,* and in a flash it's over, leaving you driving back to the office hoping it went well, with little or no idea what you said or how it was received.

As they say in television, let's take that again, only in slower motion, with some explanations along the way, which should make you more comfortable.

First of all, television cameras tend to spread out or enlarge a space as you see it on the screen, and therefore your chair will be a lot closer to the host than it would be in a social setting. Be assured that this proximity is strictly for optical reasons, rather than a plot to make you uncomfortable.

Remember, if you don't look good neither does their show. The person who places the microphone will attempt to tuck the cord out of sight and keep it from pulling on you or your garments. If the microphone or cord is making you uncomfortable somehow, ask to have it adjusted; they will be glad to help.

Particularly for male guests, your visit to a television studio is usually the first time someone will offer you makeup. I'd strongly suggest you take them up on that offer, because once those lights go on and the temperature climbs to tropical levels, your host will look as comfortable as ever while you perspire enough to look more like a suspect than a guest. Wear the makeup!

Don't Buy into the Host's Preshow Behavior

Meeting the interviewer usually goes one of two ways. Either he or she will be almost overly friendly and put you at ease, or virtually ignore you to the extent you take an instant dislike to your seemingly arrogant host. Don't buy into the behavior of the former type and don't be offended by the latter.

A friendly host can be just that and help get you in the mood for a pleasant exchange. But you can be certain that that same interviewer is capable of looking you in the eye once the cameras are on and asking you, out of the blue, to comment on the drug problem in your company.

If you remain neutral and unaffected by preshow banter or the lack of it, you will not be lulled into a false sense of security and will be better prepared to handle an adversarial interview.

As for those interviewers who generally avoid talking about the interview before it begins, this is usually a way of keeping the material fresh and spontaneous, since the chat that takes place before the interview should be of less consequence than the interview itself.

Of the hundreds of on-camera interviews I have conducted, I am least comfortable when I meet the guest before the show and am lulled into an extended conversation. The result is that both of us have to sit there trying to remember which part of the interview is new and which has already taken place, instead of simply having an "on the air" conversation, which I find to be the best form of interview.

Once the Interview Begins

Look at the Person You Are Talking To

Where or what do you look at while on television? On a set where there are three or more cameras, the question of where to direct your eye contact can seem confusing. Most of us have a vague notion of the fact that the camera with the red light (tally light) is the one that's on. The confusion is heightened when your host spends some time looking at you, some time looking at the camera (particularly at the opening of the show), and some time looking at notes.

The rule here is simple and applies to all television interviews at which the interviewer is present: *Look at the person you are talking to,* not at any camera, or at the wall or the floor, just at the person to whom you are directing your remarks. Even if you are talking directly to the viewing audience, look at the interviewer and say something like "Your viewers would like to know that . . ."

By looking at the person you are talking to, you enable the director to give you the best coverage. If you attempt to play to the cameras, the director will have to guess where your eyes will turn up next, and you'll look either shifty or comical.

If there is a monitor on the set (a television used for viewing the program by crew members), avoid looking at it during the program. If you have a burning desire to see how you look on TV, do so after the taping or have someone tape your appearance. (TV news operations will often, upon request, provide you with a copy.) Looking at a monitor while you are being interviewed is very much like having lunch with someone while you focus your eyes on a person at the next table.

Begin by Greeting the Host and Thanking Him or Her for the Invitation

This is a subtle way to take charge at the opening of an interview, or at least to let the host know that you are thinking and in control of your own agenda.

For years, at the opening of television interviews I've conducted, I've often greeted guests with the usual and somewhat perfunctory "Welcome to the program!" As I analyze that habit and why so many hosts do it, I have come to the realization that it's not just a polite greeting, but an important "test question."

If my "Welcome to the program!" is met with a blank stare and a mild affirmative nod or nervous smile, it's a clear signal that the guest is very nervous and that I'll have to provide some help in lightening the conversational load. On the other hand, if I'm an adversarial host and my "Welcome" brings that same blank expression, I know that I am definitely in charge and that nailing this guest on the issues will be an easy task.

Regardless of the host's approach, begin your first response with a remark such as "Before I begin, I want to thank you for inviting me here to talk about . . ." Once again, it's a clear signal to your host that you are in charge or at least on an equal footing.

Don't Produce the Show

You will notice a number of people on the studio floor whose purpose it is to give cues and time signals to the host, or to hold up cue cards or other messages related to the smooth running of the program or interview. Remember that you are not a member of the production staff and that none of these signals, cues, or cards applies directly to you, nor do you know what they mean.

For example, some guests will be in the middle of a response and see a card being held up that says ":10 seconds." Suddenly that guest becomes a self-appointed "producer" and hurries his or her response.

The fact is that if someone holds up a card that says ":10 sec" or gives a hand signal that seems to suggest a speed-up in the proceedings, you don't really know what it means. Are there ten seconds remaining to the next commercial? The end of the program? Or even thirty seconds remaining, but the host likes an early reminder? You don't know and you shouldn't care.

Have a conversation with your host and concentrate on getting your target issues in, as well as your theme. If you let the host and the production staff do their jobs, yours will be a more effective and credible appearance.

Handling That First Question

In a nonadversarial interview, or at least one in which the interviewer wants you to feel comfortable, you might be told what the first question will be; or if there is more than one guest, the host may let you know who will be getting the opening question. It's been my experience that this relaxes guests and lets them do a better job, particularly in the opening of the program.

Let's take a look at the opening of the show from another perspective, one in which the host is adversarial. Assume that you are the spokesperson for a company that has had an environmental accident and that you are there to explain the situation and provide reassurance for the viewers. Realize that the interviewer will be biased toward the audience and, at least for a portion of the program, even hostile to you.

One trick such a host will play is to soothe your nerves just before the show by telling you that he or she will open the program with a question about your company's history. As you may have already guessed, as soon as the theme music subsides, the opening question you are likely to get is (remember that audience bias), "How long do you and your band of polluting rip-off artists intend to go on destroying the environment?"

In the event of such a question, a strong and immediate denial is the best solution ("Bill, you've got your facts wrong. First of all . . .").

Don't Bring Notes

One unfair tradition that has evolved over the years in TV interviewing is that guests don't get to use notes. The host can be encamped at a desk covered by note cards, in a studio festooned with cue cards reminding him or her of everything from your name to that of the sponsor, but you are left to sit there "naked" without a desk or so much as a legal pad.

You may view this situation as a disadvantage, but given the level of information usually covered in a television interview and the fact that you are the expert, there is really little need for you to have notes. If there is a number or set of dates that are important, do your best to remember or approximate if that won't cause difficulty. Realize that the viewer remembers little of the content of a television interview, so keep your remarks general and nontechnical.

Once again, your emphasis should be on accomplishing your informational goals and getting your theme or agenda across, not on presenting an oration that explores the most minute details of your position(s). Relax and remember that you are the expert.

If yours is a business or issue that requires data or graphs for an adequate explanation, these should be professionally produced as 35-mm slides or cards that will be integrated into the interview; but such arrangements must be made in advance. Remember that not all studios or programs are set up to handle graphics and that their successful use in an interview requires some rehearsal as to when they will be used.

What's Your Phone Number?

Don't get tripped up by this obvious question. You may have seen an old episode of the classic Jackie Gleason sitcom, *The Honeymooners*, in which Ralph Kramden, after exhaustive study and preparation into even the most obscure operatic aria, fails immediately and dismally as a contestant on the quiz show *Name That Tune* because he can't recognize the melody to "Swanee River." Poor Ralph did what many interview guests do: Despite elaborate preparations, he forgot the obvious.

For you, the most obvious and very common question is, "It's been a pleasure to have you with us today, and I know our viewers will want to know more. Is there a phone number they can call?"

It sounds like the simplest of questions, yet since you never call yourself, or if your company has a customer 800-number that you never use, it's altogether possible that you'll have no idea what number the viewer should call.

Worse, if you respond by saying you don't know or can't remember the number, especially since this question usually occurs at the end of a show, your authority and credibility as a spokesperson will suffer.

The solution? Prearrange with the producer to have your phone number superimposed on the screen during your appearance. If you aren't precisely sure of your number, suspend the "no notes" rule, and write the number on a small index card. When asked the number, just mention that you've written it down to make sure you get it right and read it off the card. Accuracy is crucial at a moment like this, and both your host and your viewers will appreciate this attention to detail.

If You Make an Error

Over the course of a five- and especially a fifteen-minute or longer interview, you may make some kind of content error, such as getting a number wrong or substituting a word. What should you do?

First of all, what you shouldn't do is make that error the focus of your thoughts for the rest of the interview. If you do so, you will no longer be listening fully to subsequent questions and your performance for the rest of the interview will suffer.

The solution here is a judgment call. If the error was minor, let it go uncorrected. As I've pointed out before, audiences remember little of the content they hear in a media interview unless it's out of the ordinary, and your saying that you made an error is out of the ordinary. You have to weigh the importance of correcting the error against saying that you made a mistake and what that costs in terms of credibility. Once again, unless it is a serious error, my advice would be to let it go.

If you're uncomfortable with that advice, you can use the final seconds of the interview, if you get the "Anything you'd like to add?" question. Do not, however, in these crucial closing seconds of your appearance use words such as "I made a mistake earlier." Instead, use a remark such as "I'd like to *clarify* something I said earlier . . ." In this manner, the viewer's impression is likely to be that you are interested in making your message as clear and accurate as possible, rather than that you screwed up and are trying to cover yourself or at least a part of yourself.

The Very End

One of my goals in this book is to prevent you from making many of the embarrassing errors made by speakers of all skill and experience levels. It happens that one of these errors commonly occurs at the very end of a sit-down media interview.

As the theme music comes up and the lights dim and your host has said the last good-bye, a technician is *supposed* to cut power to your microphone so that any words you say will not be heard over the credits. More than one media personality has ended a career or become a feature of blooper albums by making a remark, sometimes off-color, while thinking the mike was dead.

For example, there is the oft-told story of "Uncle Don," who in decades past was the host of a popular children's television program. At the end of the final broadcast (and it was this remark that made it his final broadcast), Uncle Don, after saying good-bye to his young fans, thinking his microphone was off, became a broadcast immortal, albeit an unemployed one, by saying, "That ought to hold the little bastards."

Your potential blunder here is not likely to be of such catastrophic proportions, but I have had guests say things over the credits such as, "Are we done?" or "That wasn't so bad," or "How did I do?" (Fine until you asked that question!)

The usual rule? Don't utter a word during the closing credits or when the lights dim, until a studio crew member says "Clear" (the usual signal that a studio is off the air).

Also watch your nonverbals at the end of the show. Sometimes, just to relieve pent-up tension, guests may shake their heads, laugh, or even bury their heads in their hands in mock exhaustion. The problem is that after the viewer sees and hears a credible, effective interview, your non-verbals could undermine your entire performance.

All in all, it's best to assume that the TV interview ends when you leave the studio or even the building.

The Stand-up or On-the-Scene TV Interview

Sometimes you don't go to the media, they come to you, in the form of a stand-up or on-the-scene interview. These are often pretaped, but with currently available technology, they are just as easily done live. Stand-up interviews, like press conferences, tend to occur under negative circumstances.

In addition, if it's a breaking story, reporters are likely to be more aggressive than usual in the hope of giving the story a "late-breaking" or exclusive quality. A few important rules and strategies will help get you through what many consider to be a very stressful situation.

Maintain Control of the Interview

This is not as difficult as it sounds. First of all, if a bunch of reporters come at you with thrusting microphones and shouted questions all competing for recognition, don't even try to respond (but don't walk away either).

Instead, calmly tell the reporters to please move back, ask one question at a time, and to slow down or you can't possibly continue the interview. Making these requests calmly will change the tone of the interview from a veritable shouting match (which you will lose) to more of a press conference where you have a better chance of telling your story.

You also want to appear calm and in charge, in the event that your interview is being fed back to the studio for live broadcast. Realistically, no one will move back (they need the tight shots) but you will get gentler treatment if you *calmly* express your discomfort.

Know to Whom You Are Speaking

Especially if you are not the regular media spokesperson for your company, ask reporters to identify themselves as they question you. In this instance, you'll have a bit more think-time, and it's been my experience that people (even reporters) tend to be a bit more polite after they have just told you who they are. By the way, never hesitate to ask for press credentials (usually issued by local police departments or governments). Especially when you are new at talking to the media, you have the right to make certain that you are talking to a reporter and not an investigator for a competitor or legal adversary.

If You Can't Talk Now, Say Why

Don't just walk away, or they'll put your "escape" on the air. Reporters who come on the scene to get a story are in serious pursuit of news, and they don't like meeting up with a smug, uncaring spokesperson. If that's the way you play it, that's the way you'll be covered.

If there is a good reason you can't talk now, simply say why and tell them when you will have more information. Reporters won't like this response, but if it's the truth, it won't do you any harm. If you say "no comment," it will be used on the air and do about as much for your credibility as pleading the Fifth Amendment.

Don't Treat the Interview as an Audition

Your goal should be to answer the questions asked concisely and honestly. That means you might have to think about a response or that you may have to repeat a response or even take a second shot at having the words come out just the way you want them.

Unfortunately, many spokespersons are intimidated by the immediacy and largely self-imposed pressure of having to think "on your feet." Therefore, the stand-up interview runs the risk of becoming an audition in which you try to answer every question with total fluency and dazzling brilliance, topping off each with your most engaging smile.

If you can manage to pull this off, you're making two mistakes. First, and most seriously, you are no longer thinking, you are performing. Second, you are focusing on image rather than on content, and you can be virtually assured that in so doing you will make serious misstatements.

Take your time, think about your responses, and don't let the reporter or the presence of cameras or lights cause you to rush your answers. If none of that motivates you, remember that the more time you spend on each response, the fewer questions you'll have to answer, especially in a live interview.

If You Make a Mistake, Stop Talking

While you need not slip into apoplexy, if you misstate your case or get halfway through a statement that you realize is incorrect, hopelessly awkward, or laced with a piece of information you suddenly realize you shouldn't have revealed, simply stop talking *immediately,* and, without saying why, ask to repeat the response. The reporter will have little choice but to let you do it again, and you will end up with a better interview.

If you make the mistake of completing a response you don't want used, you'll have to depend on the reporter not to use it. Compounding the problem, the story may be assembled for broadcast by someone other than the reporter who did the interview and the wrong response may be aired against your wishes.

Therefore, waiting until the conclusion of the interview to ask for a retake of one of the responses will bring only a polite refusal, or, as they pack up to move on to the next story, a chillingly insincere reassurance that "It was fine." This response will, of course, leave you frozen in terror until the story airs.

Once again, if you make a serious error in a stand-up interview, protect your interests by stopping your response immediately and asking for a retake. The same rule applies even if you find yourself uncomfortable or just too tense to continue the response. Stop and begin again. You'll be more relaxed and better able to give a correct and effective response.

Conclude and Exit Gracefully

I am frequently asked how you know when the stand-up interview is over or how to end the encounter. If there is only one reporter present, the interview will probably end with a thank you and a request for a number at which you can be reached for further information.

Once the questions become repetitive, it is a good time to end the proceedings. However, do not simply walk away, leaving any of the reporters in midquestion. If you do, you run the risk of having a snubbed reporter go back to the studio, play the tape of your exit, and claim that you refused to answer his or her question.

Avoid this trap by saying that you'll have to end the interview at this time but that you will be available in the event of further developments. If you have no more time to submit to questions, by all means say so, but exit gracefully and on a courteous note.

A Final Word on Stand-Up Interviews

If you are a regular media spokesperson, you will become quite facile at handling the stand-up interview. If you are not the usual designee for such interviews, you will find your first stand-up interview rather unnerving. (Many first timers report that they had no idea what they said until they saw themselves on the evening news.)

Avoid or lessen your level of anxiety by practicing these interviews in advance. An afternoon spent with your colleagues conducting and videotaping mock stand-up interviews will pay handsome dividends when it comes time to face the cameras for real.

The Remote-Camera Interview

This is an interview in which the reporter or interviewer is not there in front of you and may be in the next room or even in another city. If you have trouble visualizing this scenario, think back to the last time you saw ABC's *Nightline,* which makes frequent use of this technique.

Typically, you will be seated in front of a camera, hooked up to a microphone, and given an earpiece through which you will hear the audio portion of the program (including questions for you as well as statements of the other guests). Whether you are able to see the program depends on whether there is a monitor present.

You're Always "On the Air"

The key to an effective performance in the remote-camera interview is twofold. First, once you sit in the chair, assume you are "live" and on the air. You might be told that you'll be on in five minutes and literally find a question coming at you five seconds later. This is why more than one subject of this type of interview has popped onto the screen in the middle of a contact lens or toupee adjustment and spent the rest of the program wishing he or she were on one of Saturn's rings instead of in that chair.

Listen Closely, Very Closely

A second key to an effective remote camera interview is listening to the *entire* program, including segments in which you are not supposed to appear. This becomes difficult, because after you are introduced you might find yourself off the air for quite an interval as other guests talk and even as commercial breaks of several minutes' duration go by. Unless you actively listen and become involved in the conversation, when it's your turn to participate, your responses won't be as sharp as they should be, as you struggle to get up to speed.

As you participate in the interview or discussion, look directly into the camera, both while you are questioned and as you respond. As you may have observed, some guests have a tendency to feel that they are alone or to act as if they are talking on the telephone during this type of interview, and will perhaps look to the heavens during a question as if checking with the deity on how to respond. Once again, look at the camera as you are questioned and as you respond.

Don't Be Too Polite

If the program on which you are doing the remote-camera interview is a debate or you are teamed with a guest that opposes your interests, remember that this gathering has been arranged by the producers in the hope that some verbal sparks will fly.

If the situation is adversarial, in addition to telling your side of the issue, a further objective should be to get the most air time. One obvious way is to disagree immediately with your adversary by interrupting him or her at any time an error of fact is made, even if you are not on camera. Interrupting will usually get you on camera and, if you don't carry things so far as to elicit an admonition from the host, you'll end up with most of the air time to promote *your* point of view.

Producers and interviewers often appreciate this kind of spirited debate, but the specifics of how much is tolerable is a function of the usual policy on that program. If you do interrupt another guest, do so deliberately but unemotionally, because, just as in any other debate, if you lose your temper, you've lost the debate, even if the facts tend to be on your side.

A more subtle way to get air time and steal your opponent's thunder is to react nonverbally to your adversary. This tactic was used to great advantage by Ronald Reagan in his televised debates with Jimmy Carter. Nodding, frowning, or smiling incredulously during a point being made by your opponent is a much more interesting shot for a director who must choose from among some "talking heads."

Call-in Radio Programs

Just about when audiences had given up on AM radio in favor of the higher-fidelity sounds of the FM band, AM made a super-strong comeback with the resurgence of talk-radio, particularly in the form of the call-in radio show.

The overwhelming popularity of this format has created an equally overwhelming demand for guests, which in turn increases the likelihood of your making one of these appearances as a media spokesperson. The following simple tips will increase your chances for a successful performance.

The first immediate difference between radio and television is that radio is much more informal. Time and timing is often less crucial, especially in a nonnetwork or local appearance, and the conversations, questions, and responses are likely to be a lot less structured and free-flowing. What you have so far is a recipe for pulverizing boredom unless a few ingredients are added. These usually include a host who will make more than occasional stabs at being controversial and callers intent on putting the guest (or even the host) on the griddle.

In talk-radio, the game is as much one of entertainment as it is information, and if you are the guest, you might find yourself the victim of that entertainment as the host sides with an irate caller against you.

Don't be put off by the way the host promotes your appearance on the program as you hear statements such as, "And, after the news, someone from Metro Transit Railway will be here to tell us why lateness is their most important product!"

Sure, you should disagree with such foolery on the part of your host, but his or her objective is to keep people from dialing around, and it's been proven that controversy, even if simulated, is a much better audience-grabber than a verbal love fest.

While it may be the host's job to stir up controversy, as in any media interview it's your job to get your message across. In the talk-radio arena this means not just rolling with the punches, which are certain to be there, but having a theme to which you can keep coming back, so that while the audience is entertained, it is also exposed to your message and your theme.

As in other mass-media forms, repetition builds retention. (This is how you learned the lyrics to that song you hate but they keep playing on the radio.) The same type of imprinting goes on with your audience if you have a theme and come back to it whenever possible. ("Amalgamated Power Company has low electric rates!")

Bring Your Notes

You are likely to be asked a wide array of detailed questions on a call-in program and, especially in local markets where the demand for program material is high and guests are not that plentiful, program segments are likely to run anywhere from one half to one hour.

Make sure your notes are on index cards (large cards are easier to read) and arranged according to subject. Using cards is important, because listeners will find it difficult to believe they are talking to an expert if they hear paper rattling each time you are asked a question.

What should your notes contain? Any type of detailed information that you have difficulty remembering, such as dates, prices, phone numbers, hot-line numbers, and the like.

Also be sure not to put too much information on a card. Stick to short phrases and key words so you'll converse rather than read.

Treat Callers with Respect, Even If They Don't Do the Same for You

The people who call radio programs have widely varying informational needs. As any host will tell you, those same callers also seem to have just as widely varying degrees of intelligence, sanity, and even sobriety.

No matter what kind of caller you get, you are better off trying to give a serious response than tossing out a line such as "Have another beer and call later, Bill." In an awkward moment with a difficult caller, your main concern should be the rest of your audience, not just that caller. You want to leave the impression that you are a serious spokesperson with a worthwhile message.

If things get out of hand, count on the host to deal with obnoxious questioners. He or she might let an irate caller batter you a bit for the sake of entertainment, but ultimately that host wants the show to be taken seriously and will come to your rescue. Remain respectful and informative and let your host handle the verbal fisticuffs that sometimes typify talk radio.

The Press Interview

An interview by a newspaper reporter from the print media may be held in your office and have a predetermined running time and agenda. These are factors that should serve to make you more comfortable, but they are also factors that could serve to trip you up if you're not careful.

Plan Ahead

The comfortable surroundings can have you off your guard and make you a lot more casual (and talkative) than you would be on a TV news set. As in the other interviews, have a theme and target issues to which you can keep coming back. Not having a preset theme for the interview will result in your bringing up many more issues than you intended. More important, lack of planning and focus in the issues area will give the reporter's perception a much larger role in deciding which aspects of the story should be emphasized.

Tape Your Interview

Many print reporters, with your permission, will routinely turn on a tape recorder at the beginning of their interview and state that they do so for the sake of accuracy and as a backup for their notes. Should this bother you? Not at all. In fact, if the reporter can go back and check the tape as he or she writes the story, quotes are all the more likely to be accurate.

I'd further recommend, whether or not the reporter records the interview, that you make your own recording, with the explanation that it's your policy to record all such interviews. Not only does your own copy of the interview provide a valuable reference source, should you need it; the reporter who goes back to the office to write the story is likely to be extra careful in assembling that story, knowing that you have a taped copy of the session.

Control the Agenda

Losing control of the interview happens when you forget that *you* and not the reporter are the expert and fail to establish a viewpoint as to what is and is not important to the story being covered.

Remember, in an interview with a TV or radio reporter, the material that goes on the air consists mainly of your voice and words, so you have some control over the emphasis and direction of the story.

In a press interview, its conversational format can obscure the points that you want emphasized. In fact, if the reporter's perception of what is important differs from yours, and you fail to correct it, you're inviting a story that will bear little resemblance to what you said in the interview.

Executives I've spoken to who have had a negative experience with a print reporter often admit, if grudgingly, that the problem was largely because they failed to control the agenda by specifically labeling some facts as being more important than others. Instead, they just sat there answering questions, a sure way to let the reporter decide what's important and what's not.

Remember, even if the reporter has a preconceived slant on the story, you, as the expert, have the power to change it by emphasizing *your* side of things.

To summarize the planning process for the print interview, make sure you have an agenda and a target issue or issues you want to get across to the reporter. Attempt to work those target issues into your responses.

Once the interview is underway, be certain to advocate your position by emphasizing those responses that you consider to be central to the issue being discussed.

Also, don't hesitate, particularly with underinformed reporters, to tell them if their approach or perspective in covering a story is simply wrong. Finally, give the interview emphasis through repetition of important responses and clarify technical or complex issues.

It Ain't Over, Even When It's Over

Unlike a baseball game, a print interview is always an extra-inning affair—that is, the reporter doesn't stop thinking when the notebook closes, but the interview subject usually does. The reporter may still be looking for an angle or a way to get into the story, such as an interesting quote or headline.

On the other hand, you are so relieved that the interview is over and has concluded successfully, your guard is down, and that degree of self-inhibition that served you so well during the interview—what I call your "edit circuit"—is shut down. It's at a moment such as this that you blurt out that headline.

For example, an electric-company spokesperson told a reporter of a power failure caused by a squirrel that had gotten into a transformer. While leaving the interview, the reporter ventured the line, "You really fried that sucker." The spokesperson's nodding agreement of that remark made it the headline for the story: "WE REALLY FRIED THAT SUCK-ER"—hardly a comment to endear that company to animal lovers.

The point here is to be careful. It's the reporter's job not just to get the story, but to present it with an angle that will grab the reader's attention. Sometimes adding a bit of flash to a headline may be at your expense.

Remember, the print interview is over when the reporter has left your presence, not merely when he or she has closed the notebook or shut off the tape recorder. That reporter is always thinking, so be certain to do the same, remembering your agenda, target issues, and not to kid around at the end, lest your frivolity end up as a headline.

What To Do About Reporter Errors

Despite your best efforts and even those of the TV and print reporters who cover your story, mistakes such as factual errors, wrong names, and mis-quotes sometimes get into print and on the air. Just before writing these words, I viewed some television coverage of the crash of a military jet in which the reporter described the severity of the fire as being a result of "all that high-octane fuel." (Jet aircraft burn kerosene.)

If you are wronged in print or on the air, assess how serious the error is. If it's an item such as a mispronounced name or a wrong title, it may not be trivial to you, but most viewers or readers are not that concerned about your story. In such cases, call the reporter and ask him or her to cor-rect the item in the file for future reference.

If it's a more serious error, such as a statement that, if left uncorrect-ed, could cause damage to your product, company, or company image, call the reporter and request that a correction be aired or printed. Be polite but firm. That is, point out the seriousness of the situation and request that it be corrected, but don't expect more than a correction of the error, espe-cially since it was undoubtedly just that, an innocent error.

If these steps fail, contact the editor (print) or producer or news direc-tor at a TV or radio station and repeat your request. Complaining about reporters has much the same effect as complaining to a department chair-man about an ineffective college professor. The fact is that one complaint doesn't usually get results. But if a reporter's name keeps popping up in sentences that also contain the word "inaccuracy," you can be assured that some action will be taken.

Summary

The people who occupy the anchor desks, particularly those with seven-figure salaries, would probably like you to believe that participating in a media interview is difficult or at least a highly specialized activity—right up there with vascular surgery or night-carrier landings. There is nothing all that difficult about the media interview. Sure, for most of us it's a different environment, but nothing that should inspire any degree of awe or reverence.

If you remember that *you* are the expert, and they are not, and practice a few media interviews, treating them more as conversations than as inquisitions, you should be well equipped to handle things once the "on-the-air" light flashes.

Quick Review:
Successful Media Interviews

1. Don't buy into the host's preinterview behavior.

2. Look at the person you're talking to, not the camera (except in the remote-camera interview).

3. Once on the air, ignore time signals. They are for your host, not for you.

4. Begin any in-studio interview with a "Thanks for inviting me" statement.

5. Use notes on radio, but not on television.

6. Keep your answers brief.

7. Try to direct your interview to your agenda or target issues.

8. In stand-up interviews, know to whom you're talking.

9. Don't let reporters rush you.

10. Make your own tape recording of all print interviews.

Chapter Eleven

Preparing to Be an Effective Witness

At-a-Glance Summary

This chapter is intended to give you the information you need to be an effective communicator on the witness stand, whether in a legal proceeding or in a regulatory or legislative hearing. You discover how to avoid the various traps and tricks the opposition may set for you and still maintain your credibility.

Most important, this chapter encourages you to listen to your counsel and leave the strategizing about the case to him or her while you answer only the questions you are asked.

Preparing to Be an Effective Witness

In Chapter 10 I pointed out that it is increasingly likely that in your capacity as a corporate manager or executive, you will be interviewed by the media. This is a type of exposure some of us not only welcome but actually relish.

Unfortunately, another communicative forum that you are also increasingly likely to encounter is the witness stand. If you work in a regulated industry, you'll probably end up testifying before a legislative or regulatory committee or commission.

The witness stand requires a special set of communicative skills for you to survive and prosper in an adversarial system in which the wrong word or phrase, the impression you leave, or even what you don't say can have dire consequences.

This chapter does not give you legal advice (you should get that from your lawyer), but acquaints you with some of the strategies that can be employed against you on the witness stand and how to best combat them. With the advice of your counsel, plenty of practice, and application of the information provided in this chapter, you should be able to greatly improve your chances for a credible, effective appearance on the witness stand.

Getting the Most from Your Legal Counsel

Let Your Attorney Handle the Case Strategy

Remember, witnesses don't win cases, attorneys do. Everyone loves winning. It's a natural tendency when you're involved in a legal case to try to do what you can to contribute to a victory. As a witness, however, it's not your role to strategize. Rather, it's your role to answer the questions you are asked, truthfully and to the best of your ability. It's your attorney's job to object and attempt to prevent certain lines of questioning or present witnesses who can refute testimony that may be damaging to your case.

When, as a witness, you attempt to help with the case by giving an evasive or partial answer or saying you don't know, when it can easily be proven that you really do, you may feel that you are helping your own cause but you may actually be interfering with your counsel's planned strategy. In addition, you are also tampering with your most valuable asset on the stand, *your credibility.*

Particularly if you are a witness in a large, complicated case such as a regulatory hearing, which may last for weeks, you are likely to be present for only a small part of the proceeding and hear only a limited portion of the testimony. This puts you in a poor position to have a grasp on the overall strategy in the case and hardly in a position to score points for your side.

Trying to win the case as a witness by being uncooperative with the opposing counsel can also backfire in another way: Perhaps your area of testimony is one in which your counsel expects to incur some damage that he or she intends to counter later in the proceeding. Telling a witness this would be like telling a boxer that he is likely to get knocked out in the next round but to get in there and fight.

Trust Your Legal Counsel

They might actually help you by not telling you the whole story. For example, if your testimony is a problem part of the case, you might never know it. You will be most helpful in such situations if you merely answer the questions asked and call less attention to this part of the case than you would by being contentious with your questioner.

A legal proceeding can be compared to a checker game with the witnesses being the checkers and the attorneys being the players who move the checkers around the board. As such, you really can't see the other checkers, nor do you have a firm idea of your position on the board. If checkers on a board could make their own moves, the result would be chaos. When witnesses start acting on their own, the result is much the same; maybe not chaos, but certainly not victory.

Trusting your counsel to provide the game plan and answering the questions you are asked is your job as a witness, not trying to win the case yourself.

Tell the Truth

Aside from ethical considerations and the fact that you are generally under oath as a witness, or even with the threat of a perjury charge, there is another reason to tell the truth that should impress even the most ruthless and expedient witness: Lying doesn't work.

Have you ever noticed that while most people will tell you that they are basically honest, they will also admit to telling the occasional "white lie"? We've all heard them, from "My dog ate my homework," to the more elaborate but equally ridiculous, "We'd love to have dinner with you on Friday, but we are having a small memorial service to commemorate the death of our goldfish." While these little lies may be a part of life, they never really fool us, even as we nod in mock sympathy at the tellers of such fibs.

Though most of us are good at spotting deception, whether the signal is an averted glance or a slight quaver in the voice, we invariably spot it, but for the sake of politeness, let it go. Juries, judges, and regulatory bodies, however, make their decisions outside the bounds of the social politeness that permits us to accept a certain degree of deception. Honesty is definitely the best policy, especially on the witness stand.

Now that I've convinced you to listen to your attorney and impressed you with the need to tell the truth, here are some techniques you can use in depositions and trial hearings to enhance your effectiveness as a witness.

Depositions

Most of our images of witnesses and witness behavior has been shaped by television courtroom dramas, from *Perry Mason* to *Matlock.* There are some interesting and fact-based situations portrayed, but one thing the media attorneys never seem to do is conduct a deposition.

A deposition is an information-gathering interview conducted by the opposition in the presence of your attorney prior to a court proceeding. It's not the giveaway it seems, because as the other side is asking you questions, they may be giving clues to your attorney as to the areas in which they lack information as well as their overall strategy in pursuing a case.

Your attorney will be present at a deposition to object to and prevent you from answering questions that he or she feels you should not have to answer. At the same time, you should remember that you are there to provide information and to answer questions under your counsel's guidance.

The deposition is a research expedition in which the sides in a case find out about each other. The best course is to seek the advice of your attorney in answering questions, not by waiting for a nod of approval before each of your responses, but by pausing for a possible objection in which you will gain information on the problem with the question being asked.

Your attorney will generally allow greater latitude in a deposition than in a trial or regulatory proceeding because he or she is also gaining information on areas the opposition intends to explore. As you respond, an experienced attorney can spot strategies being developed by the opposition, so don't feel that you are giving away the store by responding to their questions.

As in any legal proceeding, you should tell the truth (you will be under oath) while keeping your answers brief and to the point.

Remember that if you yourself object to a question or inquire as to its relevance instead of responding, you are also informing the other side that this particular area is a sensitive one that you'd rather not talk about. Also remember that this kind of defensive behavior on your part, or any argumentative behavior, for that matter, is a sure way to invite more questions on and greater interest in that very area.

Remain matter of fact, listen to your attorney's objections, and respond truthfully, briefly, and unemotionally. In this manner, you'll provide the information to which the opposition is entitled, while serving or at least not damaging your own interests.

Depositions often begin with a standard series of "identification" questions that include your name and address or prior addresses. Further questions might range into such areas as your educational background and credentials (particularly if you are testifying as a corporate official or in some other professional capacity), your marital status, and details about prior legal proceedings in which you have participated.

In some depositions, the questions may seem not only irrelevant but even trivial. In such cases, your best strategy is to avoid becoming irritated or argumentative and to continue responding. One possibility here is that the opposition will gather a body of information in which they hope to find the tiniest inconsistencies or inaccuracies. These discrepancies will then be used to question your credibility during later proceedings or your ability to provide accurate testimony. This strategy can be employed when the evidence is not on the opposition's side.

Three Ways to Safeguard Your Credibility

There are three ways to combat such attempts to reduce your credibility.

The obvious first one is to aim for total accuracy (which is easier if you keep your answers brief).

Second, take your time in responding and refer directly to documents rather than relying on memory. (Be sure and check with your attorney on documents to be present at a deposition or any proceeding as they can sometimes become evidence.)

Third, especially in detailed areas of testimony in which you are relying on memory, you should make frequent use of such phrases as "As best as I can remember" or "To the best of my recollection."

Such phrases are particularly important when the opposition tries to deliberately fragment your response by asking, "So that's your entire answer?"

"As best as I can remember" gives you some latitude in a subsequent proceeding, should you need it. A simple yes or no response will give the opposition an opportunity to imply that you deliberately omitted information in your deposition, thus diminishing your credibility.

Truthfully including such phrases as "to the best of my recollection" or "if my memory serves me correctly" will give your attorney room to maneuver and counterattack, should your credibility be questioned based upon your deposition responses, especially in the case of inadvertent inconsistencies caused by lapses in memory.

Once again, in deposition testimony, your attorney will lay out the basic structure and probable content of the session for you. Look at this session as you would any other interview. Answer truthfully, concisely and unemotionally, and your counsel will probably gain as much information about the strategy of the opposition as the opposition gains for its case file.

Testifying at Trials and Hearings

Be an Active Listener

As a witness, you should listen carefully and actively to the questioner. This means looking at and even turning in the direction of that questioner and being fully tuned in to what that questioner is saying. Allowing yourself to be distracted or noticing that someone at the opposition's table is writing furiously each time you speak (that could be a planned distraction, or just the lunch order) is also allowing yourself to not focus on the question being asked.

If you don't listen fully to the question, you are more likely to answer it incorrectly and give the opposing counsel the chance to say, "You still haven't answered my question," followed by a more strident version of that question.

By not actively listening, you permit the opposing counsel to make you appear uncooperative, and you answer not only the question you misunderstood, but also the question that was actually asked.

Seek Clarification

While you should answer the question you are asked, you shouldn't ever answer a question you don't *fully* understand. If there is a term you don't fully comprehend, or you are just confused by the question, say so.

Do not respond by saying "If I understand your question . . ." In so doing, you are doing the work of the opposing counsel and you shouldn't be. It's possible that that questioner doesn't fully understand the issue and is merely on a fishing expedition. Instead, respond by politely saying "I don't understand your question" and look silently and directly at the questioner. You have now put the pressure on the questioner either to clarify the question or, if he or she is unable to explain the issue, to move on to another area.

There are some nonadversarial situations in which, as an expert talking to a regulatory board member or legislator, you might want to provide your own clarification and respond, for example. "If your question refers to vehicle emissions, what we have done in arriving at that number is . . ." In such cases, it might be the wise course to educate your questioner in a constructive, nonthreatening manner.

In adversarial situations, however, let the opposition construct their own questions and don't respond until you fully understand the question. Otherwise you'll end up answering two questions: the one they asked and the one you thought they asked.

Refute Negative Language

Don't allow yourself or a situation you may be describing to be labeled in a negative way by the questioner. For example, if the question is phrased as follows: "When did you first become aware of the *complete mess* your accountants had made of the books?" and your response is "The problems with our books were noticed on . . . ," you have tacitly admitted that you have no disagreement with the "complete mess" description.

Instead, your response should refute the negative language, without repeating it, as follows: "First of all, I'll have to disagree with *your* description of our books as I point out that I reported the problems on May nineteenth." Your attorney may object even before you respond, but putting the opposition on notice that you won't passively accept their attempts at negative characterizations and descriptions will certainly cut down on their attempts to play this game.

Leave Your Temper at Home

As a questioner, if I can get you angry about questions that have no central purpose to the case or if I can get you to dislike me, when it comes time for your substantive testimony, you are more likely to react emotionally than logically. As your adversary, this is just where I want you.

This is why, when you are asked simple establishing questions about your credentials, instead of "When did you receive your bachelor's degree and what was your major?" you might hear a more antagonistic version of the same question, such as, "Exactly what is it in your background that specifically qualifies *you* for the job you have?"

If the opposition continues to ask you such simple questions in such antagonistic ways, you are more likely to dislike the questioner and become anxious as to just how rough things will get. If sufficiently antagonized, you might find yourself locked in a game of trying to beat the questioner rather than simply answer the questions asked. As you try to win this battle of wits, you are more likely to give partial answers, enabling the questioner to attack your credibility. Furthermore, to the jury, judge, or other decision makers, you are likely to appear needlessly defensive or hostile.

If you are upset, you are no longer listening and no longer in control of the situation. In your angered state, you may open up new areas and show emotions that give rise to doubts about both your capability and your credibility—all this a consequence of becoming needlessly irritated by the questioner.

The best way to keep your cool on the stand is to remain psychologically neutral and not buy into the behavior of the questioner, be it hostile or overly friendly. (The overly friendly types suddenly turn on you at some point during the proceedings and achieve much the same result as the openly hostile questioner.) You may encounter such tricks as having the questioner turn his or her back on you as you respond, even conspicuously glance at a watch as you make your point. Once the opposition realizes that you can keep your emotional distance from behaviors designed to distract, they are more likely to stick to the case itself and allow you to do your best job as a witness.

Don't Anticipate Questions; Answer Them

When watching a film or play, many of us like to try to figure out what will happen before it actually does. Readers of the "whodunit" mysteries take a particular delight in these sorts of mind games. Playing this game on the witness stand, however, is a mistake, with results that can be somewhere between unfortunate and disastrous.

On the stand, you may find yourself listening to and at the same time analyzing the questions. You may begin thinking, "I wonder where he or she is going with this line of questioning?" or "I hear this question but I know what it really means!"

The problem with either of these lines of thought is that while you are thinking, you are not fully listening to the questioner. Remember that the opposing counsel not only has the right to employ a particular strategy, but is going to get to that all-important pivotal question whether you worry about it, anticipate it, or even try to verbally dance away from that subject area.

It's best to shut off your anticipatory circuitry and try to take the questions as they come, not as you think they'll come. To do otherwise is to listen poorly and to engage in winning the case yourself, which, as I pointed out earlier, is your counsel's job, not yours.

Don't Look Back

Just as you shouldn't listen ahead to a question and try to figure out where the questioner is going, neither should you focus on a past response that might have been in error or in which you somehow misspoke. If you do, you are no longer fully concentrating on the current question and your further responses are likely to either be in error or not as you want them to be.

Being a witness has some similarities to being a relief pitcher. First of all, both witnesses and relief pitchers are used only to solve a problem. In baseball the relief pitcher comes in when the starting pitcher's performance has unraveled, or if a particularly nasty hitter needs to be retired.

As a witness, you are brought in because a legal or regulatory problem is in need of settlement. You both must operate in a pressure-cooker situation where mistakes will be costly.

Both the witness and the relief pitcher need to operate with precision and be in control of the situation in which they find themselves. As a witness, one trait you should borrow from the relief pitcher is the ability to treat questions individually, just as a relief pitcher treats batters. The really great relievers can come into a game in the late innings with runners on and no outs, give up a walk, and, without looking back, go on to neutralize the next three batters. This is not accomplished by the ones who give up a walk and begin agonizing about an imaginary twinge in their arm or what they might have done with that first batter. Relievers who solve the problem do so because they don't dwell on what has already transpired.

As a witness, don't look back and don't dwell on past errors or misstatements. Instead, stay in the present and focus on the question at hand. Worrying about a past response will only diminish the effectiveness of your further efforts. Rely on your counsel to minimize any damage caused by an errant response. Depending upon the structure of the proceeding, your counsel may get to revisit the subject area of that problem response and make up for any lost ground.

Be Careful of Humor

In Arthur Miller's play *Death of a Salesman,* the main character, Willie Loman, in explaining his declining fortunes to his son says: "Everybody loves a kidder, but nobody lends him money." This line says much about the fact that a sense of humor and credibility or trustworthiness are difficult if not impossible traits to convey simultaneously.

This is especially true on the witness stand, where so much of the outcome is dependent upon which side the judge, jury, or commission members trust and believe. If such decision makers are close to deciding in your favor and you choose to deliver a humorous response to a serious question, you run the risk of losing or greatly diminishing your credibility.

On the other hand, funny issues and situations do arise in the most serious of legal proceedings. What should you do? Sit there on the witness stand doing your best Mount Rushmore impression? Certainly not. If something funny happens, you are likely to react, just as anyone would, with a smile or degree of laughter appropriate to the situation.

The difference in your behavior as a witness, as opposed to most other communicative forums, is that *you should not initiate humor,* as in making light of a serious question or delivering a Neil Simonesque quip instead of a response. Instead, react appropriately but minimally and do your best to take every question seriously. If you do, you may not get any laughs, but the proceeding will have a much happier ending than *Death of a Salesman* does.

Be Careful of Fatigue

Despite the images fostered by the typical TV courtroom drama, the witness stand is not always a hotseat of nonstop rapid-fire verbal exchanges. Rather, it can be and often is the place from which you deliver lengthy explanations of support data or respond to numerous questions in the most minute detail. This can be particularly true in regulatory hearings where complex legal, financial, or engineering information must be explored in depth in order to begin the consideration of an outcome.

Particularly if your testimony is central to a case, you may find yourself on the witness stand for hours at a time, being asked to comment on highly specific and consequential matters. As fatigue sets in, you should be aware of its onset and ask for a recess.

Common signs of fatigue on the witness stand include:

1. Difficulty in focusing on the question or the questioner.
2. Difficulty in recalling specific informational points, even those on which you are an expert.
3. Losing your train of thought during a response, to the extent you forget the question. (If this happens, say so immediately.)
4. Reacting emotionally rather than logically to questions.

Your counsel will be on the lookout for signs of fatigue, but you should be the primary determiner of your own ability to function. If you need a break, say so immediately. You will find that even a fifteen-minute break in the action will enable you to return to the stand refreshed and ready to continue. If your counsel or judge calls for a recess, you may have waited too long, and their action may have been prompted by your having made an obvious gaffe on the stand. Recognizing and dealing with the signs of fatigue is just as important a function for a witness as giving truthful testimony.

Damage done to a case because a witness wasn't paying attention, or answered partially or inaccurately because of fatigue, is difficult to undo. When fatigue sets in, put aside that "the show must go on" mentality and have your counsel request a recess or request one yourself.

Give Your Attorney a Chance to Object

On the stand, there is a tendency for honest witnesses to want to do well. If you are testifying as part of a corporate effort, many of your peers or senior associates may be present. Such pressures tend to cause you to respond rather quickly to questions, as if to show everyone present just how sharp you really are.

This is a bad time to try to impress your colleagues, and by not pausing before each response, you are causing a serious problem for your counsel that might even damage your case. I refer to the fact that your counsel may object to a particular question and wish to have the question withdrawn. Note that the objection is to the question itself, not to your response.

If your attorney's objection is made over your response, even the most astute observer will think that your counsel was trying to shut you up. Thus, the result of the objection in the minds of the decision makers is not that there was something wrong with the question, but that you had something to hide and your attorney was concerned enough to object *over* your response. Remember, pause before you respond.

Listen to Your Counsel's Objections

The occurrence of an objection in a courtroom gets everyone's immediate attention as all eyes fix on the presiding official to await his or her reaction. For the spectator, it's largely a question of which side will win this mini-skirmish. As a witness, it's all too easy to get caught up in the drama of the moment and become one of those spectators.

As a witness, you should focus on the content of the objection itself, because it may give you important information or suggestions that can be more consequential than whether the objection is overruled or sustained. For example, an objection may contain a reminder for you to include the phrase "to the best of my memory" in your responses, or a subtle hint to restrict your responses to a specific area.

If you focus on the content of the objection rather than on the result, as most listeners will, you gain information that you can use. By focusing on the outcome, you merely gain information about the structure or direction of the proceedings, which is really noninformation for you, since, as a witness, you have no control over where the proceedings are going.

Preparing for Testimony

Your counsel will give you specific advice based upon the type of case or proceeding in which you are to testify and which issues your legal team expects to be covered.

In cases where there is a lot of written or technical evidence, it will be important to review this material, making certain to familiarize yourself with its contents. You can also help your counsel in locating areas of weakness or inconsistency that are likely to come up.

Incidentally, on the subject of written material pertaining to any case in which you are involved, be certain to check with your counsel on just which written material should accompany you to the court or hearing room or any meeting with the opposition. In certain types of proceedings, the opposition may be entitled to copies of or access to written material in your possession pertaining to the case under consideration.

Don't Memorize Testimony

Once your legal team has assembled a set of questions that they anticipate being asked by the other side, they may either provide you with a list of such questions or take you through a mock round of questioning to make sure you know the material.

Rehearsing your testimony can be an effective way of increasing your comfort level, but do so with a goal of internalizing the idea that goes behind each response rather than seeking to formulate a "canned" response. Don't memorize testimony. If you do and you have a memory lapse on the stand, you won't just forget the next word or line, you'll forget the entire response.

Memorized testimony will appear wooden, flat, and rehearsed to those evaluating it. Finally, if for any reason you are asked to repeat your testimony and those present are treated to a verbatim replay of your prior effort, your testimony is more likely to be perceived as a carefully pro-duced performance rather than the series of honest responses it should be.

Remember, You Are the Expert

Courtrooms and hearing rooms can be intimidating places, especially for the witness. The series of witness boxes, elevated squeaky chairs, and other awkward surroundings in which witnesses are placed throughout our court system seem to be designed in answer to the question, "Is there any way we can make this person more uncomfortable?"

Added to the hideous ergonomics, the adversarial nature of the pro-ceedings can make the whole scene all the more intimidating. The result is that you can easily forget that you are the master of your own information and begin to doubt what you knew as fact just before taking the stand.

Take Your Time

One way to offset the intimidating nature of the witness stand is to take your time. Of course, based upon the instructions just presented, you are going to pause, giving your counsel the opportunity to object; but beyond that, you should be deliberate and never hasty in responding.

In testimony, just as in conversations, the speakers control each oth-er's delivery. For example, if as a questioner, I come on loud, strong, and aggressive, you are more likely to respond quickly and with a louder and more rapid delivery than you might normally employ.

As a witness, once you are aware of this game, if you maintain a nat-ural, conversational, and deliberate style of responding, the questioner who continues with his or her loud or aggressive ways looks like little more than a bully unless he or she quiets down.

So don't be bullied or rushed; rather, pause and respond in a natural conversational tone. You'll have more control over your responses and over the person who's asking the questions.

Be Wary in Referring to Documents

If you are asked to refer to a document in responding to a question, you should also take your time in locating the *exact* portion of the material to which the question refers. Take as long as you need. If either side feels a recess is appropriate, they will request one. I point this out not as a delaying tactic, but rather, because witnesses, in an attempt to be considerate of everyone's time, tend to let themselves be rushed at a moment like this.

The consequences of such haste can be devastating. For example, you may be referring to the wrong information or responding to a question that is constructed on a false premise. In your haste, you may misread the material and give a damaging answer based upon your misunderstanding of a document.

The rule here is to serve your own interests and take your time, both in finding the relevant portion of a document and in reading it. You may even wish to ask for a repetition of the question once you've found the relevant material.

When You Finish Your Response, Stop Talking

Police interrogators, corporate personnel interviewers, reporters, attorneys—all know a basic fact about the people they question, which they use to great advantage: Interview subjects fear silence, and, in its presence, they will talk, even without thinking.

This is why an attorney who questions you may, at the end of your perfectly adequate response, just stare silently at you as if to say, "That can't be all you have to say; you've got to be kidding!"

In fact, when most people answer untruthfully, when faced with such a silence, they will wrongly assume that the questioner knows something more and blurt out the truth.

It's a neat trick to get more information from you, the witness; if not to get at a concealed bit of truth, then at least to get you to reveal new areas of information. Now that you know about it, don't get caught.

In much of life, talking is success and silence is failure. On the witness stand, having the sense to let silence happen after your response is success and talking too much is failure.

Summary

As I said at the outset, this chapter is intended, not to give you legal advice, but to look at depositions, hearings, and trials from a communicative perspective. The best-prepared case can be lost if the evidence is poorly communicated.

Review this chapter any time you are going to participate in a legal proceeding as a witness; but at all times, listen to the direction of your legal counsel.

Among the most important pieces of advice in this chapter is that as a witness, you are there to answer questions, not to engage in verbal duels with the opposition. Strategy and tactics are best left to the legal experts, and it is by being an effective, honest, and cooperative witness that you let your legal team get their job done with minimum difficulty and maximum results.

Quick Review:
Preparing to Be an Effective Witness

1. Let your counsel try and win the case. Your role as a witness is to answer the questions.

2. Tell the truth. Lying is dishonest, illegal, and it doesn't work!

3. If you don't understand the question, say so. Don't attempt to respond.

4. Leave your temper at home. Lose it and you might just lose the case.

5. Don't think about "where the questioner is going." If you do, you're not listening to the current question.

6. If you say something you shouldn't have, don't dwell on it. Doing so will cause you to make more mistakes.

7. Pause before you respond. It gives you think time, masks hesitancy, and gives your attorney time to object.

8. Listen to your attorney's objections. He or she may be trying to tell you something.

9. Never let yourself get hurried into a response. Take your time.

10. Once you complete your response to a question, stop talking. Don't let a stare from your questioner accompanied by a long silence cause you to say more.

Chapter Twelve

Getting What You Want in Negotiations

At-a-Glance Summary

This chapter helps you understand the negotiation process and develop effective attitudes for successful negotiation. It also provides tactical tips for use at the negotiating table.

A major misconception about negotiation is that by merely applying certain tricks and strategies, you can walk away from the table with anything you want. It doesn't work that way.

Reaching agreement should be your goal, although there are strategies and tactics you can use to your advantage. Real negotiation has taken place only when *both* sides can walk away from the table feeling they have achieved a fair settlement.

Getting What You Want
in Negotiations

A major key to successful negotiation lies in understanding what negotiation is and what it isn't. Negotiation is the *attempt* by two or more parties to arrive at an agreement upon an issue or problem, an agreement that all sides view as being generally in their best interests.

You will note that nowhere in that definition is there any mention of winners and/or losers. True, negotiation is an adversarial process in which the involved parties will have opposing positions and interests, but its adversarial nature is balanced by the fact that agreement rather than continued disagreement is the goal. When true negotiation takes place, *both* sides leave the session with the feeling that they have gotten a fair settlement.

Avoiding Confrontation

Confrontation means that you have an advantage that gives you the power to make demands and set conditions, and that the other party, when confronted, will agree to your conditions. If you are literally in charge and this is a one-time situation, confrontation may be the way to go. But if you'll be seeing these people again and the balance of power shifts, you could live to regret your confrontational ways.

Negotiation should not be confused with confrontation, as it so often is. Literally volumes have been written on the subject of negotiation. Some of the titles imply that by following a certain set of strategies you will be able to pummel your adversaries into submission.

The only truth here, and it's a half truth at best, is that anyone can make a lopsided deal or negotiate an outrageously favorable agreement. The problem is, you can do it only *once*. As soon as your opposition finds out that he or she has been had, to put it in the politest of terms, that party will be back at the negotiating table with a vengeance to take back everything he or she shouldn't have given away in the first place.

What the authors of most of those "negotiate your way to total victory" books also never point out is that their books are not restricted for sale to people who are on your side. If you sit down to negotiate armed with a series of strategies geared toward verbally nuking those who sit across from you, you will simply have a confrontation in which you will either be the loser or face a standoff.

No one likes to lose, nor, in a business relationship, can you afford it on a regular basis. If you confront rather than negotiate, the kinds of long-term relationships that spell success, repeat business, good word of mouth and customer loyalty become impossible.

The negotiation pointers that follow are based upon a philosophy that in negotiation, victory is not victory, agreement is victory. Work for agreement in an atmosphere that recognizes the existence of "next time," and both agreement and long-term success will be the outcomes.

Assembling a Goal-Centered Team

If you are negotiating with a team, which is usually the case, make certain that every member of the team is genuinely included and has a specific purpose.

If, for example, you favor some members of the negotiation team over others so that some are highly participative whereas others have little more to do than doodle, the other side will spot the disunity among your members and even attempt to capitalize on it.

By giving each member of your team a part of the problem or area of specialty, you will assure each will have an active, contributory role in the process and will give the team a more unified appearance.

As you assemble your team, make certain that leadership roles are clearly defined. Your team should have a primary spokesperson and/or team leader (who may or may not be the same person). The important point here is to make these decisions and clear up any conflicts that may exist along these lines *before* you get to the negotiating table. Failure to do so will result in a perceived weakness in leadership that will give the other side an advantage as they seek to exploit your disorganization.

Keep Disagreements Private

Your team members should be aware that disagreement on your side of the table essentially means that you will be playing against yourself as well as trying to negotiate with the other side. It would simplify matters to say that therefore disagreements among team members on a negotiating position should not be allowed. Of course, the way to encourage anarchy in any group is to prohibit disagreement: Just look at the crumbled Soviet Union.

Since disagreement among team members will happen, anticipate it, particularly as some members will see aspects of a negotiated settlement as capitulation ("We should have held out for more."). Instruct your team to keep such feelings from becoming known to the other side.

Instead, have an escape valve, such as regular recesses, as part of the negotiation process. Make certain that your team members know that they can express disagreement in those recesses so that your team will appear all the more unified.

Preparing to Negotiate

The best negotiator is the best-prepared negotiator. Being prepared is essential for any negotiation session, and most negotiators are well prepared in terms of knowing *their* side of the case. A better approach is to know both sides and, if time permits, to hold a simulation using real numbers and facts presented from the opposing point of view.

With this kind of double-sided preparation, you are more likely to unearth facets of the other side's case that you normally would not have discovered until negotiations began.

Another benefit in prior simulation using a model of the other side's case is that your positions can be worked out in advance, instead of under the deadlines that are usually a part of the negotiation process.

Set Objectives and Fall-Back Positions

When real negotiation takes place, resulting in an agreement, it is because each side has agreed to make concessions. Whether you are negotiating the purchase of an automobile and manage to have them throw in floor mats and a power antenna, or a union contract in which the length of an afternoon break for the employees becomes a sticking point, there are always items on which there can be some degree of flexibility (hence the term negotiable). If you don't systematically and carefully define your objectives in advance, however, you will fail to get the best agreement possible.

Objectives and fall-back positions should be realistic; otherwise you will waste time and lose credibility. For example, setting a unit price on a manufactured piece at $280, when you and those sitting across the table know that a more realistic price would be $150, will just cause them to question your sense of reality and increase the level of tension in the session as well as its duration. Additionally, once you back away from an unrealistic position, you will reach a settlement, but will be stuck with the reputation as a negotiator who engages in posturing that need only be waited out to gain an agreement.

Make firm decisions about fall-back positions in advance and back off only in stages, not revealing the entire range of your fall-back position at any time.

For example, if you are currently allowing employees a ten-minute break as part of an agreement, and productivity increases and automation actually will allow for a twenty-minute break, it would be a negotiating error (giving up more than required) to put the twenty-minute figure on the table when you might only have to offer fifteen. Such items sound small until you realize that if you are talking about five hundred employees on three shifts, that is the equivalent of 7,500 minutes or 125 hours of lost time per day—all over a five-minute break.

Once a negotiation session is under way, however, being lax on seemingly small numbers is just the kind of error that, if made a few times over the course of a session, can result in your later saying, "How did we ever agree to that?"

Establish the Right Physical Environment

As the American palate becomes more accustomed to *haute cuisine,* you may have noticed that restaurant critics consistently devote a major portion of their reviews not just to the food served, but to its presentation—whether courses are attractively and colorfully arrayed. Ambiance or atmosphere, expressed in such terms as warmth or the effectiveness of a theme of decor, is considered an essential element in the totally pleasurable dining experience.

In other words, environmental factors can make or break a dining experience, a fact that has not escaped the successful restaurateur. Unfortunately, the same degree of environmental awareness has not pervaded the business world, with the possible exception of a few executive dining rooms.

The meeting environment, especially in negotiation sessions, can and will have a profound effect on the tone, duration, and outcome of the session. Following are some of the environmental factors you can and should control.

Selecting the Place

To some extent, the place where negotiations are held is dictated by various practical considerations: availability of personnel, records, and so forth. Preparatory and preliminary sessions are likely to be held in your own offices or those of the people with whom you are negotiating. Crucial negotiations of the variety that are likely to produce a final agreement should be held at a mutually agreeable neutral setting away from your office.

The initial temptation is to hold the meetings in familiar surroundings so that your adversaries are placed in the role of guests. The argument for this tactic is that not only are you in the comfort of your home turf, but you have more immediate access to people and information that you would not normally have at a location away from the office.

Although using your own premises for negotiation sessions will give you these advantages, your adversary will feel at a psychological disadvantage. They may seek to overcome it either by being more guarded or by prolonging the proceedings in an attempt to level the playing field,

An additional disadvantage of using your own offices for formal or more crucial negotiations sessions is that the same proximity to the office that gives you greater access to information and people also gives those people greater access to you.

The result is the likelihood that, despite all the prohibitions and caveats you may have issued, you will be subject to the usual spate of interruptions and distractions that normally pervade the office environment. Therefore, any perceived home-field advantage will be quickly cancelled out.

Preparing the Site

Once the decision has been made to take the negotiation session to a mutually agreeable neutral location, specific environmental decisions become crucial.

The first of these is the shape of the table. At the end of the war in Vietnam, as the long-awaited Paris peace talks got under way, there were days of seemingly frivolous discussion about the shape of the table, with the players eventually settling upon an oval table.

There are good and bad seats in everything from football games to airliners. We place a lot of importance on where we sit. At the typical negotiating table, some seats (the head of the table) connote prestige, whereas increasing distance from this traditionally important position connotes decreasing degrees of importance. Placing any member of a negotiating team in an inferior position is a mistake.

This is why board rooms make such poor negotiation sites. There is usually a position of supreme authority at the head of the table, just beneath the most expensive painting, just over from the private entrance. Generally, all other seats are inferior to this one, and in some board rooms this author has visited, binoculars could well be provided with some of the more distant seats.

While the table-shape debate that opened the Paris peace talks may have seemed frivolous, the involved parties were correct in recognizing the importance of seating arrangements. For example, circular tables create a degree of ambiguity as to who is on which side and also increase the physical distance between opposing participants in that the distance across a circular table is greater than that of a rectangle or oval.

Oval or rectangular tables are best for negotiation purposes; but regardless of the final choice, head chairs at each end should be removed. Team leaders should sit in neutral positions on the side. Thus they will have to sit closer together.

The reason for this bit of proxemics (the study of spatial relations) is that since the team leaders represent different constituencies, they are likely to be in disagreement. If seated across a table rather than at opposite ends, they will speak more quietly to each other, and raised voices will be less appropriate, even if tensions rise.

In addition, by placing both team leaders in neutral positions at the table, neither will find it necessary to compensate for the perceived disadvantage of an inferior location by making an issue of a certain part of the negotiation problem just to counteract that perceived disadvantage.

If you have been attentive to the shape of the table and the seating of the participants, don't undo your good work by being inattentive to the chairs. They should be comfortable, and in the further cause of a level playing field, they should all be the same.

While I'm on the subject, chairs without wheels, with fixed or non-swiveling bases, are preferable because they make it more difficult for participants to turn away from the proceedings, causing them to be more focused as negotiations progress.

Don't Overcrowd the Table

How many people does it take to build a negotiation team? One of my least favorite answers is "It depends," but in this case, it's the correct answer. More fully, it depends on the scope and complexity of the problem.

If the problem is complex and multilayered and has everything from environmental and engineering to sociological and political aspects, the problem clearly is not going to be solved nor agreement of a final nature reached with all of those specialists in the room. Rather, a final team should negotiate, with recommendations and positions developed by teams of specialists.

The object here is to reduce the number of negotiators on each negotiating team to a manageable size—that is, manageable in that all of those present can actually participate in the development of an agreement.

It's been my experience that having more than eight members per team begins to reduce the effective functioning of the team. That is not to say that there might not be more people present, such as support staff, advisers and observers, but there should be only eight *fully* participative team members.

As one who has served on dozens of committees, panels, and task forces, ranging in size from five all the way up to fifty, I can assure you that the amount, quality, and consequence of a negotiating team's effort diminishes as its size increases.

Keeping the team small also increases the degree of individual and accountability as motivational factors for those who are charged with the task of arriving at a negotiated settlement. So keep the team small, well prepared, and informed, and the road to agreement will be considerably shortened.

The matter of team size should be discussed openly and frankly with those with whom you will be negotiating. If you can equalize the team size in advance, it makes for a smoother, more balanced session from the beginning. In the more intimate setting, there will also be no need for microphones, and a greater degree of informality and general comfort will help foster an atmosphere more conducive to producing an agreement.

Set up a Comfortable Schedule

Scheduling is an important part of the negotiation environment. Choose a time of day that is convenient for all of the parties involved. Scheduling flexibility in this area, even including weekends and extended sessions, is an area in which agreement costs you nothing, but signals that you wish to reach an agreement.

Schedule extensions and changes are a normal part of the negotiation process, so your flexibility in advance connotes experience and comfort with the overall process.

Schedule Recesses

There will be times in a negotiation session when you want to speak privately to your colleagues, perhaps to alter a position or to talk strategy on a particular issue. If such confabs take place at a crucial point in the discussion, they might be taken as a signal that you are quavering on a position or at least that there is disagreement on your team.

An alternative to the awkwardness of a sudden recess is a predetermined schedule of regular breaks in the sessions. This way, if a member of either team wants to caucus privately with team members, he or she knows that there will be an opportunity to do so.

If the other side requests recesses, however, let them happen. Such extra recesses often signal disunity or weakness on a position. If you keep your own recesses to a minimum and caucus during breaks, such signals of disunity will be coming from only one side of the table.

Schedule Meal Breaks

Physical comfort is important in effective communication. I've pointed out before that if an audience is too hot or too cold or somehow distracted, your message is less likely to get through. Biblical scholars will note that even Christ, in his Sermon on the Mount, fed the crowds before he spoke to them.

Similarly, if those seated around a negotiating table are hungry, or a meal has been long delayed because of a particularly knotty problem under discussion, be assured that attention levels will diminish.

Both teams should remain as comfortable as possible throughout the session, and this certainly includes regularly scheduled meal periods. In the event you decide on a so-called working lunch, which is the norm in some quarters, there should still be a scheduled break.

Breaks, meals, table shapes, and schedules—the environmental factors may begin to sound frivolous when enumerated or examined in any kind of detail, but it is just such attention to detail that makes for smooth, agreement-producing negotiation. The atmosphere of the negotiating session can directly influence the character of the sessions and the quality of the agreement and therefore should be an integral part of the planning process.

Beginning the Negotiating Session

Up to now, the tactics presented have dealt with the planning process that goes into successful negotiation, researching the case or issue, assembling the team, and the various environmental factors that affect the negotiations process.

The following tactics deal with the actual process itself—how to handle things once negotiations are actually under way.

Start with Introductions and a Summary Statement

Most communicative encounters begin with such ritual conversation as the weather, your trip to the office, local news, or other such banter. Prior to a meeting that is going to air disagreement on the way to reaching an agreement, the positivity established in this ritual conversation should be continued in the form of brief personal introductions from each team member, culminating in a summary statement of the negotiation problem from each side's perspective. This statement should be delivered by the designated spokesperson for each side.

In this manner, discussion begins in a structured but non-threatening and noncrucial manner; leaders and other team members are clearly identified as the negotiations begin in a more positive atmosphere than a simple listing of demands.

Let the Other Side Talk First

If you can manage it with some subtlety, let the other side begin first, presenting their position on the problem under discussion. If you are asked to begin first, do so, since seizing or attempting to seize *every* advantage will give the other team more of a need to retaliate than to agree.

If you are successful in having the other side begin, however, you gain several helpful pieces of information. Among these is the mood of the other side, particularly if you haven't met previously, or if your only knowledge of the other team comes from media accounts of the issue or other second-hand sources.

Are they angry? Agreeable? Are they realistic in presenting their side of the issue, or are they posturing and talking about impossible demands right at the outset? Is there flexibility on a part of the problem that you thought would be difficult? Should you adjust your positions in reaction to what you heard in their opening statement?

The answers to all of these questions become apparent as negotiations proceed, but having them sooner rather than later can be helpful.

Begin with Easy or Minor Issues

When the goal of a session is to produce an agreement, as is the case in negotiation, talking about how far apart you are or how much disagreement exists is not helpful in producing the agreement. That is why attempting to handle the most difficult parts of the problem at the outset is a mistake.

Instead, begin with minor issues or those that are peripheral to the main agreement. For example, in the negotiation of a labor contract you may have significant disagreement in such typically major areas as wages or health-care benefits, but such items as uniform allowances or the number of paid personal days may be a fairly *pro forma* item.

By considering and agreeing upon such minor items early in the process, everyone at the table has seen that the parties are capable of agreement, and momentum in the direction of agreement is established.

In some sessions I've found it helpful to use flip charts located around the negotiation table to post items of agreement in phrase form. In this manner, all of the negotiators are literally surrounded with visual reminders of their areas of agreement as the negotiations proceed.

Don't Underestimate the Other Side

Don't underestimate the other side by assuming that they are at a disadvantage, or that just because your side happens to be called management and they are labor or that your group has the highest cumulative salary or the longest titles, things will go your way.

Particularly in labor negotiations, line employees who suddenly find themselves at the bargaining table often have insiders' perspectives and deep understandings of the issues, which can make them tough negotiators. Similarly, long-term employees often have outstanding historical knowledge of a company or a knowledge of obscure passages of prior versions of labor agreements with which they can dazzle the most prepared and astute attorney.

In international negotiations, there may be a language barrier that may make the other team slow to respond or even to seem confused by the process. But remember, more than one non-English-speaking negotiator has developed a heretofore-unrevealed command of the language when the negotiations reached a particularly crucial stage.

A good general rule to remember in not making the mistake of underestimating the other side is to remember that they would not be involved in the negotiating process unless they had some ability, strength, or advantage to offer those who are responsible for putting them there. An airline doesn't put a baggage handler at the controls of a jumbo jet. A renowned restaurant doesn't let a busboy try his hand at giving the béarnaise sauce that special touch. Similarly, a corporation, a labor union, a government, or any similar group doesn't send a bunch of amateurs to the negotiation table. Never underestimate the opposition.

Use Inclusive Language

I have often been amused by the fact that when you enter a church to attend a wedding, or even at some wedding receptions, an usher will walk over to you and say, "Whose side are you on?" Supposedly, the bride and groom are forming an alliance in which they pledge to share all aspects of their lives from this day forward, yet there is a guy standing in the back asking you which side you're on.

The negotiation table starts out at a disadvantage to the wedding in that there isn't even a pretense of unity, only the hope of an agreement after the airing of some differences.

One way of mitigating this situation is to use what I call *inclusive language,* or language that doesn't aid in the creation of an us-versus-them atmosphere.

Here are some examples of inclusive-versus-exclusive language:

INCLUSIVE	EXCLUSIVE
All of us	Our people, your people
Everyone here	Our side, your side
Both teams	The opposition
The entire group	Enemies and friends (even stated humorously)
We	You people
You (plural)	Those of you seated across from us
Every participant	Jim's crew (needlessly personal)

The conceptual framework behind the use of inclusive language is to minimize divisive references to either side that will accentuate and foster the us-versus-them mind-set. It is also helpful not to refer to individual team members in terms of disagreement, or to separate members from a team, as in "Jim's idea is our only problem."

This makes the negotiation process a personal rather than a team matter, which then creates disagreements among individuals in addition to the disagreements between the teams.

Express Disagreement in an Open-Ended Manner

Open-ended language is that which elicits or encourages a response from the listener or receiver.

For example, in a negotiation context, an open-ended statement would be the question, "How can we get closer on this?" rather than "We're really far apart on this issue"; or "I'd like us to agree here, what will move things along?" rather than, "You people are way off on this."

Here are some examples of open-ended versus closed statements:

CLOSED	OPEN-ENDED
"That's impossible!"	"It's difficult to meet those terms."
"You're way off!	"That's a big difference to overcome."
"That's an insult!"	"You're far off our target price, but we are interested in your business."

CLOSED	OPEN-ENDED
"Take it or leave it."	"That's a firm but fair offer that we'd be happy to fully explain."
"Are you kidding?"	"We take every offer seriously, but this doesn't look promising. How can it be improved?"

In each of the open-ended statements, there is a distinct lack of emotionality and an opportunity for the other side to respond with a counter-proposal. The result of each open-ended statement is likely to be discussion, whereas the closed-ended statements, there is no clear conversational option other than silence or the terse expression of disagreement. Often, when negotiation reaches an impasse or stopping point, the strategic use of open-ended language can get things moving again.

Avoid Asking Yes-or-No Questions of the Other Team

On the witness stand, an attorney may find it helpful to box in the witness by asking a series of yes-or-no questions such as, "Isn't it true that you signed the contract?" He or she is after a specific, singular outcome and is in a confrontation with that witness.

At the negotiating table, what-where-or-how questions will elicit substantive rather than one-word answers and will lead to further discussion rather than the blunt expression of disagreement.

For example, a question such as, "We're still pretty far apart on the salary issue, aren't we?" or "Can't you do better on the renewal dates for the orders?" will elicit a yes-or-no response and may serve to crystallize the other side's position into that yes or no.

However, an open-ended question, such as *"How* can we get closer on the salary issue?" or *"Where* do you think we could make some changes to move forward on the salary issue?" will provoke discussion and show that you're interested in reaching agreement.

Handling Numbers in Negotiations

Much of negotiation, especially in a business setting, involves numbers. Prices, financing terms, deadlines, contract expirations and extensions, and even solutions to legal matters usually involve negotiations about numbers.

In negotiations where numbers are a crucial factor in the discussion, they should be held off until later. This is not to avoid the issue, but rather to discuss it in an atmosphere where agreement on some of the lesser issues has already taken place.

Blurting out the wrong numbers (too high or too low) can literally end the meeting and with it the opportunity to do business. Therefore, many negotiators are uncomfortable when it comes to discussing numbers.

Once you get to the numbers, replace your discomfort with directness. For example, develop your price, including a fair profit based upon what is typical in your industry, and present it in a direct and matter-of-fact tone.

In most negotiations, there is some ritualistic bargaining on the subject of price. For example, a retailer may want to go back to his or her office and be able to say, "I was able to get an extra 15 percent." If you anticipate such goings on, you will want to add in that 15 percent, just to take it away. If you build in a discount, make sure you don't let the negotiations end without giving that discount. Otherwise, you will end up with that extra 15 percent—but only once. As your counterpart becomes more familiar with pricing, he or she may find out that your price was high and that you may not have been completely forthright. Your momentary advantage will taint the atmosphere of future negotiations with that client.

In pricing or any numerical negotiation, don't have more than two fall-back positions or you'll suffer a severe credibility loss. If your numbers keep receding as the negotiations continue, you will begin to appear that you base pricing on how dumb you estimate your opposition to be and make adjustments based upon how far off that estimate was.

Be willing to define and explain any numerical position. Also be willing to advocate that position. For example, if your price isn't the lowest, say so, but explain why in a nondefensive manner.

Avoid Discussing Ranges

Many negotiators make the mistake of using number ranges instead of numbers. This means giving away your *entire* position and almost inevitably ending with the worst deal, from your perspective.

For example, if I am told that a product will be manufactured and in my stores between thirty and forty days from my order date at a price of from thirty-eight to fifty dollars per unit, as a good negotiator, I will fight hard to get that product on my shelves in thirty days at thirty-eight dollars.

I'll do battle to make sure that I come away from the table with the lowest end of those ranges (thirty days and thirty-eight dollars).

Conversely, if I am presented with a single position, let's say forty days at forty dollars, as a negotiator, I have no idea how firm each of those positions is. Therefore, I will attempt to gain better terms, but without a firm idea of how well I can do. In fact, I am unlikely to get at the lowest number in each range.

In negotiating any numbers issue, be open and direct, have no more than two fall-back positions, use realistic figures, and avoid stating ranges in discussing numbers.

Using the Give-to-Get Strategy

A briefly stated but highly important item, this tactic embodies a way of thinking when negotiating. You may wish to apply it when attempting to arrive at prices, deadlines, monetary settlements, or any other crucial numerical issues.

Basically, a give-to-get strategy is one in which you will make no concessions without getting something in return. This is a strategy for the aggressive negotiator when you have a definite advantage over the other side and thus can afford to take this position. Some examples in which a give-to-get strategy would be appropriate would be:

1. You are the *exclusive* supplier of a product or service and there is no alternative.
2. There is a court-directed settlement that entitles you to make a one-time agreement in which you are directed to negotiate the best mutually agreeable settlement you can.
3. Any negotiation exists of a one-time agreement in which a next-time or renewal of the agreement is not likely.

In using the give-to-get strategy, the outright concession on any negotiation issue is replaced by a question such as, "If we deliver the order early, how much extra will you pay per unit?" or "We'll approve the lower price—but on one condition. . . ." The idea is never to give without getting something in return.

Give-to-get is also an effective strategy in the final portion of a negotiation when momentum picks up as negotiators on both sides have an agreement in sight. A subtle shift to this tactic, politely and nonconfrontationally expressed, can be highly effective.

For example, a statement such as: "We're all anxious to wrap things up, so here is what I propose: We'll guarantee thirty-day delivery, and you give us the right to in-factory inspections on a weekly basis. I believe that's fair to everyone, and it will help end the day. Also, we'll give you use of our trucks for delivery, and you give us an additional 2 percent discount on the entire order. That should be more than fair for everyone."

Note that our negotiator employed the give-to-get here, and on the end of each statement tacked a tiny sales pitch ("I believe that's fair to everyone, and it will help end the day").

Also note that our negotiator tried to settle two issues in quick succession. This is clearly risky, as someone might accuse you of rushing things (which you are).

On the reward side, you are attempting to capitalize on three factors:

1. Momentum (agreement tends to produce more agreement)
2. Time (everyone likes the session to end at some point and therefore tends to rush toward the end)
3. Fatigue (negotiators are human and are more willing to agree because they are tired and lack the energy to pursue the matter further)

Once again, the give-to-get strategy can be employed throughout a negotiation if you are in a situation of clear advantage, but it also can be useful if applied selectively, especially toward the end of a session.

Avoid Being a Victim of Give-to-Get

Now that you know about the use of the give-to-get strategy, use it, but try to avoid having it used on you and your team on a consistent basis. That is, there is no particular harm done on a minor item if you hear such phrases as, "Give us fifty extra units and we'll let you have a five-day extension on the delivery date." Beware, however, of allowing those across the table from you to use the give-to-get on major items.

Responses to a give-to-get should serve to break up the momentum of this tactic with an immediate and firm refusal to link the items. For example, "We can't possibly tie the production schedule to a new delivery date. Let's examine each area on its own and make our decisions in each area separately."

Additionally, while you may want to attempt to "stack" items toward the end of a negotiation ("While we're settling delivery dates, let's see if we can also agree on a start-up date for the new plant."), don't let this tactic be used on you and your colleagues. Rushing the process because of the lateness of the hour usually results in the phrase, "How did we ever agree to this?" being heard around the office at a later date.

More Winning Strategies

Tell the Truth

Some negotiators think that a certain amount of exaggeration of positions is necessary. This kind of posturing usually takes the form of indignant reactions toward your positions, or insultingly high or low terms meant to startle. Others approach the negotiation table with proposals based upon the ridiculous "It's so crazy, it just might work!" approach, or an outlandish pricing strategy seemingly predicated on the concept, "But if we can sell just one . . ."

Even if the outrageous proposal is dismissed or the insultingly low offer is politely ignored, they will still detract from your credibility if you employ them. Such histrionics are not only time-consuming, but notoriously ineffective.

The honest approach works best and is the shortest path to agreement. Bluff positions and obfuscatory responses or nonresponses to questions are postponements of the more realistic positions you need to attain in order to achieve agreement. So why not start out closer to agreement and shorten the proceedings for all concerned? You'll not only gain a faster and less painfully obtained agreement, but you'll also have laid a good foundation for next time.

Be Attentive to the Other Side's Nonverbal Behavior

In observing the other side, you'll want to look for signs of disunity within the other team which you may be able to exploit. Members of the team who have little or nothing to say; nonverbal behavior such as shaking one's head as another team member presents, or turning away from the proceedings; a sudden decision to disassemble and clean one's pen or glasses, or other such behavior is often a sign that there is disunity among team members as to a position taken.

While such signs are not infallible, you can use them to make educated guesses as to the positions to which the opposition is less committed. If your guesses are on target, the rewards may be well worth the effort of observing and listening closely to the other team.

In the same vein, make your own team aware of the need to be verbally and nonverbally supportive of one another to prevent the other team from gaining and using information about your team and the strength of its various positions. Remind them that there will be plenty of opportunities for disagreement during planned recesses. If those who need that escape valve know it is there, they are more likely to present a unified nonverbal front to the other side, and you will have smoother sailing.

Don't Gloat When You're Winning

Sometimes, negotiations will go well, unbelievably well. Once in a while, regrettably not that often, you do run into a team that is underprepared, overly flexible, and perhaps not that motivated to come up with an agreement that benefits its side.

If you want to motivate the most unmotivated opposition, just give them some inkling of the trouncing they are taking. The temptation here is to become jubilant, perhaps to remark about how delighted you are to be achieving agreement so easily.

If members of the opposition have egos, and they undoubtedly do, you run the risk of sewing the seeds of discontent or at least a degree of discomfort among your opposition, which will cause them to utter the most dreaded phrase of those who are close to a negotiated agreement: "Maybe we should take a closer look at the terms of . . ."

So save your celebration, smiles of glee, and approving winks and nods until the agreement is signed and the other team has gone home.

Watch for Fatigue

Just as the marathon runner who sees the finish line up ahead will get that extra burst of adrenaline to spur him or her on, the negotiator can have a similar reaction: "If we can just knock off these last few items, we'll be done."

The runner is free to collapse in a corner at the end of the race, to recover from the fatigue of that final push across the finish line. Unfortunately, the negotiator who pushes him or herself across the finish line has to live with the consequences of that rush job for the duration of that agreement—another cause of "How did we ever agree to this?"

Traits of the fatigued negotiator include:

- Excessive item stacking
- Frequent references to the clock
- Snap decisions
- Emotional outbursts

Once you see these traits in either team, it's time for a recess. The temptation is to think that you can take advantage of fatigue and let the other side make snap decisions, or victimize them by stacking items to be agreed upon, since the clock is winding down on the session.

The fact is, however, that as the other side becomes tired, so do you, and *both* teams are susceptible to the effects of fatigue. Both teams are likely to make mistakes that could be costly.

Anticipate this problem and set up rules about recesses for both teams so that neither side will end up wondering how they went along with certain of the terms in the final agreement. Agreement on recesses can be a good issue to handle early in a negotiation session, since it will so clearly benefit and protect both sides.

Don't Let a Bully Force Your Hand

Norman Mailer pointed out that tough guys don't dance. If you handle the situation properly, they don't negotiate well either. The basis of negotiation is conflict: a disagreement about what you are willing to pay for a manufacturer's goods; a disagreement about the terms of a lease; or even a divorce settlement. Since all of these situations involve the possibility of losing or winning, some participants may try to bully their way to a solution.

Effective management of bullies in negotiations means recognizing them and handling them early on in the session.

There are two types of bullies usually seen around the negotiation table. First, there is the elected bully, who is actually not that angry with you, but needs to put on a show for those he or she represents; he or she will make a scene, perhaps even walk out close to deadline. If the negotiations are a very public affair, the elected bully may have some unkind words to say about you to the media.

Remember that this is a show being put on for the elected bully's constituents and has little bearing on the eventual outcome of the talks. Resist the temptation to become angry. Once the negotiations resume, you may even be able to gain an advantage over your agitated and therefore less-clearly thinking adversary.

The second type of bully is a cross between Ralph Kramden and the Wizard of Oz; he or she will attempt to wow you with vocal volume and table pounding not seen since Nikita Khrushchev visited the United Nations. Attempting to out-shout this bully will result in a stand-off and agreement to disagree.

Remember that in an argument, the one doing the yelling is out of control (which is why he or she is yelling). In negotiation, the person who is in control has the advantage. Therefore, stay quiet (not silent, just quiet) and stay in control. Remain in control and you have the edge.

When this creature starts to bellow, don't tell him or her to calm down, or begin your own tirade. If you do so, you started the shouting match the person wanted all along. Rather, go matter-of-factly to the issue being discussed. You will quickly defeat the purpose of the bully's act: to get your emotions running high, your decibel level up, and have you make agreements you wouldn't normally make.

Control Your Emotions

Whether caused by the rantings of a bully or your own exasperation at the fact that you've been sitting at this table for hours and there doesn't seem to be much movement, heightened emotional states are a hindrance to successful negotiation.

The participant who has to apologize for an outburst brought about by emotions or fatigue is at a psychological disadvantage that will work in your favor if you remain calm.

On the other hand, if you jump on the emotional roller-coaster that typifies many negotiation sessions, the quiet, calm atmosphere needed to produce an agreement that both sides can live with must be reconstructed by both sides, which takes time away from reaching agreement.

Seeking Agreement Rather than Victory

In negotiations, if you win, rather than agree, you lose. Both parties need to leave the table with the impression and the reality that they benefited from having participated in the process.

Many negotiators confuse the need to win with the need to agree. This mentality causes them to begin negotiating with victory rather than with agreement in mind.

Such behavior doesn't gain anything; tempers flare as one side has to let the other know that such unfairness won't be tolerated. After the argument is settled—the participants agree that they still disagree on the matter under negotiation—they also agree that neither side is made up of pushovers and that negotiation in good faith can finally begin. Unfortunately, that beginning is often hours or even days later—a needless delay had the participants sought agreement instead of victory at the outset.

Considering Future Negotiations

As I said at the beginning of this chapter, anyone can negotiate a good or even a great deal *once.* If it's so good that the other side has taken a severe trouncing, however, they will be back, and they will be angry. If yours is a business in which long-term relationships are important, giving the other side a fair deal will pay handsome dividends in the long run.

Quick Review: Successful Negotiations

1. Don't confuse negotiation with confrontation; seek agreement, not victory.

2. Prepare your case *and* theirs. The best prepared gets the best deal.

3. Set objectives and fall-back positions *before* you get to the negotiating table.

4. Keep team member disagreement private.

5. Negotiate in a comfortable "neutral" setting.

6. Let the other side talk first.

7. When talking numbers, mention specific figures, rather than ranges.

8. Always tell the truth.

9. Don't be rushed into agreement or make snap judgments, especially when fatigued.

10. Let them lose their tempers, but keep *your* cool.

Chapter Thirteen

Handling Crisis Communication

At-a-Glance Summary

This chapter is about effective communication in a crisis situation. Depending upon the nature of your business, a crisis can take many different forms, but it's essential that you immediately recognize its onset.

Communication strategies must be in place and ready to be implemented *prior* to an actual crisis. Team planning, constituency targeting, media selection, and symbolic communication are all part of the mix in communicating your way through a crisis.

Finally, once a crisis ends, the importance of saying so, loudly and publicly, is a crucial element in getting things back on the road to normalcy.

Handling Crisis Communication

"When you're up to your ass in alligators, it's difficult to remember that your original objective was to clean out the swamp."

That old southern adage is a handy summarization of the need for effective crisis management and communication. Much of the literature on crisis management will provide you with interesting accounts of how others have managed and survived crises. But ultimately you are the best knower of your own business and will use that knowledge to manage your way around and through a crisis.

What you may not do so well in a crisis situation is communicate. One of the main purposes of this chapter is to see that you don't ignore the communication function in the midst of a crisis, because how well you communicate with your public during a crisis will quickly become as important as your management of the crisis itself.

When survival or solution of the problems that precipitated the state of crisis becomes your all-encompassing activity, such normal activities as communicating with your various constituents—customers, shareholders, the media, the general public, and regulatory agencies—can fall to a lower priority.

Once communication is put on the back burner, even as a matter of seeming necessity, all of your various constituents are left to fend for themselves in figuring out what's going on. It is at this juncture that irreparable damage may be done, even if you manage your way out of the crisis itself. If the flow of information is stopped or severely stemmed, you or your organization will be thought to be some degree of inept, uncaring, secretive, or unethical—perceptions that can be lethal in any business.

Identifying a Crisis

The definition of a crisis is clouded by the overuse of the term and the fact that we have become relatively accustomed to functioning in a so-called crisis situation with considerable normalcy.

As a long-time faculty member of the City University of New York, I am in a good position to point out that New York City has been in a state of continuing fiscal crisis for most if not all of my more than twenty years of service. Thus, the mention of yet another squall in this continuing "crisis" must usually be accompanied by the admonition, "This time it's really serious," because things have come to the point where the word "crisis" has little impact.

A true crisis can take many forms, but it can essentially be defined as any situation that drastically and negatively affects your business to the extent that survival of the organization in its present state is imperiled.

In the banking business, it can be an invisible but devastating failure to meet regulatory requirements and a loss of public confidence. In the automobile business, it can be a perceived design flaw that sends customers to competitors' showrooms, or a crippling recall and the bad publicity that goes with it. In the pharmaceutical industry, it can be a spate of deaths or injuries related to the use of a product. In other industries, the crisis may come in the form of an environmental accident or even a terrorist action or hostage situation. In any industry or organization, a sudden loss of or change in leadership can constitute a crisis.

History has proven on repeated occasions that corporations that are forthright and communicative in the midst of a crisis are the ones that survive and prosper, whereas those that stonewall, obfuscate, and engage in cover-ups either perish or spend vast amounts of time and resources in the struggle to survive.

Defining Your Specific Crises

The fact is that *before* a crisis happens, your goal should be to define just what constitutes a crisis, or specifically which situations or events could jeopardize or seriously disrupt your business. Here is a list of events that I would categorize as being in the crisis category and in need of crisis-specific communication:

- Environmental accidents
- Product failures involving a large number of units
- Product failures involving customer fatalities
- Hostage or highjacking situations
- Terrorist or sabotage situations

- Major litigation
- Severely negative media coverage
- Abrupt or controversial changes in senior management
- Bankruptcy filings or severe financial reversals

This list suggests a range of possibilities, and using this list as a starting point, you should develop an expanded list based upon situations specific to your particular field. In this manner, you can develop not only a set of crisis-management plans but also an equally important crisis-communications plan. The history of crisis management tells us that crises are usually foreseeable, and it is in this precrisis period that you should be setting up a communications plan.

Developing a Crisis-Communications Plan

The focus here is the establishment of a plan of action to be set into motion once a crisis occurs so that information will continue to flow to your constituents in an orderly and strategic manner. Of course, in planning for a crisis you will have developed a proposed strategy for dealing with the crisis itself; but the battlefield of crisis management is littered with the carcasses of those companies whose management reacted astutely and decisively to the crisis but failed to communicate any of their actions.

Select Your Crisis-Communications Team

As important as having a communications plan in a crisis is assembling the right team to execute the plan. Your team should be organized in five areas:

1. External advisers
2. Internal advisers
3. Issues advisers
4. Legal advisers
5. Constituency managers

External Advisers

At the scene of a major fire, the chief or officer in command rarely, if ever, enters a burning building. The reasoning here is that the smoke- and obstacle-filled inside of a burning building is a lousy place from which to view the fire and make effective command decisions.

Similarly, the middle of a crisis is a lousy place from which to see yourself as others see you. Yet, this is just the perspective you need to effectively manage communications in a crisis.

This is what public-relations people do best: not just know your business, but know how your public feels about it and the job you are doing in running it.

They can help you get your story out, decide which media to use, which audiences to concentrate on, and in what sequence—all details that may seem peripheral or frivolous when a crisis has you locked in a struggle for survival.

I am not suggesting that you listen to their every dictum. If you do, you're no longer in charge, and you should be. But if your organization is of sufficient size and consequence to effect or be affected by public opinion, having external public-relations advisers is a step you should consider long before the onset of a crisis. This way, when the issues climate heats up to the crisis stage, or even before, you'll have external advisers that you know and trust.

Internal Advisors

Here I am referring to your own internal public-affairs or public-relations people, who should be an integral part of your crisis-communications team. Depending on the role of this particular group within your organization, they can serve as spokespersons (they often have relationships with local media that can be extremely helpful in a crisis period) or as liaisons with senior management for your external public-relations team.

Specifically defining these tasks prior to the crisis will enable the internal and external public-relations teams to work for you instead of against each other, which will certainly be the case if you start doling out power to a group of "outsiders" in the midst of a crisis.

Plan on choosing between the advice of your legal team and your P.R. team. (They will usually differ.)

Perhaps it's a flaw inherent in both internal and external public-relations teams, especially in a crisis—and even a flaw to which this writer is partial—but the advice of many public-relations types, boiled down to just a few words, will amount to, "Tell everyone everything, immediately."

Armed with a legal rather than a public relations perspective, your lawyers are likely to give you advice which, when boiled down to its essence, amounts to, "Don't tell anyone anything, ever."

The lawyers earn their pay by telling you not to do things that will get you into difficulty, whereas the P.R. people will pull you in the direction of taking an active stance, communicatively speaking. Your job as a manager is to make a choice or seek a balance between these camps.

What your attorneys are concerned about, and often rightly so, is that a flurry of well-intentioned, forthright information on the nature and causes of a crisis, as well as what you are doing about it, will also contain admissions of what you may have done incorrectly and that you are in some way responsible for the crisis itself. You may also be blamed for the actions you took if your crisis management steps are not as effective as you thought they would be.

Lawyers have to worry about how what you say will play in court, whereas your P.R. advisers have to worry about how it will play in the court of public opinion.

I recently learned of an incident in which a customer was severely injured while using one of a company's products. The story received considerable media attention, focusing heavily on the impact of the victim's injury on his family.

Senior executives of the company decided to make a substantial cash contribution to the family in order to help with their immediate needs. The company's attorneys vigorously opposed this gesture, lest it be portrayed in subsequent legal actions as an admission of responsibility for the injury that occurred.

Senior management in this case decided to ignore or at least set aside the advice of their legal team in favor of doing what they thought to be the appropriate gesture in spite of the possibility of adverse legal consequences.

Taking a purely legalistic stance may present you as a totally self-serving concern that places its balance sheet above the public interest. The history of corporations in crisis would suggest that those who relied excessively on legal advice may survive in the courts but not necessarily in the marketplace.

In summary, your legal advisers should be an important part of your crisis-communication team, to be relied upon in avoiding or minimizing the legal consequences of the crisis in which you find yourself. However, the advice of your internal and external public-affairs teams may be in conflict.

The final decision of which advice to follow should be made on the basis of how important your legal position is compared with public perception of your product, service, or organization. Total legal victory or exoneration from any blame in the causes or consequences of a crisis will be a hollow victory if gained at the expense of your reputation.

Issues Advisers

Issues advisers are the members of your crisis communication team who are there to give you specific information related to specific areas of your company's operations. Their specialties may range from customer relations to engineering to accounting and finance. The purpose of an issues adviser is to make certain that you get the latest and most accurate information on how a crisis is affecting your operations.

In assembling your team of issues advisers, reach down into the ranks and get the input of someone at the level of, let's say, an area manager. The usual tendency in a crisis is to choose the V.P. of operations as your issues adviser for that area. Depending upon company politics and culture, you may find that those who head entire divisions might be receiving a more positive spin on the operations picture than someone who is closer to it on a daily basis.

Much has been made of GM's success in using a "team approach" to building its Saturn automobiles. In the team approach, if any worker has a better way of doing things or a suggestion on how to improve the product, he or she has immediate access to management on that suggestion. Workers also have greater autonomy on their "teams" in deciding the best way to accomplish a task.

The results of the team approach have been dramatic improvements in both product and productivity. But like so many great ideas, it was there all the time, just waiting for corporate culture to change enough to permit such flexibility. In assembling your team of crisis-issues advisers, cast a wide net, and the quality and accuracy of the internal information you need to handle the crisis will improve dramatically.

Constituency Managers

In other chapters I have pointed out the importance of not ignoring the audience.

In a crisis, getting the story out and managing and solving the crisis at the same time often are conflicting tasks. The problem is further compounded by the widely divergent communicative needs of constituencies such as shareholders, customers, regulators, the media, and perhaps even victims and their families in cases involving death or injury. They all need to hear about the crisis and what you are doing about it, but they all have different perspectives.

The risk you run here is in either ignoring a group altogether or giving them the impression they are somehow less important than another of your constituencies. You can lessen the chance of doing damage to your relationships with any of these important groups by appointing a communicative adviser to represent the interests of each constituency.

As with the rest of the crisis-communications team, your various constituencies should be defined and the team in place *before* there is any need to make use of them.

Identifying and Reaching Your Target Audience

Who needs to know what, and in what order should they be told? Not only do you need to define that audience in the absence of crisis, you must also determine priorities. It will be important to notify some constituents before others—your customers, bankers, shareholders, regulatory agencies, employees, unions, the general public. If death or injuries are involved, you'll need to communicate with victims or their families.

Informing the wrong people, or the right people in the wrong order, is all too likely if you fail to determine your target audiences and sequence of communicating with them in advance.

Selecting the Appropriate
Crisis-Communications Media

Once your crisis-communications team is assembled and you know who your audiences are and the sequence in which they should receive information, the next step is to develop a plan for reaching the various segments of your audience. Following are some methods of communication you will want to review in assembling your communications plan.

Personal Contact

With particularly important players, perhaps board members or regulatory officials, direct personal contact should be included. If they first hear of your problem from a reporter, the consequences won't be positive. Once a crisis erupts, you can be sure that the media will be in touch with such parties for their reaction to your plight.

Before you need it, draw up a list of such individuals to be contacted and designate who will make such calls should the need arise.

Executive-Employee Briefings

Handling a crisis situation often requires an extra measure of effort from employees. Don't expect heroic measures from people who have to learn what management is doing by reading about it in the newspaper or seeing a senior executive on CNN.

The importance of internal communications in a crisis situation cannot be overstated. Remember that your employees become a primary source of information within the surrounding community during a crisis. An ill-informed staffer or one who is hostile because he or she has been left "out of the loop" can do considerable damage, especially if happened upon by a reporter.

Formulate an internal-communications plan that includes communications from senior officials. Where personal briefings are not feasible due to company size or a multiplicity of locations, consider a satellite television feed.

Make internal communications, especially regularly scheduled employee briefings, a part of your crisis-communications plan.

Press Conferences

Hold them early and hold them often, or at least on a regular schedule. Except with proprietary information or legally problematical material, be open and communicative. Even if there are areas you can't talk about, tell those present exactly why you're not talking.

If you want the media off your back during a crisis, remember that the degree and kind of coverage you get, after an initial flurry in which you may be lead-story material, is in inverse proportion to your degree of accessibility. Your nearly constant willingness to share information on your actions in a crisis will ultimately reduce the degree of coverage you get.

On the other hand, if the media sense any kind of cover-up, the story can simmer for months or even years. Anyone involved in the Watergate fiasco or the Iran-Contra affair or even the Whitewater controversy can tell you that.

Reporters fancy themselves investigators, and once a story has been *completely* told, there is no dirt to dig, no dirty laundry to air, not any smoking gun to find, they are likely to fade from the scene. In fact, on a light-news day, such openness may even get you coverage on the high-quality job you're doing of getting your story across.

Hotlines

If you are in a business that involves a lot of customers and your product is one that could be dangerous if improperly used; if you have to give complicated directions; or if the situation or the nature of the crisis changes hourly, you may want to consider a "hotline." This way customers, shareholders, reporters, or any portion of your constituency can get up-to-the minute information.

Such numbers are a common tool of the pharmaceutical industry, to supply product information to patients as well as to health-care professionals. In the case of a product defect or recall, however, hotline numbers can be an extremely important tool, not just for providing vital information, but as a reassurance to your public that you are sufficiently concerned about their well-being to provide this service.

If you decide to use a hotline as one of your crisis-communication tools, give careful consideration as to how it is staffed and the method of communication—live personnel or a recorded message.

This writer recommends against recorded messages as the sole voice on a hotline. In a crisis, recorded messages can also give the impression that everyone has jumped ship and that a recording machine has been left to handle things.

If staffing demands or the sheer volume of calls you expect make the use of a recorded message necessary, provide updates on a scheduled basis and make that schedule part of the message.

Special Mailings

Mailgrams, express letters, faxes, or E-mail or Web sites are effective ways to provide information of a clarifying nature to important segments of your public. In crises requiring the communication of detailed information to a relatively sophisticated audience, an audience-tailored written message should be your choice.

Such mailings are particularly effective in supplying detailed financial, legal, or technical information that is not feasible or deliverable via the press conference or the sound byte.

One cautionary note: Don't include information in a mailing that you don't want to see in the newspapers or on the air. Expect that the information contained in a mailing to customers or stockholders or any large group will be leaked, intentionally or otherwise. The information should therefore not be inconsistent with statements made in other forums, or you'll find yourself with a credibility crisis.

As to the specific content of a crisis mailing, you should include *your* version of the facts, a reason why this letter is being sent, and a definitive statement of what is being done about the crisis, as well as a timetable in which you will have the situation under control.

Be certain to have the name of a real person on any communication. Letters signed "The Management" or even "The Executive Committee" have all the credibility of the line "You may have already won . . ."

Make certain that the special and urgent nature of the mailing is conveyed early in the message, perhaps even indicated on the outside of the envelope, but also remember that it's been said that the importance of a piece of mail is usually in inverse proportion to the amount of printing on the outside of the envelope.

Print- and Electronic-Media Ads

If your audience is both numerically large and demographically diverse, and the crisis has received widespread media coverage, you may wish to consider media announcements—print and radio and television—to state your position and inform the general public about the crisis.

In constructing a newspaper ad, include, as you did in the direct-mail piece; a specific mention of those at whom the ad is aimed, the reason for the message (the crisis situation), what specific actions you are taking, and a timetable for getting things back to normal.

If you feel that you have been wronged by the media in terms of the kind of coverage your crisis has received (and almost everyone does, both during and after a crisis), don't use your media announcements to attack the media. You'll appear defensive and embittered rather than in command of the situation.

Also, various media may choose to respond by questioning both the accuracy of your position and your motivation in running the announcements. What started out as an attempt to communicate with the public and demonstrate your effectiveness as a manager becomes the basis for another round of unfavorable media coverage.

Who Is Your Spokesperson?

In a crisis, the public will not only want to know what you are doing to solve the problem, they'll also want to know about those in charge: whether they seem capable, trustworthy, decisive, and most of all, credible. This is why, in a time of crisis, it is most important to have a senior executive as your chief spokesperson.

While many complain about the undue influence of media, it is not the highly paid anchorpeople or hard-hitting investigative reporters who have the real clout and credibility in a crisis; it's the actual people in charge, those who make the decisions and take the actions, rather than just ask about and report on them.

Lee Iacocca, Dave Thomas of Wendy's, and many others have proven that a real executive can make a highly effective, credible spokesperson.

A professional spokesperson or actor may deliver the message in the fewest "takes" and with the most fluency, but that professional spokesperson says nothing about who you are and what you're doing in this time of crisis. In fact, the use of a hired spokesperson may even suggest that you have something to hide (namely, your senior management). Having a professional spokesperson or actor deliver your media statement is equivalent to having a receptionist sign your annual message to the shareholders.

Making Use of Symbolic Communication

A vital and often neglected area of handling and communicating effectively in a crisis, symbolic communication refers to actions or messages of senior management that clearly symbolize that things are either under control or back to normal.

It's long been a tradition on the American political scene to engage in symbolic communication, for example, to have a President travel to an auto factory to deliver an address on the importance of buying American, or to a school to sign an important piece of education-related legislation.

Such moments do more than provide photo opportunities for politicians. They also deliver a two-pronged symbolic message: first, that the issue was important enough to make this special trip, and second, to convey the impression that this executive is involved and has a hands-on approach.

Such symbolic communication is especially important in effective crisis communication and should be included as part of your action plan.

Maintain Executive Visibility

An important symbol of how well a company is weathering a storm of crisis is the level of visibility of its senior management. If, at the outset of a crisis, senior management members are suddenly inaccessible and invisible, they will quickly gain an image not unlike that of mafiosi seen in newscasts, darting out of courthouses with trenchcoats pulled over their heads.

Yes, in a crisis, you'll be busy, but don't become invisible. Even as a senior executive, if you find it necessary or desirable to appoint a spokesperson, personally introduce that spokesperson to the media in his or her first press conference. This gesture will lend that new voice some of your authority and credibility.

Don't Hide from the Troops

Another important area of symbolic communication is visibility to employees. Although, like most troops, they understand that the generals are not usually in the front lines, employees need the support and visibility of senior executives, especially in a time of crisis.

Remember that any time a crisis occurs—when an airline suffers a crash, when an automobile manufacturer has a major recall—employees are out there taking the questions and sometimes the heat from almost everyone they encounter. At the same time, they may be expected to perform at heightened levels to get through the crisis period.

Don't Just Stand There Answering Questions—Do Something!

Another important type of symbolic communication lies in the actions you take as a senior executive in a crisis. Any gesture that says things are under control or are going to be okay soon is important in restoring public confidence.

Governor Mario Cuomo of New York performed an important gesture of symbolic communication after the terrorist bombing that devastated parts of New York's World Trade Center. The Trade Center business community was emotionally as well as physically shaken by the blast. Local media outlets raised questions as to the structural integrity of one of the 110-story towers, and there were reports of defections by some tenants.

Realizing the possible adverse economic consequences of such reports and the panic they might spark, Governor Cuomo announced that not only did he intend to reoccupy his offices in the building, but that he would also be the very first tenant to move in after repairs were completed. Weeks later, as the governor reoccupied his offices, the move was made with great fanfare and maximum media coverage.

As a result, news reports of tenant defections and structural problems with the Trade Center diminished to a trickle. Governor Cuomo's triumphant return to the World Trade Center symbolized to all that things were clearly back to normal, a much needed reassurance for a nervous business community.

Similarly, any message or gesture that says, "We're okay and so are our products," should be considered as soon as is feasible and credible during a crisis. If there is a question about a product, a personal message from the CEO or a demonstration of a product in use can be that important piece of symbolic communication that may be sought by your public.

Announce the END of the Crisis!

It Ain't Over Till You Say It's Over

Crises have a lot in common with meteorological catastrophes. Like hurricanes and blizzards, they can be predicted. Precautions can be taken, but even in the face of such measures, tremendous destruction can ensue.

After a storm, the return to normalcy is often rapid. It is that very resumption of routine activity that serves as a communal symbol that all is once again as it was. A corporate crisis may be well managed, and your management of the crisis may have been successful, but often there are no striking visible symbols that things are back to normal unless you create them.

Therefore, once a crisis has passed, you should say so. Once your plants are up and running or the last repair or replacement of a defective product has been made, you should say so.

Your media choices will be determined by how best to reach your various constituents; but regardless of how you do it, the announcement that things are back to normal and that preventative measures are in place must be made strongly and definitively.

Surviving and prospering beyond a crisis should be viewed as a triumph of an effective management team that is deserving of the applause. It is also a time to send a loud and clear message to those more distant from the crisis that you are back and that perceptions of your company as an organization in peril are history rather than headlines.

Quick Review:
Handling Crisis Communication

1. Anticipate and define crises before they happen.

2. Plan crisis-communication strategies *in advance.*

3. Maintain contact with the media at regular intervals if appropriate.

4. Have internal and external advisers as part of your crisis-communications team.

5. Decide *in advance* exactly who should be informed of a crisis and in what order.

6. Don't be afraid to call a crisis a crisis.

7. Plan your symbolic-communications strategies.

8. Keep your senior executives visible.

9. Talk to your employees, early and often.

10. Once the crisis is over, say so.

Chapter Fourteen

Conducting Successful Meetings

At-a-Glance Summary

This chapter shows you how to conduct successful meetings and send the most positive signals about your leadership skills. It includes strategies to increase your level of effectiveness at running meetings, from arranging the meeting itself to managing the group dynamics and the characters that surface in any gathering of colleagues.

Conducting Successful Meetings

Often considered a necessary evil of corporate life, a way of getting decisions made and policies set, meetings may get things done but few of us like attending them.

Newer members of an organization can feel that their input is unwelcome (and they may be correct), whereas senior executives may feel that the same decisions could be made in a flash without all this wasted time and input from subordinates (and they may also be correct).

Those in the middle will often use meetings as launching pads for their own agendas, constructive or otherwise, and test the water with various levels of disagreement or confrontation. Some will attempt to operate within the agenda and try to get things done so that the meeting is not a waste of time.

All these behaviors and approaches to meetings are, in reality, power struggles. Some attempt to gain power by manipulating the agenda, and others show their distaste for power or, more correctly, those in power, by not participating. Even those who do participate may be doing so only to seek the recognition of those in charge.

As a manager you can have a masterful grasp of the most complex nuances of your field; but if your meeting-management skills are not what they should be, you will be accused of alternately being a bully, wimp, a tyrant, a nit-picker, or a bumbling generalist. If you are consistently ineffective in running meetings, that failing will be generalized to other areas of your performance.

Your effectiveness in handling meetings will shape the perception of your overall effectiveness as a leader: how you handle the ebb and flow of agreement and conflict; the interaction of varying personalities; and whether you get things done or end up in ideational disarray. If you follow the steps outlined here, people may not look forward to coming to your meetings but you will get more done in less time and reduce conflict.

Using an Agenda to Establish and Maintain Control

"You're probably wondering why I called you here," is a disastrous meeting opener. It says to those gathered that you're secretive, and they will spend part of the time wondering what you're up to rather than listening to what you have to say. Agendas should be distributed in advance, in order to give those who will be present time to formulate their own ideas on the agenda items.

An agenda enhances control and productivity for a meeting in several ways. First of all, those in attendance have expectation of what is to be discussed and will usually come prepared, not with just the required materials, but also with ideas generated by an advance look at your agenda.

Agendas also help set the tone of the meeting. For example, if a meeting agenda has a wide variety of items for discussion, it can serve as an indication that there is a lot to be done and that those in attendance should be prepared for a busy session. On the other hand, if there is an item of extreme importance under consideration, having it as the sole agenda item or presenting an unusually brief agenda sends a clear signal to participants that the meeting is of particular importance.

Finally, agendas present a structure that, in more formal settings (see the section on level of formality) permit you as leader, or even permit participants, to make sure a meeting moves forward by prohibiting discussion of items that are not on the agenda. Once again, depending on the level of formality and the culture in which the meeting is being held, prohibition of discussion of nonagenda items in a politely insistent manner will ensure that meetings cover *exactly* the items or areas intended.

Before continuing, it is important to note that there are two types of gatherings that are often confused with meetings: so-called brainstorming sessions and therapy sessions. In the former, those present may be asked to focus on a single issue or problem and work together on developing new approaches to the matter under consideration. In the latter, one may freely discuss a problem on a random or even a chaotic path to an informational destination.

Obviously, brainstorming and therapy sessions have their places in the search for solutions, but they are generally unfettered by deadlines or budgetary constraints. Also, unlike traditional meetings, the lack of forward motion is not considered a failure, but merely an indication for the need for further brainstorming or therapy. The meetings considered in this chapter are strictly of the variety that requires that things get done on time with a minimum of upheaval—meetings where the lack of results indicate failure rather than the need for more meetings.

You may want to structure meetings with the following categories as a guide for your agenda:

1. Reading of the minutes (or statement of purpose and definition for a newly convened group)

2. Approval of the minutes from the previous meeting (which have been distributed in advance of the meeting with enough time for those present to have reviewed them)

3. Old business, considering unfinished items or tabled motions from the previous meetings

4. New business (agenda items submitted)

5. Elections, if required; the establishment of election procedures should be included as an early agenda item in newly convened groups

Using these basic items as building blocks, you should be able to construct an agenda for a newly established body, or reshape and systematize the agenda for a group in need of reorganization.

This cautionary note: Don't edit an agenda to avoid discussing issues or to manipulate a group; you will only make them distrustful and non-communicative. In planning an agenda, the objective should be to get business done efficiently.

Encouraging Participant Input

An effective way to gain input without giving up control of the agenda is to establish a policy that staff members will be allotted a portion of the meeting time for items they wish to discuss. This makes it clear that input is welcome and planned. The purposefulness and sincerity of staff communication will be increased, and control of the agenda can be preserved.

Don't fear loud meetings, flying feathers and all, as long as the items discussed are on the agenda.

Establishing a Regular Meeting Schedule

If you are a new manager and your company doesn't already have a meeting schedule and a mechanism for gathering agenda items, establish them. As the one who institutes this policy, you will have communicated that you want input and that you intend to seek it in an organized, systematic manner. This gesture also communicates that you are organized, in charge, and yet willing to listen.

Regularly scheduled meetings can always be canceled if circumstances dictate, but the presence of that regular meeting on a schedule says to employees that there will be an opportunity for discussion on a regular basis, an important escape valve in the presence of problems.

Begin on Time

Employees, like the schoolchildren they once were, will test the corporate culture on the starting time of meetings. A 2:00 P.M. time can quickly degenerate to 2:10 and beyond if you let it.

Exert your authority and always begin within five minutes of the scheduled starting time, even if all of those coming have not yet arrived. You thus indicate that you are there to get things done and are in charge of not only the schedule, but the group itself.

I recognize that what I've just said may be a bit harsh in less formal environments or where the atmosphere is more relaxed; you might consider building in a kind of time cushion such as "Coffee and . . . will be served at 2:00 P.M. with the meeting to begin promptly at 2:15." In this case, you've said that the meeting will begin promptly, but in a kinder, gentler way. You have communicated the same no-nonsense, let's-get-down-to-business attitude, but you've humanized it by saying to relax and have some coffee first.

End on Time

Meetings with a definite concluding time are those at which the most is accomplished.

Why? It's not only the pressure of the clock that makes us work harder (who was it who said, "The amount of time a task takes is proportionate to the amount of time available to complete that task"?). It's also the absence of the feeling that "This thing will go on forever" that makes a meeting bearable, especially for those with tight schedules.

If you schedule a meeting with a predetermined ending time, you are communicating not only your own sense of organization, but a consideration for the fact that there are schedules other than your own to be met. The trade-off is that you'll find that those present are willing to work harder and more constructively, rather than feeling that they are unwilling guests in *The Twilight Zone* in an episode entitled, "The Endless Meeting."

Planning for the Effective Meeting

A major key to successful meetings is proper advance planning, particularly with regard to items that can not and should not be decided during a meeting.

Selecting an Appropriate Level of Formality

"Move to table the motion. Is the motion seconded? All in favor of the motion signify by saying aye."

The chairperson of a meeting stands at the podium, rattling off parliamentary rules with the rapidity and dispassion of an auctioneer, changing the direction, the length, and even the outcome. This is the stuff of parliamentary procedure, so named because of the origins of such rules in the British Parliament, as outlined in *Robert's Rules of Order.*[1]

How should you proceed, formal or informal? The corporate culture and expectations of those who attend a meeting will greatly shape the level of formality that will be tolerated.

Robert's Rules, no rules, or somewhere in between? The choice you make should be based upon four factors:

1. The size of the group
2. The atmosphere of the meeting
3. The degree of legal importance of the meeting
4. Your degree of knowledge and experience with parliamentary procedure

---

[1]Carr, Marjorie Mitchell, *Robert's Rules of Order—Simplified.* Pedigree Books, 71 pp. 1991.

Informal meetings should be the rule with fewer than ten people in the room. In a group this size, everyone will generally know everyone else, and in this informal atmosphere, there is no need to start applying rules that can cut off discussion, cause division, and seem to stifle opposing points of view for being "out of order."

The resentment caused by such rules in an informal setting, or their sudden or inconsistent application, will be viewed with suspicion and justified resentment and will not be worth the time saved.

Once a group has more than ten or twelve members, however, permitting everyone equal access to debate the issue at hand or trying to gain agreement by consensus rather than election becomes too cumbersome and time consuming. If rules are introduced for the purpose of improving the flow and productivity of the meeting rather than to control or stifle the exchange of ideas, they are generally welcomed.

Understand the Legal Consequences of Your Meetings

You'll need to examine the work of the group over which you are presiding in the context of how important that group's work is from a legal point of view.

Are your decisions going to be subject to subsequent review, perhaps in a court of law? Will there be questions about how decisions were arrived at and whether the rules were consistently applied?

If your answers to these questions are in the affirmative, regardless of the group's size, you'll want to adopt a set of rules and stick by them. You should also check with your legal counsel before getting started, to avoid potentially serious errors if your work is to be reviewed or might face challenges from external entities.

Study the Rules Before You Get to the Meeting

The effective application of rules designed to keep an agenda on track, limit debate, and carry out elections in an orderly and just manner requires experience in knowing and applying the rules. You'll need to apply a dual level of attention, not only to the items under discussion, but also to how they are in compliance or violation of the rules for the meeting (such as whether an item of discussion should be ruled as being irrelevant or "out of order," as is said in meeting parlance).

Get Help if You Need It

If you are not that experienced in chairing meetings and you intend to run a meeting under strict parliamentary rules, give strong consideration to appointing a parliamentarian and keep a copy of *Robert's Rules* or some similar guide on hand. This way you can maintain compliance with a set of meeting rules while you focus on the issues at hand.

Keeping the Peace at Meetings

If certain decisions are not made in advance of meetings, making them during a meeting will be perceived as manipulation rather than effective management and could create a level of resentment that will be difficult to reverse. Here are some preventative strategies that should improve the meeting atmosphere.

Define the Group

If matters are to be decided by vote, the group should be defined in terms of exactly who the eligible voters are. For example, members of a task force or committee may have a full vote, but what about their support staff, who may be present at the meeting? If not decided in advance, and if everyone votes, you may wind up with the classic case of the tail wagging the dog if the support staff or part-time members of the group constitute the majority.

Define a Majority

What should be decided by a simple majority, what by a two-thirds vote? Should the electorate be defined as all the members of a given group, or just those present at the meeting? What about absentee voting—should it be permitted? Can those who were not present and did not hear the discussion cast an informed vote?

Your decisions on these seemingly simple questions can drastically affect the outcome of a group's work. All of these questions need to be answered at the beginning of your work, if your meetings will make decisions by casting votes. Attempting to make decisions about voter eligibility in the presence of issues and likely outcomes looks like manipulation and probably is. Set your electoral rules before you consider any other issues.

CHAPTER FOURTEEN

Don't Let a Meeting Degenerate into a Gripe Session

A meeting is normally a time to form consensus, to provide information, or to develop policy in handling an issue or problem. However, if morale in an organization is low, or if meetings in the past have been too few and far between, meetings can easily and inadvertently become forums for people to vent their anger, outrage, or whatever other negative emotion is in the air.

Once the atmosphere at a meeting becomes charged with such negativity, it can be difficult to get things back on track. As the one who presides, you may be seen as part of the problem rather than the solution if your meetings become the major forum to air complaints.

If there is a morale problem, or there are a series of negative or potentially negative situations that require discussion, consider setting up a separate meeting billed strictly as a gripe session or a forum in which complaints can be aired.

You may wish to bill such meetings as "gripe sessions," "town meetings," or even "verbal-suggestion boxes." No matter what you call them, keep these gatherings focused on the problem issue and differentiate them from your regularly scheduled meetings.

Having a separate meeting to air complaints will demonstrate that you care about employee problems and their solutions, while preserving the integrity, structure, and purpose of a meeting held to conduct company business. You can also place agenda items of a "gripe" nature on the "gripe-session" agenda, thus assuring that regular meetings can remain task or accomplishment oriented.

Don't Overuse the "Emergency Meeting" Designation

The designation "emergency meeting" should be reserved for just such occasions when a *real* crisis comes up and attendance is absolutely essential.

One department manager I know was in the habit of designating practically every meeting he held as an "emergency meeting." His memoranda were usually laced with the word "crisis." This manager was communicating to his personnel that he viewed everything as a crisis and was referred to by more than one of his staffers as being from the "Chicken Little" school of managers.

Use the words "crisis" and "emergency" sparingly in referring to your meetings. Thus, when there is a serious problem to be tackled, you'll get help and cooperation rather than a behind-your-back shrug that says, "There he (or she) goes again."

Once the Meeting Begins

Calling for a Quorum

A quorum is defined in *Robert's Rules* as the majority of all members. Therefore, in order to conduct business fairly, especially in situations where matters are being voted upon, a quorum should be present. In fact, *Robert's Rules* further states that business conducted in the absence of a quorum is "null and void."

While it is traditionally the duty of a chairperson to monitor the number present, any member of the group can, as is said in meeting parlance, "call for a quorum." Once a quorum has been called, the business of the meeting is halted and the number of voting members is counted. If the number of those present is less than the defined majority of eligible voters, the only business to be discussed is that of an adjournment time, with all other business being suspended.

Practicality sometimes dictates that this rule be suspended, which is done formally by a majority vote of those present. If the group agrees, then business can continue with all actions taken to be ratified at a subsequent meeting at which a quorum is present. Given the reality of conflicting schedules and priorities, suspending a quorum can be a highly practical measure. When crucial matters are under deliberation and being voted upon, however, conducting substantive business without a quorum can be unfair and leave you on legally shaky ground.

Maintaining Order

No, this is not a few words about alternative uses of a gavel, but clearly one of your jobs is to keep the meeting running smoothly, and a major component of this task is to keep the discussion orderly and on target.

You should inform the group *at the outset* that members are to speak when recognized by the chairperson and that extraneous or "off the point" discussion or comments will be ruled out of order and not permitted to continue.

The application of such rules should be consistent and only to advance the smooth and expeditious running of the meeting, rather than the advancement of the chair's favored causes. A chair who attempts to manipulate these rules will quickly manipulate himself or herself out of all personal credibility and authority. Be careful!

Making and Seconding of Motions and Discussion

A motion or recommendation that an action be taken should be seconded. Motions are generally accepted only from voting members of a group and must be seconded by another voting member of the group before discussion can begin. If the motion is not seconded, it is an indication that there is no other interest in discussing the motion, and there is no further consideration given it; or, as they say in parliamentary terms, the motion "dies."

If the motion is seconded, the chair then calls for discussion on the motion just seconded. During that discussion, your function as chair is to recognize those who have comments on the motion, interrupting and stopping that discussion as being "out of order" if it does not pertain specifically to the motion that has been seconded or is "on the floor."

Point of Order or Information

During a meeting, someone may spot a flaw in the procedures being followed. Perhaps a motion was not seconded or a comment is on something other than the motion being discussed. In such cases, any member may call for a "point of order" or an immediate ruling from the chair on the perceived procedural irregularity.

Similarly, a "point of information" is a request for information, often clarification of a motion under discussion or about to be voted upon. Points of order and information generally receive immediate recognition from the chair on the assumption that if they are not cleared up promptly, proper procedure cannot be maintained and fully informed discussion or voting cannot take place.

Voting or "Calling the Question"

Once everyone who wishes to speak on an issue has been heard, the chair may call for a vote by simply asking if the group is ready to vote on the motion and proceeding with the vote in the absence of any negative response.

In a larger group, or where greater formality is preferable, you may want to have the group vote on whether they wish to vote on the motion under discussion immediately or continue discussion. This is known as a vote to "call the question." If the vote (by show of hands or ballot) to call the question fails, discussion on the motion is simply continued. If the vote to call the question is successful, the motion is then immediately voted upon without further discussion.

Motions to call the question come from the floor and like any other motion must be seconded. Motions to call the question are not debatable, and once seconded, must be voted upon immediately. Motions to call the question are usually deliberate attempts either to limit discussion or to shorten the meeting by expediting the voting process.

If discussion becomes repetitive, you may want to encourage such motions by asking if anyone present would like to make a motion to call the question. But once again, in a less formal setting, you might simply want to ask if the group is ready to vote.

Though it may be fairly obvious, it should be stated that the orderly running of a meeting necessitates that there be only one motion on the floor at a time and that no other motions be accepted for consideration until the one under consideration is voted upon and passed or defeated.

Amending a Motion

Sometimes a motion is near passage but may have a flaw in wording or structure that is a problem to those who are about to vote on it.

For example, there may be a motion on the floor that says: "The executive committee will meet monthly to review overtime costs as compared to productivity figures." Let's say that union members want some input at these meetings and, as nonmembers of the executive committee, are opposing this motion.

The motion can be amended by a voting member if the maker of the motion is willing to accept that change as part of the newly amended motion. For example, the amended motion may read as follows: "The executive committee will meet monthly to review overtime costs as compared to productivity figures. Two members of the union's steering committee may attend this meeting as nonvoting members at their option."

This would be considered a "friendly amendment." In the event the maker of the motion is unwilling to accept the amendment as part of the motion, which is at his or her discretion, that motion is then to be voted upon in its original form.

Record and Read the Motion

If your meeting is of a level of formality where you are using even a modified form of parliamentary procedure, it will be desirable to have a secretary present who is responsible for taking minutes. Another important function of that secretary is to write down the *exact* wording of a motion and to read it to those present before voting takes place.

Especially in cases where the outcome of a vote on a motion might have serious consequences, it is essential to the integrity of the deliberative process that the electorate have a *precise* awareness of just what they are voting on.

Often a motion is made, seconded, and followed by extensive discussion, which can cause many of those present either to forget or to confuse the contents of the motion altogether. In the interest of clarity and to avoid the extreme disarray and finger pointing that will result if people don't fully understand what they have voted for or against, always read the motion just before the vote takes place. Also be willing to repeat the motion as necessary.

Tabling the Motion

When a motion is under discussion and that discussion generates additional issues, or the discussion reveals the need for further information that is not readily available, it may be time for someone to move that the motion be "tabled" or discussion be postponed.

Motions to table generally require seconding and a majority vote of those present for passage. Motions to table are not debatable, as such debate would defeat the purpose of the motion itself.

So that the motion to table will be viewed as a means of postponing action until a time when it can actually be accomplished rather than a means of avoiding the issue altogether, it is generally wise to include, in your motion to table, a definite time at which the motion will be taken up again; for example: "I move to table the motion until the quarterly figures are available for inclusion, with discussion to take place no later than the meeting on March 14th."

Handling Confidential Information

If you are having a meeting on a confidential or proprietary matter, be certain to begin and end the meeting with a reminder of the confidential nature of the meeting and, where possible and applicable, the consequences attached to revealing information about the meeting.

Your chances of keeping leaks of information from confidential meetings is increased by keeping the meeting as small as possible, but remember the words of Ben Franklin, who opined that there is absolutely no problem for three people to keep a secret—if two of them are dead.

Making Meetings More Efficient (as in Shorter!)

Before continuing on this topic, as a believer in full discussion and open communications, I should point out that there are times when a discussion has gone on too long and has become repetitive, overly heated, or even trivial. At such times, as the chair of a meeting, or as one of the participants, you may wish to consider the following perfectly acceptable strategies for limiting discussion or even ending the meeting.

Limit Discussion Time

A simple device that usually occurs to people when it's too late, discussion time on motions or agenda items should be decided upon by vote *at the beginning* of a meeting before any discussion has taken place. This way no one will feel singled out by this restriction as they would if you attempted to introduce it in midmeeting. Depending on the complexity of the matter under discussion, you may wish to set the limit at anywhere from five minutes to even thirty minutes (someone should keep time), after which a vote should take place. Such limits are especially useful when you are under severe time constraints.

Motion to Adjourn

Once the business of the agenda is completed, there may be additional business; but beyond the legitimate interests of those gathered, there are sometimes a few people present who actually like meetings, or at least like making them longer than they need to be.

Many times, meetings will be adjourned simply by the clock or by people getting up to leave. As chair, you may wish to expedite things by asking for a motion to adjourn. Especially in handling the filibusterer, the motion to adjourn comes in very handy. Motions to adjourn are not debatable and will end the meeting with a majority vote of those present.

Voting and Secrecy

Be Willing to Use Secret Ballots

This is a courtesy those present will appreciate. Many meetings, particularly the more informal ones, rely on a simple show of hands for voting purposes.

If sensitive issues are being decided, you may wish to use a secret ballot, even in a small group. It's been my rule over the years to try to anticipate when sensitive issues would be under consideration and simply announce that voting for this particular meeting will be by secret ballot. This way confidentiality is assured without its becoming an issue.

At other times I have made it clear that if anyone present requested a secret ballot on any issue, the request would be granted without vote or deliberation. In this manner, everyone's privacy is protected with a minimum of bother.

If you expect a request for a secret ballot, you'll need to have ballots at the ready. Where voter anonymity is a particular necessity, you may even wish to have pencils or special pens available for the vote.

Set a Policy About Minutes and Other Forms of Recording

Minutes are generally a good idea to help keep a record of what went on at prior meetings, not only to refresh the memory of those present at the previous session of a group, but also to provide orientation for those who may be new and for whom a sense of the history of the group is required.

Following are samples of the various styles of minutes and some questions that should be answered as you decide which style best suits your purposes.

Detailed Summary Minutes

Resembling a court record, detailed summary minutes contain complete descriptions of what was said and by whom.

Here is a sample of how detailed summary minutes might look:

> The meeting began at 2:30 P.M. The first item of business was a report on the lawsuit against the Compton City zoning board headed by Gordon Pruett, vice-president for legal affairs. Mr. Pruett, in his summary, suggested the possibility of collusion between the realtor and the city council in denying the permit and pointed out that . . ."

Action or Subject Outline Minutes

These are minutes that contain only a listing and brief summary of the items discussed without direct quotes or paraphrases of statements made.

Here is a sample of action or subject outline minutes:

> The meeting began at 2:30 P.M. with a report on the legal action against the Compton City Zoning Board. Obstacles to the progress of the suit were summarized.

Whether to use a detailed or summary form of minutes should be decided on two bases: First, if there is a frequent turnover in the attendance at regularly scheduled meetings, detailed minutes will be helpful in keeping those who read them informed of the proceedings and better able to join the proceedings "in progress."

A second consideration in whether to have detailed minutes and whether to include the names of those who speak during a meeting is the question of what happens to the minutes of the meeting. Are they widely circulated? Might the meeting be a forum where proprietary information is discussed? What about the legal or public-relations consequences of an inadvertent or even a deliberate leak of information contained in minutes? A look at the issues climate and nature of your business should enable you to reach a quick decision on the degree of detail you consider necessary in meeting minutes.

To Record or Not to Record?

That is a question that has pretty much haunted us since the Watergate era. The quality and accessibility of recording equipment has dramatically increased, with both audio and videotape gaining access to many of our nation's courtrooms.

However, as in the case of having detailed minutes of a meeting, you should examine the consequences of making a video or audio record of the proceedings. The presence of cameras or microphones is likely to scare many away from the frank discussion that is often an important part of getting things done.

This is not to imply that recordings should therefore be made without the knowledge of those present. Recording people without their knowledge is always a breach of etiquette and quite possibly a breach of law. If you are recording, make certain that those being taped know about it and check with your legal counsel before making tape recording a business practice, in or out of meetings.

There is also the question of how important it is to have an *exact* record of the proceedings. Like putting too many things in writing, having a record as specific as a tape recording can come back to haunt you or others present. As the Watergate hearings taught us, even missing or erased tapes can be a tremendous liability.

In summary, while I'm providing you with the options, I remain a fan of open, no-holds-barred, and even loud-discussion meetings, recorded in the form of brief summary minutes. I also believe in giving meeting participants the right to go on and off the record, or to have their comments appear in the minutes free of attribution.

A by-product of the freedom of operating under these rules is frank discussion of ideas in an atmosphere in which everyone will participate fully and openly, secure in the knowledge that it won't come back to haunt them.

Handling Disruptive Participants

Anyone who has ever run a meeting and tried to proceed through an agenda will tell you that meetings will go much more smoothly and end precisely on time if all those people don't show up.

It's not so much the people who come to participate and move an agenda forward as the characters—and I mean characters in the most theatrical sense, who show up complete with a particular and well-defined act—who can severely disrupt and thoroughly sidetrack the most important meeting.

If you're ready for these highly recognizable characters, they become little more than an interesting communicative challenge, rather than a threat, and even provide some comic relief. Following are a few of those characters that I've met along the way and some tips on handling their behavior in the meeting environment.

The Examiner

Usually a person who thinks he or she should be running the meeting instead of you, the examiner will ask you a question, usually toward the beginning of the meeting, designed to show that you really don't know your stuff.

SOLUTION: Fortunately, the examiner types are never as smart as they think they are, and the answers to their "piercing" questions are usually as obvious as their motivation for asking them.

If you don't know the answer to the question, say so and that you'll get the information. The key here is to go no further (as in getting the information from someone else in the room); if you do, the examiner is now running the meeting.

If the question is "out of order" or off the agenda, say so and get back to the agenda, but only after the briefest response showing that you are not afraid to say, "I don't know" publicly. Further questions from the examiner should be deferred unless they pertain to agenda items.

The Showboater

A fairly harmless character whose every comment on any issue is an embellished re-creation of his or her greatest accomplishments. He or she begins with the issue at hand, but the showboater will suddenly drop in a phrase such as, "Back in '74 when I saved the company . . ."

SOLUTION: Unlike the examiner, the showboater is not out to cause you any harm, but is more likely just seeking recognition or perhaps campaigning for the next promotion. Let the showboater speak briefly and then gently steer him or her back to the agenda. You don't want to grant limitless access to the floor, but given a bit of the recognition the showboater seeks, he or she, appreciative of that recognition, can be an ally.

The Bully

Strong disagreement in a loud voice is the bully's big weapon. The bully will also try to pretend he or she is speaking for everyone, with such phrases as, "All of us know that . . ."

Given the least bit of encouragement, either in the form of recognition or any sign that you're intimidated, the bully will attempt to take over the meeting. Further, if you get into a shouting match, his or her mission is accomplished, as the meeting is no longer a meeting but is now a full-blown argument.

SOLUTION: Do what bullies never expect—shove back verbally, but do so in a normal tone of voice, which you will maintain throughout your encounter with the bully.

If the bully tries to claim that he or she is speaking for everyone present, remind the bully that he or she has not been elected to do so. With this quick rejoinder, you have caught the bully in a factual error and also isolated him or her from the rest of those present.

Once business is being conducted on *your* terms and not those of the bully, you should proceed and respond in a brief, matter-of-fact, unemotional manner, not giving the floor back to the bully. For further useful tactics to be used on particularly adversarial souls, see the chapter on handling tough questions and questioners.

The Gadfly

A person who consistently stirs up trouble or criticizes just to see what happens, the gadfly will interrupt multiple times with comments that begin with a seemingly polite, if not apologetic, "It may be just me, but I think . . ." If only the gadflies of the world would realize that it *is* just them and shut up. But of course, they never will and never do.

SOLUTION: The gadfly, like any insect, may be annoying but is relatively harmless. You can use all kinds of parliamentary procedure to call him or her out of order (as the person often is); and, just like insects, you'll never eliminate or control the gadfly completely. Instead, learn to live with this character, safe in the knowledge that he or she tends to self-destruct.

The gadfly's constancy of criticism is like living near a railroad track. At first, you can't believe anyone could live with all that noise. After a few days, you're likely to say, "What train?"

The rest of those present see the gadfly for what he or she is, an annoyance that shouldn't take up too much of your energy. Let the gadfly speak, have him or her stick to the agenda, and politely move on. At the same time, don't treat the gadfly with total cynicism—sometimes even gadflies have a point.

The Cicada

A close cousin of the gadfly, I've named this character for the insect that comes out of the ground only after years of hibernation and upon doing so makes a shrill and very disturbing sound. At meetings, this is the type of person who—just when the finishing touches are being put on the motion and it's about to pass—vigorously, often indignantly, objects to what has transpired, even though he or she seems to have been ignoring the proceedings up to that moment.

SOLUTION: Once the cicada comes out of the ground it lives a short life and so is not really a problem unless you make it one. Listen patiently to the objection, state your regret that it did not come sooner, and attempt to "have the question called" (see parliamentary procedure) at first opportunity.

Don't respond directly to the cicada's last-minute attempt to derail the proceedings and look to the rest of those present for support. As with the gadfly, the key tactic is not to engage in extended discussion.

The Mad Bomber

This character will hurl a verbal bombshell into the proceedings with the hope of causing an explosion, mostly in the form of your reaction. Outrageousness and even profanity are not beyond the mad bomber—a false accusation or a harshly critical comment about the meeting, about you, or about others present, is typical fuel for the mad bomber's attempted pyrotechnics.

SOLUTION: It's up to you to defuse the bomb as quickly as possible. Remain calm; part of what the mad bomber is counting on is an angry, out-of-control reaction from you. Don't interrupt the mad bomber, either. Let the verbal assault wind down and then respond with a firm denial where appropriate and an offer to meet with the bomber and any other interested parties after the gathering.

The point in letting the bomber unleash his or her wrath all in one shot is to avoid giving the bomber the floor again. This way, if the bomber interrupts you during your response, you can tell him or her, quite firmly, not to interrupt, since the bomber's statement went uninterrupted. This strategy is most effective if you avoid giving the floor back to the bomber and get back to your agenda as soon as possible.

The mad bomber is not to be confused with the bully. The bully is just out to gain some control and, depending upon the issue, may not be all that harmful. The mad bomber, like the real mad bombers in history, are out to be destructive.

By being a soothing yet controlling force in handling the mad bomber, you avoid the disruption he or she seeks. By not getting down to the bomber's level, his or her anger becomes one-sided; in fact, the more outrageous the mad bomber becomes, the more inappropriate he or she seems, until the explosion he or she sought simply fizzles.

The Ferret

Inspired by an animal bred for the singular purpose of burrowing deep into the earth to find its prey, its human counterpart will sit in front of you at a meeting and do the same type of burrowing; only its prey is usually an utterly obscure piece of information instead of the hapless mole. The ferret will interrupt you in midsentence with a question such as, "But just how did you arrive at .006 in paragraph 27; my numbers show something more along the lines of .286."

SOLUTION: Never argue with the ferret. He or she will gnaw you down with an endless stream of minutiae. If you solve the mystery of the seeming error in paragraph 27, the ferret will undoubtedly find something wrong in paragraph 29 or 32 or 45 and on and on.

Instead, throw him or her a piece of meat in the form of tentative agreement and the offer of a later meeting on that pesky number. "You may have a point on that figure, it gave me some trouble as well," is a far better ferret-repellent than a statement such as "That couldn't be . . . you're wrong—I double-checked the figures myself and . . ."

While in the preceding pages I've highlighted the major members of the psychological menagerie I've met in conducting meetings over the years, I hasten to add that even with the most difficult of groups or toughest of issues, not all of those characters have ever been present at one meeting: a ferret here, a gadfly there, even one or two mad bombers. But, by and large, the vast preponderance of people wanted to accomplish something and move things forward. They are willing to work, cooperate, and even to argue when they feel they have a point. These are the people before whom most of us conduct meetings.

Summary

Prepare for meetings by boning up on your parliamentary procedure and the meeting management techniques discussed in this chapter. But above all, encourage frank, free-flowing, and open discussion; show that you welcome it and listen to the participants' ideas and even challenges. You'll learn from them.

Use parliamentary procedure judiciously and always to fight the clock, not the people in the room; your meetings will improve in tone, atmosphere, and level of accomplishment. Once the "characters" I've described realize that their communicative antics aren't having the desired effect, even they will drop or at least tone down their act. Is there a motion to adjourn?

Quick Review:
Conducting Successful Meetings

1. Set an agenda and stick to it.
2. Hold regularly scheduled meetings.
3. Place time limits on all meetings.
4. Begin and end on time.
5. Don't let meetings become gripe sessions.
6. Don't overuse the designation "emergency meeting."
7. Define membership in the group and voting procedures before you get into issues.
8. Always be open to using secret ballots for elections.

9. Make an early decision about the degree of detail contained in meeting minutes.

10. Use parliamentary procedure to fight the clock, not the people in the room.

For More Information

Cann, Marjorie Mitchell, *Robert's Rules of Order—Simplified* Perigree Books, 71 pp. (1991).

Robert, Henry M., *The New Robert's Rules of Order* (revised edition by Mary A. De Vries), New American Library, 258 pp. (1990).

Chapter Fifteen

Thirty-one Quick Fixes to Improve Your Communicative Power

At-a-Glance Summary

The previous chapters have taken you from the speaker's podium to the TV studio, and even into the courtroom, providing you with suggestions, techniques, and tips. Some of them take more time to implement fully than others, particularly those that require practice or a change in your way of thinking.

This chapter is intended as a review of the most easily implemented tactics and techniques. Their use lead to immediate improvement in your communicative power and impact in a wide array of situations.

Thirty-one Quick Fixes to Improve Your Communicative Power

At the Podium

1. *Start your speeches with silence.* Whenever you approach a podium, some members of the audience will be talking among themselves or otherwise not paying attention. If you begin right away, sure, they'll gradually tune in, but they'll also be thinking about that prior conversation and not really listening to you. Talking over the noise also suggests that you're nervous, afraid of silence.

Instead, after you approach the podium and arrange your notes, *don't speak*, but wait ten or even fifteen seconds. At this point, everyone will be listening and the attention will be focused on you and your message instead of whatever was going on before you began speaking.

2. *Don't waste the first few seconds.* Most speakers walk up to a podium, place their notes on it, adjust the microphone, and then utter the ridiculously redundant and totally boring words, "Today I am going to talk to you about . . .

It was perfectly obvious you were going to talk about something even before you said anything. Don't waste that opening moment. It may be the last time during your speech that everyone is paying attention, so say something that will grab and hold their attention. Even if it's controversial, at least they're listening.

3. *Always mention your audience specifically.* Public speaking is less intimate than conversation; speeches often take on the generic and impersonal quality of a government brochure.

To make the audience feel "You're really talking to *us*," mention your audience by name, or even mention specific audience members. "Everyone knows that the federal budget is . . ." becomes, "As CPAs, you especially know that the federal budget is . . ."; "Many of you" becomes "From Alice in the Legal Department to Mary Kay in Public Affairs . . ."

Even if you're giving the same speech a number of times, this small language adjustment keeps it fresh and increases listenership.

279

4. *Once you conclude, stop talking.* As I point out in Chapter 4 or the speech-writing, chapter, you should begin the end of your speech with a concluding transitional phrase, for example, "In conclusion," or "To summarize."

Most speakers seem to know this, but too many will use one of these closing phrases and then drone on for five or ten minutes. Once you indicate you're wrapping things up, never talk for more than two additional minutes; to do so is to lose all of their attention and some of your credibility.

About the Words You Use

5. *Simpler is better.* Without talking down to an audience, use terms with which they are all familiar and define any that are in doubt. If you use acronyms or abbreviations, explain them the first time you mention them if there is any possibility that someone present might not follow you. Speakers who say of an audience, "They'll figure it out," are correct; but while they're figuring, they're not listening.

6. *Name names.* Forgetting to mention your company name is an amusing and sometimes revealing error. In the dozens of hours that make up your work week, you may never have any reason to mention it at all. The problem occurs when you maintain this internal mind-set while speaking to an external audience. They don't know you and need to be reminded of who you and your organization are.

The error of leaving out the company name also shows up when a negative issue needs to be discussed publicly. In a lame attempt to disassociate themselves and their organization from whatever is going on, many spokespersons will all too conveniently omit the company name.

This error, even if it's subconscious, makes you look like the little kid who explains having missed the school bus with the blame-shifting statement, "The bus left me behind."

7. *Watch your pronouns.* English is a sexist language in that it generally reflects, and some would say perpetuates, the male dominated nature of the corporate and professional world.

The feminists among us are distracted, if not offended, by the exclusion of female pronouns, particularly when referring to positions of power, expertise, or authority. So such sentences as, "Talk to any expert and he will say . . ." is a surefire way to offend the more socially aware members of your audience. Talk to any expert and just listen to what *he* or *she* has to say.

Handling Audience Questions

8. *Never say, "I'm glad you asked me that question."* No one believes you; they know that you'd rather not be answering their questions at all. The same is true of that other equally ineffective stall used by many speakers, "That's a good question." Instead, pause before responding and, if you must stall for time, try saying something like, "You've raised a very important issue."

9. *If you don't know the answer to a question, say so.* Many speakers fear they'll be asked a question to which they don't know the answer. Actually, no audience expects you to know everything about any subject.

"I don't know, but I'll find out," or "I don't know but let me tell you who does," are answers that will do nothing to reduce your stature. And besides, once you've said, "I don't know," and you're being truthful, no one can argue with you.

10. *Don't look at a Q&A session as a battle to be won.* Instead, look at it as an information-sharing session in which you are likely to have to talk about some problem issues. Trying to win or weasel your way out of the tough questions will only leave the impression that you're defensive and embattled rather than informative and in charge.

In the Job Interview

11. *Prepare for the "Tell me about yourself" question.* It's always there. It's usually at the beginning and sets the tone for the entire interview. Because it's so obvious and deceptively simple, many interview subjects fail to anticipate this question and turn in a fumbled, poorly structured response.

12. *Decide what your strong points are and don't be modest in discussing them.* A job interview is a self-sales presentation, and success in sales presentations or job interviews does not go to the meek. Focus on a couple of strong points that relate to the job for which you're being interviewed and practice working these points into your responses.

13. *Know more about the company than the other candidates do.* Achieving a positive outcome on a job interview is often a matter of differentiating yourself from the competition. One relatively easy way to do so is to read such publications as the annual report, employee newsletters, and even recent news items. (This doesn't mean reading them in the reception area as you wait for the interview to begin.)

Most candidates don't know as much as they should about their prospective employer, its problems and objectives. Doing some homework here will separate you from the crowd.

In the Sales Presentation

14. *Don't be ashamed to sell.* If you've done any of it, you don't need me to tell you that selling is tough, especially because of the frequent rejection that's part of the job.

In selling, you quickly learn that most presentations go well and most prospects are awfully polite (they seldom reject you to your face). You also learn that most encounters result in no positive outcome or no sale.

This reality may turn you into a member of those hordes of so-called sales professionals who approach prospects with the "I'm sorry to take up your time, but I'll be brief and let you get back to work" strategy.

If you ever hear yourself saying words such as these or thinking such thoughts, you, too, have begun to substitute apologizing for selling. Don't apologize, sell! Take up their time with your presentation and make it worthwhile.

If you are there to sell and want to close that day, say so and work toward that *exact* goal. You'll make more sales by selling than you will by apologizing.

15. *Plan on coming back.* The rejection that is an inevitable part of selling means it may take more than one shot to succeed. Sometimes, even before you enter the room, they've decided to go with another vendor—this despite your super, all-cylinders-clicking, all-barrels-blazing presentation.

In light of this possibility, a secondary objective of your sales presentation should be to get invited back. This means being careful about knocking the competition and not making your prospect nervous or defensive about going with another vendor. Accentuate your positives, tread lightly over the competition's negatives, and be invited back.

In the Media Interview

16. *Have an informational goal or set of target issues for any media interview.* Prior to many media interviews I've conducted, I've said to guests, "What would you like to talk about?" Many respond by saying, "Anything you'd like." This is a mistake, especially if the interview is potentially adversarial.

You should always try to anticipate and control the subject areas covered in media interviews, either by planning to mention some target issues or by being directive when asked that preinterview question, "What would you like to talk about?"

17. *Remember, you are the expert—they are not.* Most reporters have somewhere between a surface idea and no knowledge at all about your interview subject. Yet even the foremost experts tend to be intimidated in the presence of reporters, answering unfair or ill-constructed questions in the hope that the reporter will "go easy."

If there is something wrong with a question or you just don't understand it, politely say so and get yourself a better question or an admission that the reporter is merely fishing. Remember, *you* are the expert.

18. *Never say "No Comment" to a reporter.* Sometimes you will be asked a question you shouldn't answer. You might think a quick solution is to say "No comment!" A reporter's audience views that statement much the way most people erroneously view taking the Fifth Amendment: you've got something to hide and you're probably guilty.

Instead of saying "No comment!" tell the reporter why you won't be responding to a question: "It's proprietary information;" "It's a matter to be decided in court, not here and now;" or "I don't have sufficient information to make any intelligent comment" are all ways to say, "No comment" without actually using those unintentionally incriminating words.

Conducting Meetings

19. *Use agendas for meetings and stick with them.* An important part of your perceived effectiveness in running meetings is the orderliness with which things proceed.

Most of us remember to generate and distribute an agenda, but many fall short on sticking to it. Especially if you're just beginning a leadership role, you'll find that any group will test your willingness to be led away from your planned agenda. Sticking with that agenda, except under the most extreme circumstances, will get you through that test with your leadership skills intact.

20. *Begin and end meetings on time.* Another test you'll face, particularly in the early stages of a leadership role, is the tendency of groups to push back the starting time of meetings with tardy entrances. Once such patterns become the accepted routine, meetings can be delayed and efficiency greatly undermined.

By beginning at or very close to the scheduled time, you are sending a signal that there is work to be done and that it will be done even in the absence of those who are overly lax about starting times.

Ending meetings on time is an important symbolic communication that you are as considerate of their time as they have been of yours. Besides, little or no business is conducted when everyone in the room has somewhere else to go and can't get there because your meeting is running late.

Once you've established a reputation for getting things done in the allotted time, you'll find the atmosphere more conducive to accomplishment and a positive commentary on your leadership skills.

21. *Don't let meetings become gripe sessions.* The chronic complainers in your midst can use meetings as a platform to air their complaints. This behavior can snowball to the extent that your meetings are not to be directed toward productive ends, but instead become a verbal dumping ground for all that's wrong or might be wrong with your organization.

The solution to this problem is twofold: first, stick to your agenda and don't let yourself be derailed by those who would make your meetings a gripe session. Second, don't shut out the complainers altogether. Consider the scheduling of a separate meeting to air their concerns. These steps will keep your meetings more productive, while giving those with something negative to say a place and time to do so.

On the Witness Stand

22. *Don't let them rush you.* The witness stand is an uncomfortable place for most of us because we spend so little time there. To make matters worse, what you say can have far-reaching and sometimes devastating consequences.

As a corporate witness, your peers and superiors are also likely to be watching. All this pressure and I haven't even mentioned the opposition yet.

Of course, the opposition will want to increase the pressure by getting you to respond immediately to each question. You may be questioned by someone who shoots words at you like an automatic weapon, all so you'll feel hurried and compelled to speak without thinking (which is just what the opposition wants you to do).

Instead, pause before responding, even on easy questions. As you respond, speak deliberately and slowly. In this manner, you'll set up a pattern to give you more think time for each response and also to mask your reaction as to the degree of ease or difficulty of each question.

23. *Greet silence with silence.* When a questioner wants a witness to say more, all he or she usually has to do is look directly at the witness at the end of a response and say nothing for a few seconds.

Under the pressure of the moment, most witnesses will start talking again and often say things they wish they hadn't said. Remember, this extra verbiage was in response to silence. Now that you know this trick, don't become its victim.

24. *Just answer the questions.* Let your attorney win the case. Sometimes witnesses see themselves as soldiers on a field of battle, determined to lash out at the "enemy" at every opportunity. This is just how the opposition wants you to feel: combative, angry, aggressive, and most of all, not thinking. With you in this emotional state, they'll have a much easier time getting you to say things you shouldn't.

Instead of trying to win the case, concentrate on answering the questions truthfully and succinctly. Your attorney will do the strategizing and take the actions necessary to counter any problem testimony. Your role as a witness is just to answer the questions you are asked.

During a Crisis

25. *Maintain media contact at regular intervals.* During a crisis, the kind and degree of media coverage you receive will be a major component in shaping both the public perception of the severity of the crisis and your effectiveness in dealing with it.

If you do not make yourself available, you increase the chance of building the perception that you are avoiding coverage because you have something to hide, possibly your inability to manage the crisis.

Part of your communications plan in a crisis should be regularly scheduled media briefings. Your public will get *your* story, rather than the multitude of versions arrived at by reporters who did their investigating without your input.

26. *Don't forget to talk to the troops.* Your employees will become a major source of information in a crisis, not only for the media but for anyone they encounter outside the workplace. Facing constant inquiries as to what's happening at your company, as well as the extra effort employees may have to make during a crisis, can be tough on morale.

Make your employees a top communications priority; they have a special stake in any crisis. As informed sources, they can make good ambassadors as the public at large and the media seek to find out what's going on.

This reliance on employees as communicators will boost morale, as well as provide reliable information to those seeking it. It also will shut down that most notorious and unreliable information center during any crisis—the rumor mill.

27. *When a crisis is over, say so.* If you look at the history of corporate crises—be they financial, product-related, or even crises of public confidence—you will find that all of these situations had a beginning; the particular event that precipitated the crisis; a middle, the phase in which a crisis management plan was implemented; and finally, an end, the phase in which business is getting back to normal.

The problem is, if you don't declare an end to the crisis, the public perception will persist that you are still mired in crisis and that your products or services may somehow be affected. If the crisis is severe enough, some people may even assume that you are no longer in business.

So, once a crisis has ended, be sure to declare to all your constituents that the crisis is over and that normalcy has returned.

At the Negotiating Table

28. *Seek agreement, not victory.* If your primary objective in negotiation is to beat up the other side, they'll soon recognize it and try to do the same to you.

Too often negotiators forget that the purpose of negotiation is to arrive at an agreement. If you enter the session with the idea of achieving "total victory," you are poised for war, not negotiation. In real negotiation, each side gives, gets, and agrees; but no side should win at the total expense of the other.

29. *Don't get angry, get an agreement.* In the negotiations chapter I pointed out that the one who yells the loudest in negotiations tends to lose out when it comes to getting the best agreement.

The negotiation process can be particularly frustrating when the other side is full of bluster despite your attempts to be fair and open. The opposition may even pull a stunt like walking out or changing an item already agreed upon.

In such situations, rather than losing your cool, look at the reasons behind the other side's belligerence. Such negotiators are usually playing to an audience beyond the negotiating table—either their superiors or perhaps a union membership that elected them.

In any event, don't take such behavior personally; it's not aimed at you and will impede your ability to function if you buy into it. Don't get angry, get an agreement.

30. *Let the other side begin.* If possible, let the other side talk first in any negotiation session. If they do, you'll gain valuable information as to their perspectives and priorities on the issues involved, their emotional state, and their degree of preparedness. Getting this information will keep you from getting off on the wrong foot and will usually shorten the proceedings.

31. *Begin with easy issues.* In negotiation, one of the best creators of a climate conducive to agreement is agreement itself. Conversely, discussing focal or major issues first will emphasize the distance between the sides.

Therefore, find out what you can agree upon and do so early in the negotiation session. The momentum gained by this agreement will serve both sides when it comes to agreeing on major issues. It is too seldom said, and too little understood, except by seasoned negotiators—negotiation is the search for agreement, not victory.

Summary

So there you have it—thirty-one quick fixes to help make you a more powerful communicator. Having taken you through hundreds of pages and tactics for all sorts of communicative encounters, I remain vividly aware that listeners and readers tend to remember what they hear (or read) last.

Therefore, I want to encourage you at this closing moment not to be hypercritical of your abilities—as so many of you are. As I cautioned earlier, don't use the information contained on the preceding pages to give yourself a communicative makeover. Instead, accentuate and build on your strengths.

You may have come to realize that truly powerful communicators exude confidence with their every look, movement, and word. You, too, can communicate that degree of confidence, not by building an act, but by communicating with comfort and consistency, regardless of the situation or issues climate.

Consistency builds comfort, and that comfort communicates the confidence you need to achieve your full potential as a powerful and confident communicator.

Index

T